CÉSAR CHÁVEZ, THE CATHOLIC BISHOPS, AND THE FARMWORKERS' STRUGGLE FOR SOCIAL JUSTICE

CÉSAR CHÁVEZ,

THE CATHOLIC BISHOPS,

AND THE FARMWORKERS'

STRUGGLE FOR SOCIAL JUSTICE

Marco G. Prouty

The University of Arizona Press   Tucson

The University of Arizona Press
© 2006 The Arizona Board of Regents
All rights reserved

First paperback printing 2008
ISBN 978-0-8165-2731-1 (pbk. : alk. paper)

Library of Congress Cataloging-in-Publication Data
Prouty, Marco G., 1973–
César Chávez, the Catholic bishops, and the farmworkers' struggle for
social justice / Marco G. Prouty.
p. cm.
Includes bibliographical references and index.
ISBN-13: 978-0-8165-2555-3 (hardcover : alk. paper)
ISBN-10: 0-8165-2555-2 (hardcover : alk. paper)
1. Chavez, Cesar, 1927– 2. Church and labor—California—History—20th
century. 3. Catholic Church—California—History—20th century. 4. United
Farm Workers—History. I. Title.
HD6509.C48P76 2006
331.88'130974709046—dc22   2006006863

Manufactured in the United States of America on acid-free, archival-quality
paper containing a minimum of 30% post-consumer waste and processed
chlorine free.

13 12 11 10 09 08   7 6 5 4 3 2

To my parents

CONTENTS

ILLUSTRATIONS

ACKNOWLEDGMENTS

This project began to take shape during a 2002 meeting with Ronaldo M. Cruz, executive director of the Secretariat for Hispanic Affairs at the U.S. Conference of Catholic Bishops (USCCB), who knew César Chávez and volunteered for the UFW. After securing permission for me to access the USCCB's archives, Ron spent the next three years generously sharing his time and insights to help me better understand the Catholic Church and La Causa. This book could not have happened without him.

Similarly, I owe an enormous debt of gratitude to Dr. Leslie Tentler. Her counsel, patience, and firsthand knowledge of U.S. labor history made both my Ph.D. and this book possible. It has been a privilege to be her student and a guest at her family's table.

Dr. Richard T. Hughes, my M.A. thesis advisor, has continued to be a source of guidance, inspiration, and encouragement. I am indebted to him, and grateful for his friendship.

My dissertation's readers, as well as the professional staffs at the various archives, were especially helpful. Special thanks to Dr. Tim Meagher, Dr. Jim Riley, John Shepherd, Dr. Joseph Turrini, Heather Morgan, Jane Stoeffler, Patrick Cullom, Kathy Schmeling, and Nancy Patterson for their support and enthusiasm for this project.

Many thanks to the excellent team at the University of Arizona Press —especially Senior Editor Patti Hartmann, Director Christine Szuter, Adam Duckworth, Alan M. Schroder, and Leigh Johnsen.

All photographs are courtesy of the Monsignor George G. Higgins Photographic Collection, The American Catholic History Research Center and University Archives, The Catholic University of America, Washington, D.C..

My love and appreciation to my family, friends, and contributors for helping make this work possible.

Above all, to my parents: words can express neither the scope of your contributions nor the depth of my gratitude. Thank you for your unconditional love.

ABBREVIATIONS

ACTU	Association of Catholic Trade Unionists
AFL	American Federation of Labor
AFL-CIO	American Federation of Labor-Congress of Industrial Organizations
AWOC	Agricultural Workers Organizing Committee
CALRA	California Agricultural Labor Relations Act
CALRB	California Agricultural Labor Relations Board
CNS	Catholic News Service
CSD	Committee on Social Development
CSO	Community Service Organization
CWM	Catholic Worker Movement
FPS	Farm Placement Service
GSVA	Grower-Shipper Vegetable Association
NACFL	National Advisory Committee on Farm Labor
NAWU	National Agricultural Workers Union
NCCB	National Conference of Catholic Bishops
NCCML	National Citizens' Council for Migrant Labor
NCWC	National Catholic Welfare Conference
NFLU	National Farm Labor Union
NFWA	National Farm Workers Association
NLRA	National Labor Relations Act
SAD	Social Action Department
UFW	United Farm Workers
UFWOC	United Farm Workers Organizing Committee
USCC/NCCB	United States Catholic Conference/National Conference of Catholic Bishops
USCCB	United States Conference of Catholic Bishops

CÉSAR CHÁVEZ, THE CATHOLIC BISHOPS, AND THE FARMWORKERS' STRUGGLE FOR SOCIAL JUSTICE

INTRODUCTION

From 1965 through 1977, César E. Chávez led his union, the United Farm Workers (UFW), in two major conflicts: the Delano Grape Strike (1965–70) and the Battle of the Salad Bowl (1970–77). During this epoch, the Catholic Church, through the Bishops' Ad Hoc Committee on Farm Labor, played an invaluable role in bringing peace to California's valleys and victory to César Chávez's movement—La Causa (the Cause).

Drawing upon rich, untapped archival sources at the United States Conference of Catholic Bishops (USCCB), this book reveals the internal debates among the American Catholic hierarchy's top leadership during the farm labor crisis of the 1960s and 1970s. In reading this story—based on the hierarchy's (at times confidential) communications—the audience can acquire a better understanding of the Catholic Church's decision-making process and a more complete account of the struggles César Chávez and the farmworkers faced in the final decades of the twentieth century.

The first conflict covered in this book, the Delano Grape Strike, pitted Catholic farmworkers against Catholic agriculturalists. There is scant evidence to indicate that the second clash encompassed such an intrafaith conflict; however, the Battle of the Salad Bowl reveals the Catholic Church's gradual transition from reluctant mediator to outright partisan of César Chávez and La Causa.

A soft-spoken and devout Catholic, César Chávez labored for years to construct a viable farmworker union. Three principal factors enabled him to become the first person to successfully organize California's farmworkers: the 1964 termination of the bracero program, the rise of the Civil Rights movement, and the support of the Catholic Church. The engagement of the Catholic hierarchy became so critical that Chávez pronounced it "the single most important thing that has helped us."[1] Only briefly mentioned in the existing literature on the UFW, the partnership between Chávez and the Catholic Church is the focus of this work.

Initially, the Catholic hierarchy resisted intervening in the 1965–1970 conflict amongst its faithful. The dispute encompassed social justice for the farmworkers, but it also impacted the growers' economic interests. Often these agriculturalists were politically well-connected, and provided major financial contributions to the parishes in California's Central Valley. The crux of the problem was that many clerics felt they had an obligation to both parties. Exacerbating the situation, both the growers and the farmworkers believed the Church should support their respective side. After all, both parties were an integral part of the Catholic flock. The farmworkers filled the pews, and growers enriched the coffers.

Dismayed by this stark choice, the hierarchy in the Central Valley remained on the sidelines during the first three years of the Delano conflict (1965–68). However, by 1969 the national spotlight glared upon the long-running strike. Questions arose as to why the Catholic Church had not taken action to resolve this intra-Catholic dispute. Chávez petitioned the Church. Twice. The public pressure became overwhelming, and the Catholic hierarchy decided that the most effective way to assuage their critics would be to establish an Ad Hoc Committee on Farm Labor to investigate the conflict.

The hierarchy organized the Bishops' Ad Hoc Committee in November 1969, and the group swung into action shortly thereafter. Comprised of five bishops and two priests, Monsignor George G. Higgins and Monsignor (now Cardinal) Roger Mahony, the committee tirelessly traveled California's Central Valley during the first half of 1970 to bring peace between the warring factions. The team quickly grasped the idea of transforming the liability of intra-Catholic divisions into an asset. The committee decided to act as a mediator and achieved a settlement within months of entering the five-year conflict. The hierarchy intervened and brokered a peace quicker than anyone, including the bishops themselves, imagined. By July 1970, the Delano Grape Strike had ended. Calm settled upon the land owned by Catholic agriculturalists and worked by the hands of Catholic farmworkers. The clergy had brought peace . . . if only for a day.

As the grape growers and farmworkers negotiated contracts, another conflict festered. Lettuce growers took note of the trouble Chávez incited in Delano and decided to circumvent the UFW. Fortunately for the lettuce farmers, an alternative union appeared in the fields—the Teamsters. Blatantly "raiding" the UFW's jurisdiction, the Teamsters Union moved to organize the fieldworkers. AFL-CIO president George

Meany called this action "union busting."[2] Lettuce growers disagreed. For them, it simply reflected an opportunity to cut sweetheart deals with a less-contentious union. Exhausted from five years of battle in Delano, Chávez had no time to rest. He shifted gears and prepared to fight a war on two fronts—against the lettuce growers and the Teamsters. This would be a major undertaking, and Chávez needed help; he again turned to the Catholic Church.

The Bishops' Ad Hoc Committee agreed to enter the Battle of the Salad Bowl and attempt to broker peace among the UFW, the lettuce growers, and the Teamsters. This seven-year struggle became even more contentious than the Delano Grape Strike. Importantly, the Catholic hierarchy experienced a major transformation during this period. From 1970 to 1973, the Ad Hoc Committee attempted to play the role of conciliator—much like it had successfully done in Delano. However, the Battle of the Salad Bowl was different.

In Delano, economic pressure from Chávez's nationwide boycott of the fruit of the vine made grape growers receptive to the Ad Hoc Committee's overtures of mediation. This time, the lettuce growers and Teamsters were not inclined to compromise. They wanted to destroy the UFW. The Catholic Church, traditionally a conservative force, drew upon its rich tradition of social teaching and transformed the words into action.

By 1973, liberal clergy had gained significant influence within the U.S. Catholic hierarchy. The Church observed the injustices being perpetrated against Chávez and the farmworkers, and made a conscious decision, based on the advice of the Bishops' Ad Hoc Committee, that the institution could no longer be a neutral mediator. The U.S. Catholic Church officially endorsed Chávez's grape and lettuce boycotts, and placed the hierarchy squarely against the powerful Teamsters Union.

Because of the bishop's backing, Chávez and his union emerged victorious in the Battle of the Salad Bowl. The UFW's triumph in 1977 cleared the way for the union to reach its organizational apogee of an estimated one hundred thousand members by the late 1970s. Peace had again come to the fields of California, and the farmworkers finally enjoyed, if only briefly, a significant improvement in wages and working conditions.

The epilogue to this story is not joyous. Indeed, it is tragic. Ultimately, Chávez and the farmworkers lost. The Catholic hierarchy teamed with Chávez in a quest for social justice, but only briefly. The UFW became a powerful force in the fields, but only for a short while. The farmworkers enjoyed a higher standard of living, but only for what seemed like a moment. The growers struck back, the UFW imploded, and the Bishops' Ad Hoc Committee faded away.

The national mood began to change during the 1980s. Social concerns gave way to an emphasis on improving one's material wealth. The grower-backed George Deukmejian succeeded the pro-Chávez Jerry Brown as governor of California. Ronald Reagan, notoriously hostile to Chávez, took the White House.[3] George Higgins retired, the U.S. hierarchy withdrew from the UFW, and the Church embarked on a more conservative agenda.

Against the backdrop of these larger changes, the UFW began to implode. Chávez, a charismatic leader, neither delegated authority nor established the administrative framework necessary to effectively manage a full-fledged AFL-CIO union. Marching and fasting worked well for Chávez during the 1960s and early 1970s, but by the late 1970s his organization was no longer a social movement. He needed to structure the organization to operate independent of his presence. He didn't, and the UFW collapsed from its pinnacle of one hundred thousand members to less than twenty thousand by the time of Chávez's death in 1993.

1 ROOTS OF THE CONFLICT

The Farmworker in California

Growers built California's agricultural industry on the backs of migrants: first the Chinese, then the Japanese, and, finally, the Mexicans. Large-scale farms in the Golden State began to appear "in the nascent days of the robber barons, and it was they who seemed to suggest the tone for the evolution of California agriculture."[1] During the 1849 Gold Rush, Anglos swarmed the Pacific Coast and shifted the region's population from Mexican to Anglo.[2] Along with the demographic transformation came a radical shift in the area's economy from the small traditional ranchero farms to sprawling acres of industrial agriculture.[3] Through fraud, forgery, and bribery roughly eight hundred grants were used to provide grantees with an astounding eight million acres of California land.[4] By 1870, the Golden State had been transformed into feudal fiefs requiring a large labor force to work the soil.[5]

The Chinese became the first ethnic group to cultivate these vast plots. After being barred from many of the gold camps and out of work after the transcontinental railroad's 1869 completion, the Chinese moved to the fields, and by the 1870s they comprised more than three-quarters of the state's farmworkers.[6] To the disappointment of many agriculturalists, this access to inexpensive Chinese labor did not last. Congress passed the Chinese Exclusion Act in 1882 over grower protests.[7] Over the next decade, Anglo thugs attacked Chinese businesses and labor camps; the Chinese became scapegoats for hard economic times.[8] When confronted with angry protests regarding the ethnicity of their workforce, growers responded that "they only hired Chinese because they could not pay the wages demanded by domestic workers."[9] As a deadly combination of "fiat and terror" forced the Chinese out of the fields, growers began to look elsewhere for a hardworking, yet inexpensive, labor force.[10] Enter the Japanese.

Between 1898 and 1908, California experienced a major influx of Japanese farmworkers.[11] The Japanese initially underbid agricultural workers from other ethnic groups and rapidly dominated the fields.[12] However, after establishing themselves as the premier farm workforce, the Japanese began to command higher wages, and worse, from the grower perspective, started to exhibit signs of labor militancy.[13] Moreover, much to the chagrin of domestic agriculturalists, the Japanese formed cooperative farms and became a financial threat to domestic growers.[14]

The Japanese practice of family wage economy—a system where all members of the family contributed their earnings to the collective— became central to the farms' competitive edge vis-à-vis the established agricultural interests.[15] Dismayed by the resourcefulness of the Japanese, domestic growers successfully lobbied for the passage of the Alien Land Law in 1913—a law that barred Japanese from purchasing or leasing land for more than three years.[16] Undeterred, the Japanese began circumventing the punitive legislation by forming cooperatives in the names of their American citizen children.[17] Outraged by this defiant show of entrepreneurship, domestic growers struck back in 1920 by convincing legislators to pass an even harsher Alien Land Law that "barred 'aliens ineligible to citizenship' from leasing land or from acquiring it through corporations or in the names of the American-born children."[18] The final blow to the Japanese came with Congress's enactment of the Immigration Act of 1924, which barred all immigration from Japan.[19]

With the Chinese and the Japanese out of the fields, agribusiness began yet another search for cheap, hardworking, and docile labor. Since the late 1870s, the advent of the railroad had begun to modernize Mexico and had incited a significant transformation in the Mexicans' traditional way of life.[20] These changes, and the reactions to them, contributed to the Mexican Revolution in 1910.[21] In order to survive the effects of modernization and the Mexican Revolution, many Mexicans became economic migrants and left their homeland to seek a better life in the United States.[22] Between 1900 and 1930, an estimated 10 percent of Mexico's population departed north in order to find gainful employment.[23]

Domestic agricultural interests welcomed this influx of inexpensive, and often desperate labor.[24] Growers collaborated with labor contractors and the railroads to develop a highly organized system to expedite delivery of Mexican workers to large farms.[25] Lax enforcement of the border in early 1900s, combined with the services of labor contractors and the railroads, made for a relatively easy journey between Mexico and the United States.[26] Moreover, agriculturalists developed an effective recruitment campaign to make Mexican workers aware of opportunities to the north, and in the process made a significant contribution toward increasing the volume of immigration.[27]

During the First World War, agriculturalists successfully lobbied politicians to provide conditions favorable for Mexican immigration.[28] Growers argued that the First World War created a labor shortage, and that a steady supply of Mexican labor would be necessary to keep food on American tables. The U.S. secretary of labor responded to the farmers' entreaties and exempted Mexicans from the 1917 Immigration Act's head tax and literacy restrictions. Although created under the auspices of alleviating a wartime labor shortage, grower pressure kept the exemption in force until 1921.[29]

Throughout the 1920s, Congress continued to erect barriers to European and Asian immigration, but frequently exempted Mexicans from such anti-immigrant legislation because growers valued their docility and inexpensive labor.[30] In an effort to assuage Anglo fears that Mexicans would "destroy the culture," agriculturalists developed a "bird of passage" myth.[31] Growers maintained that Mexicans would head south for the winter and not disturb white culture; incidentally, this tale also served to bolster the myth of the agrarian ideal because the Mexican workers allegedly were only needed to provide periodic assistance on family farms.[32] Apparently comforted by the story that Mexicans would only remain for the harvest, Anglo society accepted their presence.[33] While Americans became addicted to an inexpensive food supply, those who harvested the bounty were generally unwelcome in white neighborhoods and lived in separate barrios.[34] Moreover, because they were perceived as temporary, they could be, and were, politically marginalized.[35]

As America sank into the Great Depression, the farmworkers who helped enable high U.S. standards of living were sent back to Mexico for "threatening" the "American" way of life.[36] The reaction to Mexican workers shifted from a warm welcome to a curt goodbye.[37] By the 1930s, it appeared that America wanted to send the "birds of passage" back home.[38] Clearly, growers were displeased to lose their inexpensive, docile, and hardworking labor force; nonetheless, popular pressure incited a mass deportation of immigrants during the 1930s, which included many Mexican farmworkers.[39] Between 1929 and 1931, an estimated three hundred thousand Mexicans and Mexican Americans returned to Mexico.[40]

With immigrant labor no longer in ready supply, agriculturalists had little choice but to hire the more expensive and combative Anglo farmworkers. By 1936, Americans of European lineage comprised two-thirds of the agricultural workforce.[41] These Anglo farmworkers made some attempts at organizing between 1938 and 1939, but their efforts collapsed under violence at the hands of grower goons.[42] In fact, agriculturalists went so far as to collaborate with the local police to conduct clandestine operations that successfully undermined efforts to organize the farmworkers.[43] From the agribusiness perspective, these steps were necessary; unlike Mexican farmworkers, the Anglo laborers could not be threatened with deportation.[44]

Experiencing a tortuous withdrawal from their addiction to Mexican labor, growers rejoiced at the opportunity presented by the Second World War's labor shortage. For agriculturalists, the need for additional workers in 1942 offered an ideal opportunity to bring back Mexican farmworkers. However, this time the financial benefit to growers would be even greater: the U.S. taxpayer would help cover the expenses.[45]

The U.S. government initiated the bracero program on August 4, 1942, to alleviate the wartime labor shortage; it expired on December 31, 1964—nineteen years beyond the end of the Second World War.[46] Throughout the bracero program's twenty-two year run, the U.S. government maintained that the Mexican contract workers must be treated fairly, and that the braceros not to be used to replace domestic workers or to depress farm wages.[47] As the bracero program evolved during the 1940s, the government's oversight diminished and reports of farmworker mistreatment increased.[48] By 1951, the allegations of abuse became so widespread that the government of Mexico threatened to abrogate the agreement unless reforms were implemented.[49] The U.S. Congress reacted swiftly and passed Public Law 78 in 1951. The new legislation mandated increased government supervision of the bracero program and provided employers with clear guidelines regarding the treatment of Mexican contract workers.[50]

Growers welcomed Public Law 78, and successfully pressed Congress to renew the legislation five times until its December 1964 expiration.[51] Like previous immigrant farmworkers, braceros became a docile, inexpensive, and hardworking labor force. During the program's entire history there was not one recorded instance of braceros initiating a strike.[52] Braceros who complained about wages or working conditions were free to leave the farm, but would likely be deported if they did.[53]

Moreover, growers ensured an ample supply of Mexican contract workers by frequently making exaggerated requests for braceros.[54]

Attempts to organize the farmworkers during the bracero era proved feeble. In 1946, the American Federation of Labor (AFL) chartered the National Farm Labor Union (NFLU), with Ernesto Galarza as president.[55] Growers quickly crushed Galarza's organizing attempts by calling upon their virtually unlimited reserve of bracero labor to break strikes.[56] Of course, technically the braceros could not be employed as strikebreakers, but inconsistent law enforcement emboldened growers to flout such prohibitions.[57] Exacerbating the fledgling union's difficulties, the American Federation of Labor-Congress of Industrial Organizations (AFL-CIO; the AFL merged with the CIO in 1955) provided little support to the NFLU.[58] Apparently the AFL-CIO neglected the NFLU because several AFL-CIO affiliates had food production and distribution relationships with agribusiness, and it was in the economic interest of the aforementioned parties to preserve the status quo—even to the detriment of the farmworkers.[59]

By 1952, it became clear to Galarza that he could not successfully unionize the farmworkers as long as the bracero program existed. In that same year, the NFLU changed its name to the National Agricultural Workers Union (NAWU) and, importantly, redirected its efforts toward eradicating the bracero system by highlighting Public Law 78's catastrophic impact on the wages and working conditions of American farmworkers.[60] Through meticulous chronicling of the bracero program's injustices, the NAWU raised the public's awareness of the farmworkers' plight and ultimately contributed to the demise of Public Law 78.[61]

NAWU's attempts to discredit Public Law 78 inflamed already-strained relations with the AFL-CIO. In an effort to further undermine the NAWU, the AFL-CIO established the Agricultural Workers Organizing Committee (AWOC) in 1959.[62] According to Franz Daniels, assistant director of organization for the AFL-CIO, President George Meany "just got tired of going to international conventions and being needled by labor people from smaller, poorer countries, who could point out that at least they had organized farmworkers, while the American labor movement hadn't."[63] Fatigued by such criticisms, AFL-CIO president Meany simply "set up AWOC to get them off his back."[64]

Given such an inauspicious beginning, it comes as little surprise that the AFL-CIO demonstrated about as much enthusiasm for AWOC as it had for the NAWU. Norman Smith, a man without any experience organizing farmworkers, and apparently "little connection with the labor movement in general," was selected to head the organization.[65] Predictably, AWOC did not encounter immediate success, and the AFL-CIO, disappointed by AWOC's slow progress, decided to slash the union's funding.[66]

With organizing attempts stifled and the labor supply heavily weighted in the growers' favor, farmworkers accepted substandard wages and working conditions; however, their suffering did not go unnoticed. Religious organizations began to voice their objection to the bracero program. A young Catholic priest by the name of George Higgins spearheaded the Catholic Church's opposition. His efforts, guided by Catholic social teachings, contributed to the bracero program's demise, opened the path for Chávez's ascension, and paved the way for the partnership between César Chávez and the Catholic Church during the 1960s and 1970s.

George G. Higgins and the Farmworkers

Papal encyclicals provide the intellectual framework for the Catholic Church's engagement with America's labor movement. Therefore, to understand Catholic social action, we first must examine the Church's social teachings. The Magna Carta of encyclicals is Pope Leo XIII's 1891 letter, *Rerum Novarum* (the Condition of Labor).[67] Leo XIII's encyclical argued that workers, as the creators of a nation's wealth, deserve adequate compensation and reasonable working hours.[68] Toward this end, society must seek an equitable partnership among government, labor, and business.[69]

In 1931, Pope Pius XI penned the next Catholic social encyclical, titled *Quadragesimo Anno* (the Reconstruction of the Social Order). Written during a global economic depression, the letter condemned communism (a "dictatorship of the proletariat"), capitalism's injustices, and unregulated competition.[70] Pius XI exhorted business owners to demonstrate compassion and provide their laborers steady work, fair compensation, and the right to unionize.[71] *Quadragesimo Anno*, like *Rerum Novarum*, asserted that workers deserve compensation sufficient to "acquire moderate ownership."[72]

Pope John XXIII updated the teachings of Leo XIII and Pius XI with his 1961 encyclical, *Mater et Magistra* (Christianity and Social Progress).[73] A powerful teaching, *Mater et Magistra* warned the faithful that "it is not enough [to] merely formulate a social doctrine. It must be translated into reality."[74] Pope John XXIII's exhortation for the unionization of rural and agricultural workers inspired César Chávez and became a significant moral force in Chávez's effort to organize the farmworkers.

The two encyclicals that followed, *Gaudium et Spes* (the Church in the Modern World), in 1965, and Pope Paul VI's 1971 letter, *Octogesima Adveniens* (A Call to Action), seemed to speak directly to La Causa. *Gaudium et Spes* insisted that "God intended the earth for everyone," therefore, private property should be used for the good of all humankind.[75] *Octogesima Adveniens* supported labor's right to organize, and emphasized the importance of a "preferential respect for the poor."[76]

During the first half of the twentieth century, the director of the National Catholic Welfare Conference's (NCWC) Social Action Department (SAD), Father John Ryan, became the American Catholic hierarchy's point man for transforming encyclicals into social action. Prior to the First World War, the American hierarchy, for the most part, did not know each other and collaborated on few matters.[77] The Great War necessitated a unified voice, and in 1917 the hierarchy established the National Catholic War Council in Washington, D.C.[78] After the cessation of hostilities, the bishops decided to maintain the organization, but softened its name to the National Catholic Welfare Conference.

The NCWC's structure consisted of a board of directors and various departments. Bishops sat on the board and supervised the departments' staff. The NCWC's mission focused on promoting the Church's social agenda, supporting a variety of church-related institutions, fostering dialogue among the bishops, and serving as a venue to formulate official positions on issues of public debate.[79] From the outset, the U.S. Catholic bishops restricted the conference to an *advisory* role despite the fact that prominent bishops occupied the administrative board. Power within the U.S. Catholic hierarchy rested squarely with individual bishops, and the NCWC could not supersede the local authority.[80]

Father John Ryan took the SAD's helm in 1919, and by the time of his retirement in 1944 had become one of the Church's most respected labor priests. Born in Minnesota, Ryan attended seminary in St. Paul during the 1890s and continued his education at the doctoral level at The Catholic University of America in Washington, D.C.[81] During his studies, Ryan became captivated by *Rerum Novarum*'s message, and decided to spend his life advancing the social gospel.[82] In 1906, Father Ryan published his first major work, *A Living Wage*. Ryan's piece argued that laborers had a "moral right" to a respectable living and advocated basic worker protections such as a minimum wage, unemployment insurance, health and retirement benefits, and the right to organize.[83]

By 1919, Ryan had gained respect as a relentless advocate for the working person. Boldly speaking his mind, Ryan argued that "a small number of very rich men" had oppressed "the masses of the poor" via "a yoke little better than slavery itself."[84] Seeking change, he designed the Bishops' Program of Social Reconstruction, and assumed the directorship of the NCWC's SAD.[85] For the next twenty-five years, the SAD became Ryan's platform to implement his vision of a more just society. Under Ryan, the department became a major clearinghouse for Catholic thought on social and industrial relations.[86]

Soon after its inception, the SAD came under fire during the 1919–20 Red Scare.[87] The ensuing decade of the 1920s brought the department considerable challenges as the roaring twenties drowned out thoughts of social justice from the American psyche.[88] Despite these lean years for progressive causes, the SAD's staff of like-minded progressives persevered, and when the Great Depression struck, Ryan and his team were prepared to bridge the Progressive Era with the New Deal.[89]

The economic hardships of the 1930s made clear the need for social action.[90] The market had crashed, but John Ryan's standing rose. Pope Pius XI's 1931 encyclical *Quadragesimo Anno* gave Ryan near-prophet status because it reinforced his long-standing prolabor ideas.[91] Ryan's pronouncements were now understood as church policy, even if they had not received the hierarchy's blessing.[92] Much to the chagrin of conservative Catholics, Ryan's pronouncements went so far as to defend sit-down strikes and support the use of "force against the unjust aggression of an employer who refused to pay a just wage or who forced his workers to toil under dangerous conditions."[93]

Politically active, Ryan made great strides toward moving the Catholic Church from a marginalized faith group into mainstream America—in no small part due to his enthusiastic endorsement of Franklin D. Roosevelt's successful bid for the presidency. Ryan wanted social reform, and FDR delivered. In gratitude for Father Ryan's support, the Roosevelt administration called upon the priest for advice on resolving the depression era's most pressing social issues.[94] Pleased to serve FDR and the nation, Ryan readily assisted the administration's efforts to shape Social Security policy.[95] Ryan believed the government to be "the most important agent of social justice" and supported the New Deal reforms.[96] Some American Catholics opposed Ryan's activism due to concerns about increasing the power of a government dominated by Protestants; however, the majority of Catholic faithful supported FDR's social policies, reasoning that the New Deal encompassed the Catholic ideal of a "common good."[97]

Father Ryan's skillful melding of secular New Deal policies with Catholic social justice earned him the moniker "Right Reverend New Dealer."[98] Throughout the 1930s, Ryan continued to speak out against social inequalities. He argued that the Great Depression resulted from an income disparity between workers and business owners, and that the economic crisis could have been avoided if capital had provided labor with a living wage. If business owners had paid their laborers higher wages, the workers' increased consumer spending would have provided sufficient economic stimulus to avoid the collapse.[99]

To some people, Ryan's stand might have appeared controversial, but he was not a revolutionary. The Right Reverend New Dealer wanted peace and stability achieved through cooperation—not competition—with capital owners.[100] Ryan clearly supported the concept of private property, and he insisted that "capital had a right to a fair share of the profits after labor received its due."[101] Under Father Ryan's stewardship, the NCWC's SAD, and by extension the Catholic Church, had firmly established a prolabor tradition qualified by a solid defense of the right to private property.[102]

By the 1940s, an intense hostility toward communism suffused the nation, the labor movement, and the Catholic Church. There exists serious disagreement among scholars regarding the role of the Catholic Church in the labor movement during this era. For the purposes of this history, suffice it to say that anticommunist objectives influenced, but did not overwhelm, Catholic social action during the period. The deeds of progressive, prolabor clergy like Monsignor George Higgins, Father Raymond McGowan, Monsignor Francis Haas, and Charles Owen Rice serve to remind us that purging leftists did not become the hierarchy's sole focus during the 1940s.[103] Nonetheless, fighting communism did become a passion for some in the Catholic Church, and the Association of Catholic Trade Unionists (ACTU) served as a conduit for the bishops' efforts to purge unions of communist influences.[104]

ACTU had its roots in Peter Maurin and Dorothy Day's Catholic Worker Movement (CWM). Maurin and Day founded the CWM in response to the Great Depression's economic dislocation.[105] In 1933, the organization launched its newspaper, *The Catholic Worker*, and Day's writings on labor and race quickly attracted a significant following.

Between 1933 and 1935, circulation expanded from just twenty-five hundred to sixty-five thousand.[106] Although the CWM considered itself radical, even anarchist, it did not claim adherence to any specific ideology.[107] Instead, Maurin and Day exhorted their CWM members to act according to their "informed conscience," but always to maintain an "orthodox" respect for Church authority.[108] Above all, action became the CWM's hallmark. The Catholic Workers brought hot meals, clean sheets, and hope to the underprivileged through their network of soup kitchens and Houses of Hospitality.[109]

In 1937, an assortment of clergy, labor, and social activists inspired by the CWM founded the ACTU.[110] ACTU members, known as Actists, were mostly Catholic Workers who sought to help others by promoting organized labor.[111] These inaugural Actists diligently studied papal encyclicals and grounded their philosophy squarely in Catholic social doctrine.[112] This pleased many U.S. bishops, and the Actists delivered the gospel of unionism to working-class Catholics knowing they enjoyed the backing of the U.S. hierarchy.[113]

A decidedly progressive attitude initially permeated the ACTU, but, according to some scholars, the organization quickly moved to the right after breaking from the CWM.[114] While the CWM emphasized working with the underprivileged, some Actists found a greater sense of mission in purging leftists from the labor movement.[115] To achieve this end, Actists operated as a Catholic pressure group within existing unions; they reached out to non-Catholic members and urged them to expel communist influences. [116]

Despite its relatively small size (membership peaked in 1940 at fifteen hundred), ACTU played an important role helping to assure many Catholics that industrial unions were a legitimate means to social change.[117] Some scholars argue that by the late 1940s ACTU's efforts to fight leftists became such a singular focus that the organization collapsed after the CIO's successful purge of communists.[118] Indeed, by 1951, ACTU became, according to its leaders, "a very inactive organization."[119]

Out of this tumultuous decade of Catholic social action emerged Monsignor Higgins, a student of Father Ryan and an eventual friend of César Chávez. George Gilmary Higgins, the eldest son of C. V. Higgins and Anna Rethinger Higgins, entered the world on January 21, 1916.[120] From the Higgins's home in Springfield, Illinois, C. V. shaped his son's interests by exposing George to intellectual pursuits, politics, and church life.[121] After eighth grade, Higgins entered Quigley Preparatory Seminary and moved on to Saint Mary's Seminary in Mundelein, Illinois.[122] Seminary endowed George Higgins with a "sense of personal responsibility and an overwhelming interest in the social teaching of the church."[123] After ordination in 1940, Higgins left Illinois to enter doctoral studies at The Catholic University of America in Washington, D.C.

Higgins relished his time in the nation's capital—the center of national and American Catholic politics. While at The Catholic University of America, Higgins met the leading priests in Catholic social action, including Monsignor John Ryan, Father Raymond McGowan, and Father Francis Haas.[124] Inspired by such figures, Higgins, who eventually became known as the Labor Priest, decided to write his dissertation on "Voluntarism in Organized Labor in the United States," and graduated with his Ph.D. in 1944. Higgins's mentors at the Social Action Department recognized the young priest's talent, and invited him to join their cause. Enthusiastically accepting his new position, Higgins immediately put his "warm and gregarious people-skills" to work.[125]

As part of his outreach, Higgins began in 1945 to write a regular column, the "Yardstick." By the time Higgins finally quit his musings on social issues in 2001, his weekly column had appeared in the Catholic News Service and more than twenty newspapers.[126] The hierarchy recognized Higgins's excellent work, and it promoted him in 1955 to director of the Social Action Department.[127] As his reputation grew, Higgins increasingly became known as "the leading Catholic liaison with organized labor," and the "bridge that linked the social teaching of the late 19th Century and the present."[128]

During the 1950s, Higgins increased his involvement with migrant worker issues—an interest that played an important role in bolstering the Labor Priest's credentials as a friend of farm labor, and by extension, enhancing the reputation of the Church as an advocate for social justice. Higgins harshly criticized the bracero program and spearheaded the Church's successful efforts to terminate Public Law 78.[129] The National Citizens' Council for Migrant Labor (NCCML), an organization founded in 1947 to bring worker's compensation, social security, and health care to farmworkers, became the conduit for Higgins's initial foray into migrant worker justice.[130] In September 1947, Higgins joined the nascent NCCML, and although the Labor Priest did not assume a proactive role in the organization, he closely followed the organization's writings and criticisms of the bracero program.[131] Unfortunately, the NCCML folded three years later, but the experience peaked Higgins's interest in migrant worker issues.

Soon after the NCCML's demise, the National Advisory Committee

Both Monsignor Higgins (left) and Eleanor Roosevelt served on the National Advisory Committee on Farm Labor, which sought to improve the wages and working conditions of both foreign and domestic farmworkers. Richard Nixon (right) did not possess Monsignor Higgins and Mrs. Roosevelt's zeal for the farmworkers' cause. The three are pictured at the United Nations. (Photo courtesy of Catholic News Service)

on Farm Labor (NACFL) invited Higgins to join its board of directors.[132] The Labor Priest accepted and became part of a membership that included several senators, representatives, and Eleanor Roosevelt.[133] Much like the NCCML, the NACFL sought to eradicate the injustices suffered by both foreign and domestic farmworkers.[134] Toward this end, NACFL members launched a concerted public awareness campaign, much as César Chávez would do years later, to educate the populace about the farmworkers' plight. NACFL's media blitz included high-profile congressional testimony by several noted labor authorities on bracero abuses.[135]

In 1958, Monsignor Higgins testified before Congress on the bracero program's deleterious effects on wages and working conditions.[136] The Labor Priest contended that growers manipulated Public Law 78 to their advantage, mostly by inflating the labor supply so that agribusiness could leave American farmworkers jobless while exploiting Mexican laborers through low wages and poor working conditions.[137] Higgins's congressional testimony brought a deluge of letters, both supportive and condemnatory, from Catholics around the nation. Swimming in mail, Higgins must have realized that through his service at the NCCML and the NACFL, and because of his work with the NCWC's Social Action Department, he had become a recognized authority on migrant labor.[138]

One significant political figure, President Dwight D. Eisenhower's secretary of labor, James P. Mitchell, recognized Higgins's expertise and called upon the Labor Priest's services. In an action that signaled a shift in the national mood toward social concerns, Secretary Mitchell decided to scrutinize Public Law 78.[139] In January 1959, Mitchell formed a Committee on Migratory Labor to provide an expert opinion on the continued viability of Public Law 78.[140] Mitchell's team consisted of Edward J. Thye, a former U.S. senator from Minnesota; Dr. Rufus B. Bon Kleinsrnid, chancellor of the University of Southern California; Glenn E. Garrett, chairman of the Texas Council on Migrant Labor; and Monsignor Higgins.[141] Higgins, always holding Mitchell in the highest regard, felt privileged to serve a man he considered to be "a great humanitarian."[142]

Higgins and Garrett performed the bulk of the committee's work, and they traveled extensively to examine firsthand the impact of the bracero system on farmworkers. Troubled by their findings of "inhuman living conditions, and a program that simply did not work," Higgins became even more adamant that Public Law 78 should be drastically revised.[143]

At his core, Secretary Mitchell agreed with Higgins's assessment; however, Mitchell had to work in Washington, D.C., with a rough and powerful agribusiness lobby. In such a situation, a veneer of neutrality is critical to survival. For example, at one particular committee meeting Higgins began to forcefully express his opinion, when Mitchell cut him off and snapped, "Wait a minute, who do you think you are? Do you think that just because you're a priest you . . . [can] come in here and dominate this meeting?"[144] Stunned, Higgins quietly sat back. The Labor Priest had little fear of challenging people, but ever respectful of hierarchical authority, he did so quietly, one-on-one.

Later in the day, Higgins returned to Mitchell's office. As the atmosphere relaxed, Higgins turned to the secretary and fired off a sarcastic salvo, "Thanks a lot, Jim."

The secretary replied, "My God—couldn't you see what was up? I was just playing a little game. Of course I agreed with you."[145]

Mitchell's performance didn't win any Oscars, but it did make him a highly effective secretary of labor—and one whose methods Higgins would later attempt to imitate when the Bishops' Ad Hoc Committee on Farm Labor worked as a neutral mediator between growers and farmworkers.

The Mitchell Committee presented the secretary its report in October 1959. The document denounced the U.S. government's provision of an inexpensive, submissive labor force used to depress domestic wages, condemned Public Law's 78 deleterious impact on working conditions, and criticized the programs' detrimental effect on domestic workers.[146] Well aware of the potent agribusiness lobby's likely negative reaction to an outright abolition of the bracero program, the committee suggested that Public Law 78 be phased-out through a series of reforms.[147] Drawing upon the committee's recommendations, Secretary Mitchell testified before Congress in 1960 "that the [bracero] programs should be discontinued because of their adverse effects upon domestic workers."[148] Mitchell accepted his committee's pragmatic phase-out strategy and advised Congress that Public Law 78 "be drastically amended so as to prevent any adverse effect on American workers, ensure utilization of the domestic work force, and limit the use of Mexican contract workers to unskilled seasonal jobs."[149]

Mitchell and his collaborators did not directly abolish Public Law 78, but they did cast a sizable cloud of doubt over the bracero program's viability. Soon thereafter, the cloud burst into a torrent that eroded the system's foundation and swept away the "temporary" program created to alleviate a "wartime" labor shortage.[150] Monsignor Higgins, representing the Catholic Church's commitment to social justice, was at the center of the storm.

The 1960s was a watershed decade in Higgins's career. The U.S. bishops sent the Labor Priest to Rome as a *peritus* at all three sessions of the Second Vatican Council, where he participated in a committee that examined the layperson's role in the Catholic Church.[151] Vatican II radically transformed the ecclesiastical landscape and expedited the integration of the Catholic faithful into mainstream society. Ironically, the Second Vatican Council, held from October 1962 until December 1965, was rather unexpected.

Following the passing of Pope Pius XII in 1958, the cardinals met to select a successor but were unable to agree on any of the leading candidates. Instead, they selected a seventy-seven year old cardinal, whom they thought would be merely a short-term caretaker pope, named Angelo Roncalli from Venice, Italy. Cardinal Roncalli chose the name

Vatican II—Second Session. The Second Vatican Council, where Monsignor Higgins (far left) served on the commission investigating the role of the laity in the Church, influenced Higgins's perspective on social issues.

John XXIII, and although his tenure was short (he died in June 1963), the cardinals seriously misjudged his significance. Instead of merely being a caretaker, Pope John XXIII proved to be a man of extraordinary vision and convoked Vatican II just after assuming the papacy.[152] The gathering revolutionized the Church by creating new avenues for the organization to engage the modern world.[153]

Unfortunately, the interpretation of the council's documents spawned significant controversy. Although neither conservatives nor liberals argue about the council's legitimacy, some conservatives insist that the documents of Vatican II were "misinterpreted by ill-advised bishops, permissive clergy, and power-hungry lay people."[154] Liberals, in comparison, feel that the Vatican II reforms should have gone further, and that perhaps even a third Vatican council is necessary.[155] Regardless of differences in interpretation, by the late 1960s Vatican II and the Church's ascendancy into mainstream American political life had infused key members of the U.S. Catholic Church with a newfound sense of mission. With César Chávez's arrival on the national scene, the hierarchy seized upon this opportunity to express its newfound confidence.

By the mid-1960s Higgins enjoyed recognition as a staunch advocate for migrant workers; therefore, it comes as little surprise that he also demonstrated professional respect for another farmworker activist: César E. Chávez. Some of Higgins's first public comments on Chávez appeared in the April 18, 1966, edition of the "Yardstick," where he noted, "we haven't seen anyone like . . . [Chávez] in the American labor movement in many a long day."[156] Three months later, on July 18, Higgins bubbled with praise for Chávez's "inspired, not to say charismatic leadership," and went on to note that by "all accounts, he is a man of extraordinary genius and unimpeachable integrity."[157]

The two finally met in person during the summer of 1967 at the convention of the National Catholic Social Action Conference in Boston. They instantly connected. After their encounter, Higgins described Chávez as "an extraordinarily gifted leader possessed of a happy combination of unbending toughness and calm serenity, organizational shrewdness and prophetic vision, dead seriousness and a saving sense of humor —and of legitimate pride in his own Mexican-American heritage coupled with a remarkable degree of personal humility."[158]

The Labor Priest and Chávez shared a friendship that spanned the remainder of the 1960s and the 1970s. Although their relationship ruptured in the 1980s, their collaboration launched La Causa to its organizational and political apogees, and it engaged the Catholic Church in its most fruitful effort to actualize social justice in the latter part of the twentieth century. Chávez once remarked, "I doubt that anybody has done as much for us as Msgr. Higgins has."[159] But it could also be said that few layman had done as much to transform the Church's pronouncements of social justice into action as Chávez. *Los curas* (the priests) and La Causa became a team.

The Rise of César E. Chávez

"To give birth" in Spanish is *dar la luz*, literally, "to give light." In this spirit, Librado and Juana Chávez brought light into the world on March 31, 1927, with the birth of their son, César Estrada Chávez, near Yuma, Arizona. In 1938, the Chávez family's devastating loss of the farm that César's grandfather had homesteaded in the 1880s forced the family to uproot. Librado and Juana moved their family to the barrio of Sal Si Puedes (leave if you can) in San Jose, California, where Chávez dropped out of the eighth grade and, two years later, enlisted in the navy. Chávez did not enjoy his time in the service, and in 1946 returned to the fields of California at the end of his two-year military obligation. Soon thereafter, Chávez met a woman named Helen Fabela; the two married in 1948, and became partners for life.[160]

Chávez's vocational direction began to change in 1952, when a missionary priest by the name of Donald McDonnell entered Sal Si Puedes. McDonnell, attached to the Archdiocese of San Francisco, dreamed of seeing the farmworkers unionize.[161] He became the second significant spiritual mentor to Chávez, after César's mother, and the first person to suggest to Chávez that *he* should be the one to successfully organize California's farmworkers—a feat that had never been accomplished.[162]

McDonnell met Chávez by knocking on doors in the barrio, and the two rapidly became good friends.[163] McDonnell had much to teach, and Chávez much to learn. McDonnell explained the importance of papal encyclicals to Chávez and placed the teachings in the context of labor history.[164] Chávez listened. Intently.

McDonnell continued his instruction and commended Louis Fisher's *Life of Gandhi* to his young pupil.[165] The book resonated with Chávez as it built upon the philosophy of nonviolence that Juana Chávez instilled in her son.[166] Chávez greatly admired Gandhi and decided, like Gandhi, to dedicate his life to liberation of the poor through nonviolent tactics.[167]

Reflecting on McDonnell's impact on his life, Chávez remarked that McDonnell "told me about social justice, and the Church's stand on farm labor." So important to Chávez was McDonnell's tutelage that Chávez would follow the priest to the bracero camps, the city jails, and "would do anything to get the Father to tell more about labor history. . . . [Chávez would do] anything to be with him."[168]

McDonnell's spiritual influence spilled over into Chávez's later efforts to unionize the farmworkers and became an important component of the UFW's success. Chávez studied and respected many faith traditions, and although he was devoutly Catholic, his movement attracted assistance from a wide variety of faith-based organizations.[169] La Causa's ecumenical appeal likely stemmed from Chávez's penchant for sacrifice, moderation, honesty, and humility, and his persistent belief that because the farmworkers' cause was just, "he could be divinely guaranteed of eventual success."[170]

Chávez consciously integrated the Catholic faith into his movement. By doing so, he endowed the union with a strong sense of collective identity, and he brought a powerful moral and spiritual force into the organization.[171] Although Chávez did not impose any religious litmus test on the UFW's members, he did draw upon moral principals to guide his decisions.[172]

It was only natural for Chávez to include the Catholic faith in his union. The majority of UFW members were Hispanic and, at least nominally, Catholic. The Church played an undeniably strong role in the history, tradition, and culture of Latin America, and by invoking the faith, rituals, symbols, and authority of the Roman Catholic Church, Chávez brought a sense of solidarity among his followers.[173] The Virgin of Guadalupe, the patron saint of Mexico, became a natural rallying point for the UFW's faithful, and her likeness appeared at most UFW gatherings.[174] Even the UFW's headquarters, La Páz, short for Nuestra Señora de la Paz (Our Lady of Peace), bore evidence of Chávez's connection to the Church.[175]

Chávez's strong emphasis on the Catholic faith brought his union both spiritual encouragement and political backing.[176] On numerous occasions, Chávez acknowledged the potency of the Catholic Church as a temporal ally in the UFW's struggle.[177] In some rural California farm communities the Catholic Church had a virtual monopoly on the population; Chávez's identification with the Catholic faith in such instances greatly enhanced his union's image.[178] Additionally, Chávez's close association with the Catholic Church protected him from frequent allegations of communist sympathies.[179] Chávez once commented, "I go to unions for publicity and money; to the Church for respectability; to students for bodies."[180]

Not everyone in Chávez's union shared his enthusiasm for the Catholic Church or La Causa's emphasis on faith.[181] Jerry Cohen, who for years headed the UFW's legal team, admitted, "a lot of liberals and radicals were pissed" about Chávez's inclusion of faith in the union. They felt the prayer, fasting, and sacrifice were "phony and . . . taking away from work."[182] One exceptionally harsh critic of Chávez's faith, Antonio Orendian, the UFW's secretary-treasurer, described Chávez's fasts as "an embarrassing religious display that indirectly supported the hierarchy of the Roman Catholic Church."[183] Some UFW volunteers agreed with Orendian, finding "the mystical and Catholic character of the fast so offensive that they . . . quit," complaining that Chávez had acquired "a messiah complex."[184]

Whereas McDonnell nurtured Chávez's spiritual development, Fred Ross taught him how to organize. Ross was an associate of Saul Alinsky and he introduced Chávez to the Community Service Organization (CSO). Alinsky had founded the CSO to help the poor organize and maximize their political leverage. Ross became a disciple of this cause, and went to spread the message in Sal Si Puedes. Ross sought Father McDonnell's opinion on potential leaders in the barrio, and shortly thereafter met Chávez and convinced him to join the CSO.

Chávez began his tenure with the CSO in 1952 as a volunteer, but rapidly moved into a paid staff position. By 1958, Chávez had scaled up the ladder to become general director of the CSO—a post he retained until his resignation in 1962.[185] From this position of influence, Chávez sought to terminate the bracero program and organize farmworkers.[186] "More than anything else I wanted to help farm workers," Chávez recalled. "I began to realize that a farm workers' union was needed to end the exploitation of the workers in the fields."[187]

In 1958, Chávez went to Oxnard, California, to get a first-hand look at the bracero program. He found a corrupt system controlled by the growers in league with state and federal officials.[188] Chávez became incensed as he observed agribusiness' spurious cries of labor shortages, growers employing braceros part-time at depressed wages, and the injustice of charging the braceros exaggerated prices for food and housing.[189]

Over the next year, Chávez fought the inequities he witnessed sitting down. Gathering unemployed farmworkers, Chávez walked onto Oxnard farms that employed braceros, sat down, and refused to move.[190] Chávez had tried to be reasonable. For months prior to the sit-down strikes, he petitioned California state and U.S. government officials to employ domestic laborers instead of braceros.[191] They ignored Chávez's requests. Chávez sat down. Then the officials stood up and paid attention. The strikes caught the media's eye and resulted in an investigation into the employment practices of California's Farm Placement Service (FPS). The FPS chief and two other officials resigned.[192] Another FPS worker was subsequently fired for taking kickbacks from Oxnard growers.[193]

Agribusiness took note. César E. Chávez was an emerging and potent farmworker activist. He crossed swords with growers and won. Importantly, Chávez realized that, under the proper leadership, the farmworkers *could* successfully organize.[194]

Chávez had tasted victory and wanted more. The issue of organizing the farmworkers came to a head at the CSO's March 1962 convention in Calexico, California.[195] Chávez offered to forego a year's salary for an opportunity to start a farmworker union.[196] When Chávez's CSO colleagues rejected his proposal, he simply stood up and said, "I resign."[197]

Chávez was out of a job but not out of options. Before he reached the Calexico city limits, the Agricultural Workers Organizing Committee offered him a position. Chávez politely declined AWOC's invitation; he correctly felt that the union was ineffective at organizing and doomed for failure.[198] Sargent Shriver, head of the Peace Corps, also made Chávez an attractive offer to oversee operations in four Latin American countries.[199] The work didn't appeal to Chávez, and he turned down this chance for a steady paycheck. Instead, Chávez looked to his former colleague, Dolores Huerta, to help him build a farmworkers' union.

Chávez had met Huerta through his work at the CSO, where her leadership, character, intellect, and confidence greatly impressed him.[200] Huerta had extensive experience registering voters, fighting segregation, and lobbying for farmworker rights.[201] Chávez and Huerta shared the same objectives, but often clashed over methods.[202] Despite these differences, or perhaps because of them, in 1962 Chávez invited Huerta to join his cause.[203]

Chávez decided to make his stand in Delano, California. Central to the California table grape industry, flush with farms and year-round work, Delano had a high proportion of nonmigratory farmworkers—a potential core constituency for Chávez's union.[204] Moreover, Chávez had relatives in the area that could provide necessary support.[205] For six months, Chávez tirelessly drove up and down the Central Valley planting an idea.[206] He didn't speak of a union, but rather "a vaguely defined organization of like-minded individuals."[207] If the farmworkers wanted to improve their wages and working conditions, then Chávez could provide the venue.[208]

Chávez's message touched the farmworkers. They wanted change. With the winding down of the bracero program and the rise of the Civil Rights movement, the time was right.[209] Chávez convoked the first National Farm Workers Association's (NFWA) convention in September 1962. An optimistic spirit electrified the atmosphere surrounding the 232 people gathered in Fresno, California.[210] The group elected Chávez to the presidency and Dolores Huerta and Gil Padilla as vice presidents, and Antonio Orendian took responsibility for the union's finances as secretary-treasurer.[211]

Over the next three years, Chávez and his lieutenants labored diligently in the shadows to construct a viable union. After September 8, 1965, however, Chávez's days of anonymity were numbered. On that day, eight hundred AWOC grape pickers walked out of the vineyards in Delano, upset that Coachella Valley growers had imported braceros for the harvest despite the fact that Public Law 78 had expired in December 1964.[212] The Department of Labor had issued the special dispensation using the Public Law 414 loophole of the McCarran Act.[213] California governor Pat Brown had convinced Secretary of Labor Willard Wirtz to invoke this exception; apparently, Californian agriculturalists could not find a sufficient number of domestic farmworkers to complete the harvest.[214]

Adding to the domestic farm laborers' frustration, braceros earned fifteen cents per hour more than Filipino-American farmworkers, and a full thirty cents per hour over the rate allotted to Mexican Americans for exactly the same work.[215] Although the braceros required higher wages than domestic laborers, growers apparently accepted the additional costs as insurance against unionization efforts by domestic workers—a distinct possibility with the expiration of Public Law 78.

The Filipino-dominated AWOC and the predominantly Mexican American NFWA had a common cause, yet Chávez hesitated to join AWOC's strike because he felt the nascent NFWA was unprepared for such a major undertaking. From a financial perspective, Chávez's concerns were well founded. The NFWA had only eighty-seven dollars in savings.[216] Dolores Huerta appeared not to agonize over such details and headed straight for the AWOC picket line.[217] Chávez had to make a decision. He did, and in 1965 on September 16, Mexican independence day, the NFWA joined AWOC's strike.[218]

Within a year, AWOC and NFWA joined forces to become the United Farm Workers Organizing Committee (UFWOC).[219] As the union's president, Chávez fostered solidarity between the union's ethnically diverse constituencies by incorporating symbols and rituals that accentuated the commonality of the members' Catholic faith. Altars began to appear in station wagons outside fields.[220] Catholic priests became a regular fixture at UFWOC gatherings and provided God's blessing to La Causa.[221]

Chávez also employed the services of another powerful institution to help his cause: the media. Understanding the power of print, radio, and television, Chávez regularly seized upon opportunities to develop relationships with opinion shapers. By earning their sympathy, he ensured that the farmworkers' side of the story reached the general populace. Chávez correctly assumed that the public, once aware of the farmworkers' predicament, would rally to the side of the underprivileged and become an invaluable pressure group.[222]

In March 1966 Chávez brought La Causa into the media spotlight and onto the national stage when he issued his Plan of Delano, and embarked on a march from Delano to Sacramento. Religious implications suffused the three-week procession to California's capital. It ended on Easter Sunday, and some observers drew a parallel between the march and a penitential Lenten procession focused on prayer and atonement for past sins.[223] Chávez used his Plan of Delano to explain the affair by drawing heavily upon Mexican tradition and history (major events in Mexico tend to commence with a document titled "Plan of . . .").[224] The plan envisioned farmworker justice in the context of faith, "suffering, dignity, and sacrifice," and emphasized the critical importance of the Catholic Church's support for La Causa.[225]

If the media were some of the most potent tools in Chávez's arsenal, it acted as the bow that delivered the arrow of the boycott. The boycott rapidly became the most deadly weapon in the UFWOC's quiver because consumers' decisions to stop purchasing nonunion grapes impacted growers' bottom lines.[226] The growers were businessmen, and nothing got their attention quicker than a sharp drop in profits.

Chávez announced his first boycott of California grapes on December 2, 1965, and over the next year he expanded the embargo to cover every single grape grower involved in the Delano Strike.[227] La Causa turned to the boycott when the strike lost its efficacy under the stress of unrelenting injunctions by local magistrates, routine terminations of pro-union farmworkers, and violence on the farmworkers' picket lines.[228]

Tired of the growers' crafty lawyers, Chávez and his legal team decided to beat them at their own game. Taking advantage of the 1935 National Labor Relations Act's (NLRA's) failure to extend protection of workers' right to organize and bargain collectively to agricultural laborers, the UFWOC's legal team successfully argued that because the NLRA didn't cover the farmworkers, its 1947 amendment proscribing secondary boycotts, known as Taft-Hartley, did not apply.[229] In a stroke of legal brilliance, Chávez's lawyers turned what had been perceived as a weakness (that is, the NLRA's failure to cover agricultural labor) into an asset.[230] The result enabled farmworkers and consumers to combine forces and threaten agriculturalists' profits.[231]

During the prolonged 1965–70 Delano Grape Strike, the UFW and its striking workers were fortunate to receive significant assistance from numerous clergy and laity who volunteered their money, time, and efforts for La Causa.[232] Additionally, the AFL-CIO and several unions provided strike support in the form of food, cash, and office equipment.[233]

Throughout the strike, Chávez remained committed to nonviolence; however, some of his opponents did not. Growers, frequently with the tacit support if not outright aid of local law enforcement officials, harassed, beat, and shot farmworkers.[234] Appalled by such brutal acts on the picket line, Chávez conducted a twenty-five day fast to renew his commitment to nonviolence in February–March 1968.[235] Again keeping the media close to his side, Chávez through the fast attracted considerable press and engendered notable public sympathy for the farmworkers.[236]

Chávez ended his high-profile fast by breaking bread with fellow Catholic senator Robert Kennedy.[237] During the encounter, Senator Kennedy called Chávez "one of the heroic figures of our time."[238] Both Kennedy and Chávez shared a vision of a more just society, and both realized the political value one brought to the other; therefore, it came as little surprise when Kennedy invited Chávez to be one of his delegates to the Democratic Convention. Chávez graciously accepted the invitation, and he rallied La Causa's volunteers campaign for Kennedy in precincts that would bring him the Chicano vote.[239]

By 1968, the violence and legal injunctions against the farmworkers' pickets had reached such a fevered pitch that Chávez decided to shift gears and throw the boycott into overdrive. This bold move staked the UFWOC's future squarely on the boycott's success. Chávez's new strategy entailed ratcheting up the UFWOC's boycott efforts to a national and international level. Chávez moved many of his best people into boycott offices located in major urban centers and charged them with raising public awareness of and support for the union's boycott of all California grapes.[240] This broad-based 1968 protest effort against all California grapes is now known as the famous "grape boycott."[241]

More than an innovative strategy, the national/international boycott proved to be a logistical feat. Through its strategically placed boycott offices, the UFWOC coordinated a broad coalition of students, a medley of Catholic, Protestant, and Jewish faithful, liberal activists, AFL-CIO locals, support from international labor unions (for instance, those from the United Kingdom and Sweden), and the farmworkers' families to successfully promote an extensive boycott of California grapes.[242] Students demanded that school cafeterias be rid of California grapes while shoppers excoriated their grocers for peddling the forbidden fruit of the vine. By 1969, the squeeze from consumers prompted the growers to seek, and find, assistance from two prominent California politicians: President Richard Nixon and California governor Ronald Reagan.[243]

Neither Reagan nor Nixon appeared to hold La Causa in high esteem.[244] Reagan expressed his antipathy toward Chávez's union by defiantly consuming grapes and declaring the boycott "immoral."[245] In

September 1968, Reagan characterized grape strikers as "barbarians."[246] Governor Reagan instructed the State Board of Agriculture to produce antiboycott literature, and ordered state agencies to send welfare recipients and prison inmates to replace striking farmworkers.[247] The California State Supreme Court eventually struck down Reagan's mandate to replace agricultural laborers with convicts.[248] Equally unsympathetic to La Causa, President Nixon suggested that the "illegal" boycott be crushed "with the same firmness we condemn illegal strikes, illegal lockouts, or any other form of lawbreaking."[249]

The fight in the Delano vineyards ended on July 29, 1970, due in large part to the combination of an effective boycott and the mediation efforts of the U.S. Catholic Church; specifically, the Bishops' Committee on Farm Labor. Growers covering almost half of California's table grape crop and roughly eight thousand farmworkers signed contracts with the UFWOC. These agreements provided farm laborers with wages of $1.80 an hour—40 cents more than they had requested at the strike's beginning.[250]

Chávez became the first person to successfully organize California's farmworkers. In retrospect, it seems almost intuitive that a union with a predominantly Catholic membership led by a devout Catholic would seek and receive assistance from the Catholic Church. In reality, the decision of the Catholic hierarchy to assist La Causa met significant resistance from within the Church itself. But upon closer examination, this should come as no surprise. The growers were Catholic, the farmworkers were Catholic, and both wanted the Church on their side.

2 CHÁVEZ AND THE BISHOPS' AD HOC COMMITTEE

Catholic Growers, Catholic Farmworkers

"It was awful," recalled Cardinal Roger Mahony of Los Angeles during an interview for the 1996 documentary *The Fight in the Fields*. "It was a terrible, terribly difficult situation," he continued, "because virtually all of the growers and all of the farmworkers were Catholics." "So what happened almost overnight," Mahony explained, "was both sides said, 'Well since we're Catholics, the Church must be on our side.' Well the problem was we had both sides saying the same thing."[1]

The Catholic News Service (CNS) had a similar recollection of the 1965–70 situation in California's vineyards, calling it one "of three great social battles that wracked America in the 1960s."[2] Of the three—the Civil Rights movement, the Vietnam War, and the farmworkers' struggle—"it was the farm labor battle that was uniquely Catholic."[3] CNS contends that the Delano Grape Strike "pitted Catholic Hispanic migrant laborers against Catholic grape growers in California."[4] The *Fresno Bee*, one of the Central Valley's leading newspapers, corroborates CNS's assertion, noting, "farmworker organization attempts, coupled with harvest-time strikes and the secondary boycott . . . split Catholic believers, many of whom are growers."[5]

The problem, according to a 1973 National Catholic News Service article, was that Chávez became "a thorn in the side of some Church officials" during the early 1960s.[6] The Catholic clergy in California's Central Valley initially hesitated to endorse Chávez's union because the farmworkers challenged the very growers who were the Church's largest contributors.[7] Agriculturalists were the major benefactors for many of the Central Valley's schools and churches, and in some of the area's smaller communities, an entire parish would be dependent upon the largess of one or two growers.[8] Dolores Huerta put it bluntly: "Most of the growers are Catholics," and priests in the Central Valley are "scared to death to come out for the farmworkers because [they are] dependent on local growers for big contributions."[9]

Whereas growers (many of Slavonian, Italian, and Irish descent) stuffed the Church's coffers, Catholic farmworkers (mostly of Mexican and Filipino descent) filled the pews.[10] Unfortunately, the laborers were often so impoverished that they had difficulty providing for basic necessities such as clothing, food, and shelter, much less finding money to tithe.[11] Faced with such a stark reality at the beginning of Chávez's struggle, some Central Valley clergy sided with the agriculturalists and provided tacit support for the growers' attempts to thwart farmworker unionization.[12]

During the early 1960s, the bishop of Fresno, Aloysius J. Willinger, allegedly told the editor of the diocese's newspaper, the *Register*, that there was to be "no mention of the farm labor problem" for fear "that the rich growers would stop supporting diocesan programs."[13] To his credit, the editor successfully insisted that Chávez had to be covered.[14] Throughout the decade, the farm labor struggle created "an obvious split in the Christian community within the Valley," with "many of the younger priests . . . speak[ing] out openly on the question of social justice for the farmworkers."[15]

As the Church became more deeply involved in the intrafaith dispute, and as the clergy began to shift their sympathies from quiet support for the growers (during the early 1960s) to tacit support for the farmworkers (by 1970), agriculturalists expressed their displeasure with the Church by withholding donations.[16] Catholic farmers in the Central Valley boycotted the Diocese of Fresno's newspaper, the *Register*, and forced it to close its doors in 1972—two years after the Delano Grape Strike ended.[17] Apparently, local growers were slow to forgive the clergy's eventual support for Chávez. The *Register*'s editor, Gerald Sherry, explained that the paper was "never able to regain advertising . . . nor . . . subscriptions because of the split in the Catholic community."[18]

While Catholic growers clashed with Catholic farmworkers, the bishops were reluctant to publicly choose sides in this intrafaith conflict, and frequently ended up doing little or nothing to address the battle raging at their doorstep. Bishop Ricardo Ramirez of Las Cruces, New Mexico, corroborates this perspective by reminding us that he was "not proud" that Chávez initially "encountered a lack of cooperation and even opposition from church authorities."[19] Only in 1969, a full four years into the Delano Grape Strike, did the hierarchy take action through the Ad Hoc Committee. Because of the bishops' reluctance to quarrel publicly, or for that matter even seriously address the situation until 1968, public intra-clergy disagreements on the matter are somewhat limited. The Bishops' Ad Hoc Committee on Farm Labor did have its detractors, but the majority of priests, and of course the hierarchy itself, supported the committee's work.

Two of the Bishops' Committee's most outspoken critics of the cloth were Jesuit priests: Father Daniel Lyons and Father Cletus Healy. Lyons and Healy spearheaded the clerical opposition to the hierarchy's involvement in La Causa using the *Twin Circle*—a conservative paper published independently of the Catholic hierarchy.[20] Founded in November 1967, the *Twin Circle* sought to spread its message of "faith and freedom" with an impressive circulation of one hundred thousand.[21] The paper did not contest the farmworkers' right to organize—that had become a matter of papal directive with *Mater et Magistra*; instead, the *Twin Circle* took issue with the Ad Hoc Committee's reported pro-Chávez bias, and with Higgins's alleged penchant for compulsory unionism.[22]

Lyons's writings continuously insisted that Chávez was a fraud.[23] Healy agreed, and claimed that Chávez did "not represent the majority of the workers, and [was] not supported by even one percent of the Catholic clergy."[24] The *Twin Circle* insinuated that Saul Alinsky, described as "a radical organizer who turns Church leaders . . . into blocs of militant revolutionaries," had mesmerized Chávez and turned him into a communist sympathizer.[25] Monsignor Higgins felt the communist allegations were "so grossly unjust" that he found "it difficult to respond . . . without losing [his] temper."[26] Higgins maintained his composure, and countered that the Ad Hoc Committee and "many of the growers" judged the UFWOC to be "a completely reputable and thoroughly democratic organization."[27]

The *Twin Circle* held Chávez in contempt, and it felt equal antipathy for Monsignor Higgins. The publication's editorials characterized Higgins as a one-dimensional stooge who believed "that labor unions are all paragons of virtue."[28] In a May 10, 1970, editorial, the *Twin Circle* dubbed Higgins the "canonizer of all union causes" who sought to "put all the farm workers . . . under the control of some distant big-city labor leader."[29] A week later, the paper went further and accused Higgins, the "croaking old voice of the Catholic Left" and a "perennial advocate of compulsory unionism," of imposing his uninformed "big-city" ideas on local farmers.[30]

Tired of the attacks on Chávez, the Ad Hoc Committee and Higgins himself fired off an aggressive rebuttal to the Reverend Lyons.

The Labor Priest accused his Jesuit interlocutor of going "to desperate lengths in an effort to portray Bishop Donnelly [chairman, Bishops' Ad Hoc Committee] as a prejudiced pro-union partisan."[31] Higgins accused Lyons of "recklessly tampering with the record," and took extreme umbrage at Father Healy's "persistent efforts to smear the personal reputations of Chávez and his community-organizing mentor, Saul Alinsky."[32] He called Father Healy's rhetoric "totally reprehensible," and concluded that the Jesuit had gone "off the deep end."[33]

Higgins continued his dogged pursuit of the *Twin Circle* by hounding publisher Dale Francis. Higgins told Francis that he was "out of touch" and had "a complete misreading of the situation in California."[34] Moreover, Higgins let Francis know that the Ad Hoc Committee's "role in the farm labor dispute would be made a little easier if papers like *Twin Circle* were to get off their anti-Chávez kick and try to find out what's really happening."[35] Higgins wanted to spend his "time and energy working constructively to solve a problem," and wished the "*Twin Circle* were disposed to give [the Ad Hoc Committee] a hand instead of spending so much time and energy sniping . . . from the sidelines."[36]

Higgins's intellectual combat with the *Twin Circle* earned him Chávez's gratitude. In a letter to Higgins, Chávez expressed his appreciation for the Labor Priest's efforts "to refute the vicious attacks of Father Healy . . . and to bring a just solution to the farm worker's struggle for Union recognition."[37] Higgins counseled Chávez not to "take Father Lyons and Father Healy too seriously," because ultimately, "they are fighting a losing battle."[38] Higgins called the *Twin Circle*'s attempts to destroy Chávez's reputation as "absolutely beneath contempt," and felt that Lyons, in short, had "a very sick mind."[39]

If Healy had indeed gone "off the deep end," Lyons apparently decided to follow his colleague off the pier on July 12, 1970. In a scathing editorial against the Ad Hoc Committee, Lyons directly challenged the judgment of several powerful members of the Catholic hierarchy. His opinion piece accused the Bishops' Committee of confusing "compulsory unionism" with "negotiations," and claimed that the farmworkers were not an oppressed people.[40] Moreover, Lyons implied that Chávez had hoodwinked the entire Catholic hierarchy by getting "all the Catholic bishops . . . behind him officially," when "only a few Catholic bishops are actively behind him."[41]

Outraged, the Ad Hoc Committee blasted back just three days later in a widely covered press release. "It is incredible that a publication calling itself 'Catholic' should publish such a collection of untruths, innuendos, distortions and plain inaccuracies," began the Bishops' Committee's statement.[42] The bishops' accused the *Twin Circle* of "crude attempts to pit priest against priest, and bishop against bishop."[43] The committee charged Lyons with not even having "the courtesy of seeking" the bishops' perspectives, and of selectively using sources hostile to their work.[44] Perhaps most frustrating for the bishops was the fact that *Twin Circle* had attempted to undercut fellow clergy and undermine public confidence in the Ad Hoc Committee's work.[45]

The bishops' strong rebuke sent shockwaves through the Church. In a separate interview, Ad Hoc Committee chairman Donnelly remarked that he didn't waste time on the *Twin Circle* because the publication was "either very stupid or it deliberately misstate[d] the facts."[46] "It is incredible to read this mishmash of untruths," Donnelly lamented, "from beginning to end the report is a fraud on its readers."[47] PADRES, an association of Mexican American priests, also were "appalled and disgusted at the anti-farmworkers stance of the *Twin Circle*," and suggested that the publication practiced "a subtle form of bigotry."[48] The *Los Angeles Times* took note of the controversy and commented that the Ad Hoc Committee's attack on a national Catholic newspaper was the harshest since the Kansas City–St. Joseph Diocese's 1968 blast against the *National Catholic Reporter* for allegedly being a "poisonous publication" and a "platform for the airing of heretical views on the church."[49]

The outcry prompted the chairman of the *Twin Circle*'s board, Archbishop Robert Dwyer of Portland, Oregon, to suggest "the best interests of the Church would be served by Father Lyons' resignation."[50] Father Lyons left the paper, but tried to couch his departure in terms of a misunderstanding.[51] Almost five years later, Gerald Sherry, acting in his capacity as editor of the Archdiocese of San Francisco's newspaper, provided an assessment of Lyons's veracity. Commenting on a July 6, 1975, column Lyons wrote for *California Farm Labor*, Sherry alleged that Lyons's work was "replete with untruths and gross distortions of the facts."[52] Lyons, Sherry concluded, "has prior obligations to the truth—and he hasn't told it yet."[53] Eventually, Lyons was laicized.[54]

The second notable intraclergy rift in California came from Father Mike Cross, a Catholic priest based in the Salinas Valley. Father Cross's stance against the Ad Hoc Committee began to garner media attention during the Battle of the Salad Bowl. Unlike the Delano Grape Strike, the Battle of the Salad Bowl yields little evidence to suggest that the majority of growers were Catholic. Public intraclergy debate regarding the Ad Hoc Committee's work was relatively small during the Delano Grape

Strike, but it was even less notable during the Battle of the Salad Bowl.
During the 1970–77 conflict among growers, the Teamsters, and the
UFWOC, the bishops lined up behind the Ad Hoc Committee and minimized clerical dissent. Father Cross, one of the few priests who publicly
opposed the hierarchy's position, provides a valuable alternative perspective of the Ad Hoc Committee's contribution, or lack thereof, to the
farmworkers' struggle.

Father Cross accused members of the Bishops' Committee of exceeding their authority, having a pro-UFWOC bias, and hurting the reputation of the Catholic Church. Cross believed that the work of the Ad
Hoc Committee fostered "resentment for the Church, bitterness, and
sometimes hatred with the intention of getting even . . . [with] the Catholic Church in the Salinas Valley."[55] In a letter to Cardinal John Dearden,
chairman of the National Conference of Catholic Bishops, Cross described his concern that the Ad Hoc Committee had brought the Church
in the Salinas Valley "grave injury."[56] He claimed that because the bishops had exceeded "the authority conferred upon them by the National
Conference of Catholic Bishops," they had "created a critical credibility
gap between large numbers of the faithful and their clergy."[57] Because
the UFWOC "is Catholic from all outward appearances," Cross continued, one could reasonably infer that "the Catholic Church [had] either become a tool of a labor union or the labor union [had] become a
tool of the Catholic Church."[58] Cross argued that the Ad Hoc Committee,
"while publicly proclaiming themselves 'neutral mediators' . . . were de
facto conscious and biased advocates of UFWOC."[59]

Cross did not perceive his dissent as harmful to the farmworkers'
cause. To the contrary, he supported "the papal teachings on social
justice," and favored "the Church's effort to promote the civil rights
of the Mexican-American workers, specifically their right to organize
and bargain collectively."[60] However, Cross took issue with the Bishops'
Committee's concept of social justice. In his opinion, "social justice by
definition . . . [required] impartiality among parties concerned," but
he felt that "this touchstone of impartiality . . . was tragically absent
from [the committee's] activities in the Salinas Valley."[61] To staunch the
Church's hemorrhaging reputation, Cross suggested Dearden "appoint
a commission to visit the Salinas Valley, investigate the activities of these
representatives of the Bishops' Committee on Farm Labor and report its
conclusions to the National Conference of Catholic Bishops." If for some
reason Dearden doubted his allegations, Cross offered to provide "evidence to support [his] contentions."[62]

USCC/NCCB general secretary Joseph Bernardin responded to Father Cross's letter on behalf of Cardinal Dearden, and insisted that the Ad Hoc Committee served as a bridge, not an instrument of the UFWOC. Bernardin forcefully rejected "out of hand" Cross's "harsh charges" that the Committee acted "as . . . 'biased advocates' [and] were working under conditions 'imposed by UFWOC.'" Expressing full confidence in the Ad Hoc Committee's reports, Bernardin remarked that "the National Conference of Catholic Bishops has been kept fully informed of the activities of the Committee," and that the group "has been commended by the Bishops of the Conference and it continues to have their full confidence." Bernardin politely expressed appreciation for Cross's concern and assured the priest that "if there were any evidence that the Committee has not acted properly, action would be taken to correct the situation."[63]

Unsatisfied with this response, Father Cross again wrote Cardinal Dearden to criticize the "verdict of Bishop Bernardin." Cross asserted that Bernardin gave "no consideration to the evidence substantiating [the] complaints," and went on to request that Dearden allow him "at least five minutes before the Executive Committee of the NCCB" to present his "overwhelming evidence."[64]

The USCCB archives contain the following handwritten note by Bernardin, dated November 10, 1970, that appeared to end the conference's dialogue with Father Cross: "Called [wording illegible] Church. He said Fr. Cross had become almost irrational. He feels that *no* [emphasis Bernardin's] further answer should be given—all he is seeking now is publicity. Even some of the growers have rejected him."[65]

Cross's ordinary, Bishop Harry Clinch of Monterey, California, publicly reprimanded his subordinate. "It is regrettable," stated Clinch, "that a young Catholic priest of Salinas saw fit to accuse the national Catholic Bishops' Committee of prejudice in the current mediation."[66] Clinch reiterated that the Ad Hoc Committee enjoyed "the full confidence of this diocese . . . and the National Conference of Catholic Bishops."[67]

Cross ignored the rebuke and continued his criticism of the Ad Hoc Committee. Importantly, Cross publicly acknowledged the limited extent of public clerical dissent against the Bishops' Committee. "I feel in conscience, as one priest—and one who undoubtedly stands alone—that" the role of the Ad Hoc Committee "certainly was not the role of [a] peacemaker."[68] Although mostly a lone voice within the clergy, Cross did have his supporters; namely, the Special Committee in Support of Father Mike Cross.[69] When questioned about the organization, Cross indicated that "the committee was composed of concerned Catholics in the Salinas area," but he "didn't know whether any growers were members of the group."[70]

Throughout 1970 and 1971, Father Cross stayed at the forefront of opposition to César Chávez.[71] In October 1972, the vicar general of the Monterey Diocese and a close friend of Father Cross, Monsignor Thomas Earley, publicly joined the anti-UFWOC cause.[72] Given Salinas' central location in the Battle of the Salad Bowl, it comes as little surprise that clergy in the Diocese of Monterey were sharply divided over the appropriate role of the Catholic Church in the farm labor controversy.

Earley and Cross sent an open letter to the nation's Catholic Priests supporting the *Lettuce Story*, a publication backed by lettuce growers that accused Chávez of "demanding a monopoly in agricultural unionization, and, with it, control of the nation's food supply."[73] The accompanying letter accused "poorly informed churchmen," an obvious reference to the Ad Hoc Committee's members, of exceeding their jurisdiction.[74] Not surprisingly, once Higgins obtained Earley's letter to "The Priests of the United States," the Labor Priest chaffed at Earley's claim that "as a result of involved but poorly informed churchmen, not only our farmers, but more especially our farm workers have suffered in their pursuit and right to self-determination."[75]

Higgins promptly wrote "Tom" to inform him that, although he didn't mind the disagreement, he did "question the advisability of . . . saying that we [that is, Higgins and other members of the Ad Hoc Committee] are 'poorly informed.'"[76] Although not residents of Salinas, Higgins told Earley that members of the Ad Hoc Committee nonetheless had "a substantial amount of information about the background of this dispute which apparently . . . [hadn't] yet come to . . . [his] attention"; "more specifically . . . [the bishops had] a great deal of information about the relationship between the Teamsters and UFWOC which the local growers . . . [had] yet to pass along to" Monsignor Earley. Higgins pressed the point further by adding that the committee was "present (as you were not) at the secret negotiating session in August 1970 that resulted in a one-year jurisdictional pact between the parties."[77]

Higgins mercilessly continued to pound Earley. The phrase "poorly informed" must have upset the Labor Priest, and it caused him to unleash his pen at the vicar general of the Monterey Diocese:

> You will also recall that we were present in Monterey approximately a year later when the parties renewed this jurisdictional agreement for

a period of three years. Much of what was said and agreed to by the parties at these two negotiating sessions was not put in writing and has never been made public. There is nothing in your letter to indicate that you have even heard about it. I am sorry about that. If you had taken the trouble to get in touch with us before you wrote your letter, we would have been happy to bring you up to date.[78]

If Earley decided to continue reading Higgins's letter, he would have quickly discovered that the Labor Priest was merely warming up. The best was yet to come.

"Forgive me for saying that I am sorry, for your sake," Higgins continued, "that you have permitted the Farm Bureau to use your prestige in this way for its own propaganda purposes."[79] By doing so, Higgins told Earley that he "clearly left the impression (whether you intended to or not) that you disagree with the California bishops' statement." Reprimanding Earley for contradicting his superiors, Higgins insisted that the vicar general "owe[ed] it to the bishops and to the priests of the United States to clarify [his] position on this matter." Higgins continued upbraiding Earley: "I am sorry that you don't agree with our approach to the problem"; moreover, continued the Labor Priest, "[I am] deeply disappointed that you felt it necessary to undercut our efforts (and the efforts of the California bishops) by associating yourself so closely with the propaganda campaign of the Farm Bureau Federation."[80]

Higgins also reminded Earley that publicly undercutting the hierarchy had negative career repercussions. "I think you have made an extremely serious mistake," blasted Higgins, "and I hope that you will find it possible to neutralize the harm which your letter will undoubtedly do to the farm workers' cause." Salting the wound, Higgins added, "I am also distressed by the fact that your letter will undoubtedly hurt your own reputation among many of your fellow priests in the United States. I have already received information from various sources indicating that a number of priests think that you have been taken in by the Farm Bureau Federation. If possible, I think you ought to take the necessary steps to correct this impression."[81]

Chairman Donnelly also assailed Earley, claimed that he deplored Earley's reflections on the committee, and felt that the priest had been used by the lettuce growers.[82] When confronted with the fact that by 1973 several bishops throughout the nation had issued "statements in support of [the UFW's] lettuce boycott," Earley and Cross simply dismissed them.[83] "I never saw Cardinal O'Boyle [a pro-Chávez supporter and retired archbishop of Washington, D.C.] here in Salinas," snapped Cross.[84] "We don't know what's happening, say, on the Mexican Border, or over in Utah, or places like that," Cross reasoned, yet bishops like O'Boyle have "the cannons that they're loading . . . aimed at the Salinas Valley."[85] Earley concurred with Cross's assessment and had "no regrets whatever" for the October 1972 letter.[86]

Throughout the mid-1970s, the Diocese of Monterey continued to be a bastion of clerical opposition to the work of the Bishops' Ad Hoc Committee. Higgins discovered the California Central Coast's next Doubting Thomas in February 1974 while advising a group Canadian clergy who were visiting California to examine the farm labor controversy. During the course of the meeting, one of the Canadian priests provided Higgins with a "very disturbing" letter from the chancellor of the Diocese of Monterey.[87]

Incensed with what he read, the Labor Priest fired off a communication to Bishop James Rausch, USCC/NCCB general secretary and a staunch supporter of La Causa. "I would say that it comes close to treasonous in some of its implications with reference to the role of the NCCB in the farm labor dispute," roared Higgins. Offering Rausch a copy of the letter, Higgins suggested that the general secretary might "want to bring it to the attention of the appropriate officers of NCCB."[88]

The treasonous priest in question was Monsignor Philip Maxwell, chancellor of the Diocese of Monterey. On November 30, 1973, Maxwell wrote to Reverend B. V. Gajda, secretary of the Senate of Priests in Winnipeg, Canada, providing a highly critical assessment of the Catholic Church's official stance on the farm labor dispute. In particular, Maxwell condemned the NCCB's November 16, 1973, decision to endorse Chávez's grape and lettuce boycotts. Of interest is Maxwell's account of Los Angeles's Archbishop Timothy Manning. According to Maxwell, the archbishop, who was also a member of the Bishops' Ad Hoc Committee on Farm Labor, felt the boycott "immoral."[89]

In his communication to Reverend Gajda, Maxwell indicated his pleasure at receiving Gajda's letter requesting information on the UFW-Teamster dispute, and told him that "the California Bishops are completely opposed to a boycott." Maxwell commented that he had recently attended a meeting with his ordinary, Bishop Clinch, Cardinal Manning, and Bishop Johnson of Los Angeles, and that "they were all unanimous in their agreement that a secondary boycott such as boycotting Safeway, would be both unjust and immoral." The chancellor of the Diocese of

Monterey conjectured that "many of the Mexican workers from the beginning were with Chávez and have now discovered that by going along with him they are much worse off than they were before." Moreover, Maxwell contended that "many of the small Mexican farmers are injured by both the tactics Chávez uses and by the results of his type of organization."[90]

Maxwell then addressed one of the most unique, and controversial, aspects of Chávez's union: hiring halls. UFW contracts required growers to notify the union's local hiring halls of their intention to hire laborers two weeks in advance and to provide the specific number of available positions two days prior to the hiring date.[91] The more stationary farm laborers approved this seniority-based system, illegal workers—often reluctant to associate with an established institution for fear of deportation—tended to oppose the concept, and growers generally felt outright antipathy for the arrangement.[92] Hiring hall advocates cited its numerous advantages, including greater employment opportunities, increased job security, reduced corruption, and greater transparency.[93] Growers, in contrast, felt the hiring hall unfair because it put them at the mercy of Chávez's union. They criticized the arrangement because, unlike a labor contractor, the hiring hall would not necessarily allocate a sufficient number of workers to complete the task; moreover, it constrained the growers' ability to obtain additional labor.[94] Overall, it appears that the hiring hall proved relatively equitable to the more stable sections of the agricultural workforce, and detrimental to growers.

Clearly sympathetic to the growers' perspective, Maxwell's letter noted that "when the growers go to the hiring halls to obtain the Mexicans, frequently they cannot find enough workers to come to their place to do their job." Further, Maxwell told Gajda that "the Mexican workers themselves do not like to go to a hiring hall, but would rather go directly to a grower who has treated them well in the past and would do so at the present."[95]

Raising the issue of the bishops' 1973 endorsement of Chávez's boycott, Maxwell stated that after speaking with the bishops in California, and with Cardinal Timothy Manning, he had learned that the NCCB reportedly took the vote to endorse Chávez's boycott "at lunch time when some of the California Bishops were absent." "[M]oreover, the Cardinal himself, as well as [Bishop Clinch], wished to address the floor on this subject and did not have the opportunity to do so." Although the American Bishops had voted to endorse the UFW's boycott, continued

Maxwell, "the California Bishops . . . [felt] that this was very unfair and improperly done, and therefore not really a valid vote because they were not allowed to address the issue and discuss it."⁹⁶

Maxwell explained that the conflict in California hurt "many people on both sides of the issue," including "small growers and also the workers." "[T]he main issue in California seems to be . . . which union [the farmworkers should join], the Teamsters or the UFW," the chancellor clarified, "and since some of the farmers and growers had contracts with the Teamsters years before the UFW even existed, [the] UFW has been very unjust and unfair in relating to them." Maxwell sharply accused the UFW of engaging in "dirty tactics . . . namely, the overturning of cars, the cutting of trees and plants and injury done to crops that would take years to recouperate [sic]." Maxwell closed his letter by noting that "the California hierarchy . . . [felt that], in view of the local situation . . . [the boycott was] both unjust and immoral."⁹⁷

Maxwell's assertion that Manning found the boycott immoral disturbed Higgins. The Labor Priest decided to research the evolution of Manning's position on the boycott. Higgins found that the Reverend Francis Colborn, professor of moral theology at the Los Angeles Major Seminary, drafted a memo, at Manning's request, supporting "the morality of the secondary boycott under certain conditions." In a letter to Rausch on this subject, Higgins wrote, "I distinctly recall that the Cardinal was pleased with the memorandum and so indicated to Bishop Donnelly and myself when he presented us with a copy for our files." Higgins noted that if Manning was "convinced that the secondary boycott is absolutely immoral," then he could "only conclude that the Cardinal . . . [had] revised his original position on this matter."⁹⁸

Rausch decided to address the conflict by sending a letter directly to Maxwell. In his communication, Rausch challenged the chancellor's assertions, but did so in a measured, private, and respectful manner. Rausch told Maxwell that he felt "an obligation . . . to write to you [and] . . . assure you that the vote taken by the bishops, on the farm labor dispute, was not a hasty action." Rausch explained that "lengthy discussion preceded their action with several amendments offered from the floor." He continued that he was "morally certain that no one who indicated a desire to speak was denied an opportunity to address the assembly on the questions being considered." Rausch confirmed that "the minutes indicate that . . . two bishops from California" spoke on the matter, indicating that events did not unfold "in the manner you describe in your letter." Offering an olive branch, Rausch stated: "I regret having to impugn the statement you have made in your letter. I bring this matter to your attention, to enable you to correct the false impressions your comments on the Conference's action have left. Correcting this matter appears to me to be a question of justice."[99]

Rausch's communication generously offered Maxwell an opportunity to rectify the situation with a minimum of embarrassment. The chancellor could have admitted his error and the controversy would have subsided. Instead, Maxwell inflamed the issue by writing Rausch and denying that he had ever written such a letter. Exacerbating the situation, Maxwell claimed that he was "both surprised and perplexed upon receiving your letter," and told Rausch that he was "mistaken and in error." The chancellor maintained that he had "never written to a Rev. B. V. Gajda. I do not know who he is, where he lives or what religion he professes." Furthermore, Maxwell denied having "written anything in [his entire] life about the lettuce situation or any bishops meetings." If such a letter exists, as you state," concluded Maxwell, "it most certainly is not my letter."[100]

Bishop Harry Clinch supported his chancellor and assured General Secretary Rausch that "neither Monsignor Maxwell nor I have any knowledge of who the Reverend B. V. Gajda is or where he is located." "Monsignor Maxwell has never written any letters regarding the lettuce situation," continued Clinch, "nor committed himself or the Ordinary in any way." The bishop of Monterey felt that the situation was serious and asked Rausch to "ascertain whether or not this office is being used in any way to discredit any official action of the N.C.C.B.—U.S.C.C."[101]

At first willing to let Maxwell admit error and correct the situation, Rausch then had little choice but to reveal his evidence. Unknown to Maxwell, Rausch had the chancellor's original letter. Instead of upbraiding Maxwell, Rausch delivered a nuanced communication to Bishop Clinch indicating he would send "a copy of the letter attributed to Monsignor Maxwell." Rausch expressed his concern that the correspondence "was addressed to someone outside the United States," and told Clinch that "whether the letter was written by Monsignor Maxwell or not," he hoped "something . . . [could] be done to correct" the misperceptions it created.[102]

Writing a second time to Maxwell, Rausch pointedly remarked that "perhaps I should have enclosed a copy of the letter to Father Gajda when I wrote." The general secretary asked the chancellor to understand his concern that "the letter (on the letterhead of the Diocese and with what appears to be your signature) is addressed to someone outside the United States . . . [and] the comments . . . do not do credit to the National Conference of Catholic Bishops."[103]

On the same day that Rausch wrote Clinch, the bishop of Monterey hastily drafted another letter to Rausch. Clinch told Rausch that because of the issue's serious implications, he would not let the matter drop, and had asked Maxwell to search his personal files for record of "any letter he might have written in regard to the Farm Worker situation." As a result of Maxwell's efforts, "a copy of a letter he sent to Father Gajda, which he had considered as routine and forgotten, finally came to light."[104]

Clearly flustered by Maxwell's now-implausible denials, Clinch attempted to put into context the divisive impact the farm labor controversy had had on his diocese. He explained that Maxwell had been "a highly respected Prelate, never before having exhibited anything but excellent judgement [*sic*]," but that perhaps the "emotional stress this issue has brought about among our people and priests" could have clouded his otherwise sound reasoning. Clinch left the remainder of the explanation up to Maxwell.[105]

In his clarification to Bishop Rausch, Chancellor Maxwell stated that he owed both an apology and explanation because he had great difficulty recalling the letter he had sent to Gajda three months before. Maxwell reported that he "could not recall any Rev. B. V. Gajda" and was certain that Rausch was mistaken. Perplexed and puzzled by Rausch's initial correspondence, Maxwell requested that his assistants search their files, but regrettably, they could not find "anything."[106]

"Today," however, "filed under 'Teamsters,'" Maxwell told Rausch that he had discovered a letter to Gajda. The chancellor attempted to offer Rausch an explanation for the letter that had "embarrassed" Bishop Clinch.[107] Maxwell noted that his communication "was intended as a personal letter giving this priest . . . [his] point of view and [was] not an open letter for publication." "Since it was a personal letter," continued Maxwell, "I see by hindsight that it would have been better if diocesan stationery had not been used" because it gave "an 'official' look, which certainly was not intended."[108]

"I am ready and willing to admit my point of view may not be accurate," admitted Maxwell, "and in fact, it is well known that there are many points of view. I may be convinced my view is right but I am also aware that it could be wrong." Maxwell appeared confused, but nonetheless, continued: "As a personal letter, with no thought of publication the terminology of the letter can be misleading."[109]

The chancellor felt hindered by the fact that he "was attempting to express . . . [his] conclusions without the lengthy process of complete arguments." For example, Maxwell pointed out that his meeting with Bishop Clinch, Cardinal Manning, and Bishop Johnson was "in no way" what anyone would consider "a 'technical' or 'formal' meeting."[110] "To meet with someone can be as casual as meeting them on a street," explained Maxwell. The chancellor clarified the situation: "What happened is this: I was present to these persons along with a few more, and I brought up the question of the secondary boycott in conversation. The 'consensus' which I observed, and which is my opinion and my interpretation, is what I was trying to express to Rev. Gajda. If someone believes that the bishops called a meeting and discussed such issues and promoted results, this is certainly false."[111]

Maxwell expressed empathy for Rausch's position, claiming to clearly understand "how the letter could be totally mis-leading when taken outside the situation and context." The chancellor claimed that he merely "attempted to give a feeling and conclusion and 'consensus' which" he believed existed. Unfortunately, in the attempt to be brief, Maxwell admitted that he had created "a serious misunderstanding."[112]

The chancellor thanked the NCCB's general secretary for making it clear that "this letter may have been not understood by Rev. Gajda, and that certainly in public it could and would be misleading." Maxwell told Rausch, "I do see your point of view and understand your emphasis . . . [and] I have the deepest respect for the position of the California bishops and fully endorse their policy." The chancellor closed his letter by humbly suggesting that his "speedy reaction to Rev. Gajda was intended to get him to see . . . [the bishops'] position and adopt their view." In closing, Maxwell requested the hierarchy to consider the entire incident "a passing matter and trivia."[113]

The exchanges among Father Cross, Monsignor Earley, and Chancellor Maxwell illustrate an important point: although the U.S. Catholic hierarchy may have reluctantly entered the farm labor dispute in the late 1960s, once the Church had committed to resolve the conflict and had to defend its position, the bishops closed ranks and publicly supported the Ad Hoc Committee's activist role. As critics pressed the hierarchy to define the Church's position, the bishops' support for La Causa galvanized; detractors appeared to embolden, rather than intimidate, the hierarchy's top leadership.

The bishops' deepening involvement in the farm labor dispute impacted the Church's coffers in California's agricultural areas. By 1970, the financial situation throughout the parishes in California's Central Valley had deteriorated to such an extent that Monsignor Roger Mahony, in his capacity as chancellor of the Diocese of Fresno, wrote a personal note to Most Reverend Joseph Donnelly pleading for assistance. In his November 4, 1970, letter, Mahony defended the Church's involvement in the farm labor issue, despite its deleterious effects on financial operations.[114] "Catholic Charities suffered so very much because of our involvement in the farm labor issue [that] three of our best self-help programs are on the verge of termination," Mahony wrote.[115] "Our Appeal is down almost 50 percent this year," he continued, "which has produced disastrous effects."[116]

Mahony's letter to Donnelly had a second, and very important, component: the health of his superior. Bishop of Fresno Hugh Donohoe found the Church's involvement in the farm labor dispute so emotionally upsetting that he became physically ill. Perhaps more than anyone else in the Catholic hierarchy, Donohoe felt wedged between the competing interests of Catholic farmworkers and Catholic growers. As his bishop crumbled under the stress, Mahony asked Donnelly to "give Bishop Donohoe some support and encouragement."[117] According to Mahony, his bishop felt "quite depressed because of the many resulting difficulties . . . due to his involvement in the farm labor issue," and could use some uplifting as he tried to continue with the work of the diocese.[118]

While Donohoe deteriorated, Mahony appeared invigorated. Perhaps the difference can be attributed to their respective attitudes. Mahony appeared comfortable with the diocese's financial troubles because they resulted from the Church's support of what he deemed to be an exceptionally worthy endeavor. Mahony's profarmworker bias, albeit intentionally subtle, helped carry him through the struggle's most difficult periods. In contrast, Donohoe appeared to have a progrower bias. Although in November 1969 he became the principal advocate for the Church's conciliatory role in the conflict, it appears that he did so more out of a desire to avoid the hierarchy's endorsement of the grape boycott rather than an overwhelming concern for the plight of the farmworkers. Donahoe most likely did not possess enthusiasm equal to that of Higgins, Mahony, or Donnelly, and felt enervated by the conflict.

Mahony revealed the root of Donohoe's consternation in the closing of his letter to Bishop Donnelly. Donohoe, wrote Mahony, "has been disappointed over the financial events of the Diocese, . . . but he needs to realize that it is all worth it—regardless of our drop in revenues." Mahony remarked that he admired "Bishop Donohoe so very much" that he did "not want him to feel that his efforts, and those of the Church, have been in vain."[119]

Despite the hand wringing of some clergy, the hierarchy's work with La Causa during the 1960s and 1970s brought a net benefit to the Church. Catholic clergy of all ranks, from parish priests and sisters to cardinals, were empowered to move from being associated with the stodgy (and reviled) establishment to becoming cult heroes among liberal journalists, academicians, and college students. Even Cardinal Manning, the most conservative member of the Ad Hoc Committee and the group's least enthusiastic supporter of La Causa, received fan mail from the United Mexican American Students of Loyola Marymount University.[120] Mike Farley, S.J., of Loyola University of Los Angeles, also sent Manning a supportive letter on behalf of "almost 700 students and faculty members . . . who wish to express their support for your participation in the [farmworker] struggle."[121]

In addition to praise from the academic community, the Ad Hoc Committee's work garnered letters of support from clerical colleagues. The Senate of Priests of the Diocese of Fresno praised the committee's efforts "to clarify the message of the Gospels and the social mission of Christ's Church."[122] The Senate of Priests of the Archdiocese of San Francisco also offered accolades for the Bishops' Committee by complimenting the group's peacemaking between the UFWOC and growers in Coachella Valley and Delano.[123] In addition, Richard P. McBrien of the Pope John XXIII National Seminary in Weston, Massachusetts, paid the highest compliment to the Ad Hoc Committee. "If ever there was a case of the Church's enabling the Kingdom of God to break through," McBrien opined, "it occurred in your ministry of mediation."[124] McBrien's closing, penned more than thirty-four years ago, could still be applied today: "In a time when the credibility of the Church is so often undermined, the constructive contribution of your committee makes it easier to accept the Church according to the high ideals of the Second Vatican Council."[125]

Created in the midst of struggle, the Bishops' Ad Hoc Committee implemented the Church's pronouncements on social justice, brought resolution to the Delano Grape Strike, and helped bring victory to the farmworkers in the Battle of the Salad Bowl.

1968: Chávez's First Appeal

In October 1968, César Chávez finally got tired of waiting for the assistance of the Catholic Church. He took the matter into his own hands and sent a letter to the United States Catholic Conference/National Conference of Catholic Bishops (USCC/NCCB—the successor to the NCWC) asking the U.S. hierarchy to formally endorse his union's boycott of California grapes. As Bishop Ricardo Ramirez noted, prior to the Ad Hoc Committee's creation the bishops had taken little action to support La Causa. In 1966, Fresno bishop Hugh Donohoe had issued a statement publicly supporting the farmworkers' right to organize and bargain collectively.[126] Two years later, Bishop Manning reiterated the Church's support for the farmworkers' right to organize and bargain collectively, and recognized that "the majority of . . . farm workers belong to that vast number of forgotten, neglected and invisible poor Americans."[127] These timid proclamations unleashed a firestorm of criticism from growers. Bishops Donohoe and Manning, well aware of the farmers' financial influence, had little stomach to further antagonize the Catholic agriculturalists, and opposed the Church's endorsement of Chávez's boycott.

By 1968, many religious organizations had given their outright public support to Chávez. Noticeably absent from this group was the Catholic Church.[128] Dismayed that the hierarchy had not taken a firm stand in favor of a predominately Catholic union, Chávez made a direct appeal to the highest reaches of the American Catholic hierarchy. By sending a front-channel communication to the USCC/NCCB, Chávez forced the body of bishops to finally address the intrafaith conflict in California's vineyards.

Chávez's letter began by assuring the hierarchy that the UFWOC was "not attempting to cause catastrophe in the agriculture industry, but rather, social and economic betterment." The UFWOC's "previous, non-violent attempts to gain . . . basic recognition [had] not been successful"; therefore, Chávez argued, the union had decided to launch "a nationwide boycott of all California grapes in order to gain nationwide awareness of . . . [the farmworkers'] problems." Chávez maintained that the farmworkers had "no recourse but to appeal to the conscience of American citizens" and requested that the Catholic Church "consider refraining from the purchase of all California table grapes in [its] Diocesan institutions."[129]

George G. Higgins, the driving force behind the Catholic Church's support for César Chávez throughout the 1960s and 1970s, jumped at the opportunity to respond to Chávez's plea. Higgins immediately began traipsing the USCC/NCCB's halls, pressing his superiors to endorse Chávez's boycott.[130] He argued that the "boycott is legitimate 'when the injustice inflicted by the employer is grave, and when no milder method will be effective.'"[131] For Higgins, the Delano Grape Strike served as an ideal case for legitimate use of the boycott because doing so would likely "persuade the growers . . . to recognize their workers' right to organize."[132]

The hierarchy agreed to put Chávez on the agenda for the bishops' November 14 gathering and charged Higgins with drafting a statement on the California dispute. Higgins did not want a statement; he wanted *action*. The Labor Priest wanted the Church to get off the sidelines and make a public stand supporting Chávez's grape boycott, but Manning and Donohoe outranked Higgins, and their concerns carried the day. Despite the irony of having to draft a proclamation that he, in principle, would not support, Higgins attempted to make the best out of a distasteful situation.

Higgins presented his draft statement on farm labor to Monsignor Edward O'Rourke, executive director for the National Catholic Rural Life Conference.[133] Bishop Joseph Donnelly, who became chairman of the Bishops' Ad Hoc Committee on Farm Labor upon its formation in 1969, also provided input on Higgins's draft. In a letter addressed to Bishop Joseph Bernardin, the executive secretary of the USCC/NCCB, Donnelly commented that he felt corrective action on the working conditions and wage standards in farm labor was "deplorably overdue," as "farm workers and their families have been shamelessly barred from the social and economic advances made in America during the past generation."[134] Donnelly's letter made clear that he harbored strong sympathies for the farmworkers and La Causa. During the 1970s, critics of the Ad Hoc Committee accused certain members of harboring a pro-UFW/ pro-Chávez bias. In the cases of Donnelly, Higgins, and to a certain extent Mahony, the allegations had merit.

On Halloween 1968, Higgins presented his final version of the statement to Bernardin for placement on the November agenda.[135] The USCC/NCCB proclamation recognized the farmworkers' right to organize and bargain collectively, called upon the government to include farmworkers under minimum wage laws and the NLRA, affirmed the moral teaching of the Church with regard to the right of workers to strike, and acknowledged "the difficult economic position of small farmers."[136] The Labor Priest's draft also noted that "low wage-scales, mounting health problems, inadequate educational opportunities, sub-standard housing, and a lack of year-round employment force large num-bers of farm laborers to live a life devoid of security, dignity, and rea-sonable comfort."[137] Most likely Higgins shuddered as he wrote the next line. After acknowledging that the farmworkers had to endure such sufferings, the statement continued: "strikes and boycotts, though legiti-mate and at times even necessary, *cannot substitute* [emphasis added] for the orderly democratic process of collective bargaining. . . . Positive steps must be taken to resolve the conflict which now divides them."[138] Chávez needed action from the bishops—at the very least he wanted them to endorse his boycott. At this time, the Church did neither. None-theless, the draft went on with a somewhat self-congratulatory state-ment: "as a servant of justice, the Church must speak out on contro-versial issues such as these even with the knowledge that she might be misunderstood."[139] There was little to misunderstand. Chávez needed tangible assistance from the Catholic Church, and in 1968, he didn't get it.

On November 14, 1968, the USCC/NCCB held its conference in the nation's capital. Chávez's request ranked high on the agenda of pressing issues.[140] The farmworkers' struggle offered an ideal opportunity to implement many of the Church's social teachings, addressed in such encyclicals as *Rerum Novarum* and *Quadragesimo Anno*. Chávez chal-lenged the Church to transform words into action. Despite the Church's lofty rhetoric, the bishops decided merely to sympathize with Chávez and ask the government to help the farmworkers. No action. Not even an endorsement of the grape boycott. Instead of making a meaningful con-tribution to La Causa, the bishops decided to offer words and all the assistance the wind could carry; the hierarchy acted by adopting and issuing Higgins's draft statement.[141] Needless to say, its failure to en-dorse the boycott disappointed Higgins.[142] And Bishop Ramirez. And Chávez. And the farmworkers.

In writing guidance for a 1970 press interview, Higgins commented that by declining to endorse the boycott in 1968 "the Bishops did not mean to say or imply that they were against the boycott or that the boycott is unethical. They simply took no position on the subject one way or the other."[143] That was Higgins's official response. It is fair to conjec-ture that beneath the surface Higgins felt angered that the bishops did not back the papal encyclicals with action, that the hierarchy would not endorse the boycott, and worse yet, that he had to write the words that substituted for deeds—or the lack thereof.

1969: Creation of the Ad Hoc Committee

During the first half of 1969, the AFL-CIO and the U.S. Catholic Church made common cause by petitioning the U.S. government to extend the National Labor Relations Act's coverage to farmworkers. In April 1969, the Catholic hierarchy urged President Nixon to consider extension of the NLRA to agricultural workers so that the farmworkers' right to organize would be vindicated. In his letter to Nixon, however, Cardinal Dearden appeared to abdicate the Catholic Church's responsibility for seeking a resolution to the clash by concluding that "the end of current chaos [that is, the Delano Grape Strike] requires action on *your* [emphasis added] part."[144] Apparently the hierarchy still did not feel obligated in April 1969 to find a solution to the conflict between Catholic growers and Catholic farmworkers.

George Meany, the legendary president of the AFL-CIO who was once lukewarm—at best—on the issue of farm labor, fell like Saul on the road to Damascus, and he was transformed into a strong partisan of La Causa from the late 1960s onward. Meany's change of attitude most likely stemmed from a need to reinvigorate organized labor's image after the AFL-CIO aligned itself too closely with the political establishment—a situation exemplified by the organization's enthusiastic support for the unpopular war in Vietnam. Siding with Chávez's cause provided the perfect vehicle for the AFL-CIO to enhance its standing among progressives.[145]

In this spirit, Meany delivered a bold testimony before the Senate Subcommittee on Labor. Set ablaze for farmworker justice, Meany lashed out against the myth of the small farm by characterizing "the true farm picture [as] large corporate farms, . . . wages well below poverty levels, primitive living conditions and medieval terms of employment and working conditions." Meany exhorted Congress to extend protections and benefits to farmworkers, including access to health care facilities, unemployment compensation, and coverage under the NLRA. Perishability is no "excuse for giving the grower a special legislative deal when it comes to labor relations," Meany concluded, because perishability "of grapes or tomatoes is not the issue"; instead, "perishability of people—their human dignity and economic well being—is the issue."[146] With his nearly poetic sermon before Congress, Meany became a confirmed convert to La Causa.

The intersection of the AFL-CIO and the USCC/NCCB's growing concerns about the farmworkers prompted Meany to send Cardinal

From apathy to advocate. AFL-CIO president George Meany (at lectern), who was initially lukewarm toward farmworker unionization efforts, became one of César Chávez's staunchest allies. Monsignor Higgins is seated at the far right.

Dearden a telegram. Meany's message foreshadowed the hierarchy's conciliatory role in the Delano dispute by indicating there was "a possibility that third party intervention with the grape growers could be of value in achieving a just peace in the grape fields," and that the Catholic bishops might "use their good offices to persuade the grape growers to adopt a sense of social responsibility and treat their employees as human beings."[147] With additional prompting from César Chávez, the hierarchy made Meany's suggestion a reality at the USCC/NCCB's November 1969 meeting.

In October 1969, Chávez, yet again, petitioned the bishops to endorse his union's grape boycott. In his letter, Chávez addressed the hierarchy's concerns that an endorsement of the boycott might hinder potential negotiations. To date, he pointed out, "there have been no meaningful negotiations and we who have been on strike for four years see the boycott as even more important."[148] Clearly annoyed with the Church's neglect of his predominately Catholic union, Chávez reminded the bishops that boycott endorsements had already come "from the California Council of Churches, the National Council of Churches, and the World Council of Churches." "We need vocal support of the table grape boycott," implored Chávez, "will you assist us in the passage of a resolution endorsing the boycott?"[149]

The bishops assigned John Cosgrove, director for the Committee on Social Development at the USCC/NCCB, the task of responding to Chávez's letter. On October 17, Cosgrove sent a proposed reply up the chain of command with a cover memo highlighting the Church's disagreement over an outright endorsement of the boycott. The memo noted that Hugh Donohoe, bishop of Fresno, "would not favor the Bishops' endorsement of the boycott because he . . . [felt] this would impair his usefulness as [a] mediator between the growers and the workers."[150] Cosgrove's original draft to Chávez explained the hierarchy's divisions. Because "there remains some opposition among the Bishops to endorsement of the table grape boycott," wrote Cosgrove to Chávez, "the Body of Bishops, in November, might well refuse to endorse the boycott program."[151] Cosgrove's proposed letter would have informed Chávez that the Committee on Social Development planned to ask the bishops to consider "a resolution . . . [that] would note with gratification that there is . . . increasing support . . . of the table grape boycott."[152] Realizing that his response would not be the answer for which Chávez had hoped, Cosgrove concluded, "I believe that the above . . . is the best statement we can obtain," and he acknowledged that "while the above actions are not all you or I would desire, I believe, everything considered, we should move in this direction."[153]

Cosgrove's rough draft to Chávez exposed divisions within the Church over the farm labor issue. Perhaps it revealed too much. Monsignor Hurley apparently felt that the Church's interests would be better served if Chávez were not made aware, especially in writing, of the USCC/NCCB's reluctance to support a devout Catholic labor leader and his union of predominantly Catholic farmworkers. Three days after receiving Cosgrove's proposed reply, Hurley instructed him *not* to send the draft letter because "it almost express[ed] a position by the bishops." Hurley suggested that Cosgrove "at most . . . merely . . . [indicate] that you . . . will review the request and make a recommendation to Cardinal Dearden. The letter should be noncommittal."[154]

One week later, Cosgrove produced an amended reply that mentioned nothing of the divisions within the Church. After a standard introduction, the banal letter simply told Chávez that "the question you raised is being actively considered by our departmental Committee on Social Development. We will be in further touch with you, as our work on this continues."[155] Hurley approved the draft.

During October 1969, the bishops also had Cosgrove diligently working with a small committee, including Higgins, to develop a draft resolution on the farm labor situation. Intended for presentation at the bishops'
November convocation, the memo recognized the plight of the farmworkers, expressed the Church's continued support for their right to organize and bargain collectively, and importantly, recognized "the growth
and extension of the table grape boycott as a morally legitimate weapon
of defense against injustice and exploitation." The proposed memo suggested that "the Bishops of California . . . intercede with the growers and
the union . . . in an effort to initiate negotiations where there have been
none, and in addition, to seek resumption of those negotiations which
had begun and were, unfortunately, interrupted."[156]

On November 7, Bishop Bernardin updated Cardinal Dearden on
the status of Chávez's request. After the Committee on Social Development reviewed the draft resolution on farm labor, Bernardin reported
that Monsignor Johnson from Los Angeles and Bishop Donohoe "opposed . . . any support of the boycott," whereas "a majority of the Committee strongly support[ed]" the resolution.[157] With the November 1969
gathering rapidly approaching, the bishops still appeared divided over
how to address Chávez, the boycott, and La Causa. Cosgrove and Higgins wanted an outright endorsement of the boycott, but according to
Higgins, "Bishop Donohoe . . . and Archbishop Timothy Manning of Los
Angeles said that the bishops would perform a better service if they put
off a statement on the boycott, and offered their services in some way as
mediators between the farm workers and the growers."[158]

Higgins failed to garner support for his first choice, outright endorsement of the boycott, so he embarked on Plan B. Seeking a way to
help Chávez and the farmworkers, the Labor Priest hastily arranged
a meeting between Bishop Donohoe and AFL-CIO director of organization William Kircher. Described as both a committed Catholic and
"the farm workers' best friend in organized labor," Kircher had become
deeply concerned about the Church's role in the dispute. Higgins's dip-
lomatic legwork literally changed the course of history: Kircher and
Donohoe, meeting privately, conceptualized "a committee that would
offer to mediate the dispute" in California. By the end of the USCC/
NCCB's November meeting, Kircher and Donohoe's vision had a name:
the Bishops' Ad Hoc Committee on Farm Labor.[159]

As the November gathering got under way, Bishops Manning and
Donohoe took the floor and begged the hierarchy not to endorse the
boycott.[160] Highlighting the divisions between Catholic growers and

Catholic farmworkers, Manning and Donohoe urged their colleagues to demonstrate concern for all members of the Church.[161] Donohoe insisted that his opposition to the USCC/NCCB's endorsement of the grape boycott emanated from his concern that "the Church in general, as far as the farmer is concerned, is looked upon as having sold out to the workers."[162] Evidently, Donohoe felt that an absolute endorsement of Chávez via the boycott would exacerbate existing divisions among the flock, and therefore, should be avoided at all costs.

Bishop Donohoe did raise the issue of financial pressures, but apparently only to discount such influences on his decision making. Donohoe remarked that he did not fear losing "the farmers' economic support because . . . [he had] already lost much of that."[163] This was true. By August 1968, advertising revenue for the Diocese of Fresno's official publication, the *Central California Register*, had plummeted to its lowest level in twenty years due, in large part, to the paper's reporting on Chávez.[164] However, Donohoe's insinuation that the growers' economic potency did not factor into his assessment could be questioned—especially in light of Monsignor Mahony's November 1970 letter to Bishop Donnelly.[165]

After arguing against endorsing the boycott, Donohoe presented a compromise solution (courtesy of his meeting with Kircher). "To build a bridge," declared Donohoe, "that is [the Church's] basic function and it isn't always easy to keep this stand."[166] Archbishop Manning agreed. "If the Bishops endorsed the boycott," opined Manning, "it would immediately polarize the growers and the workers, and there would be no chance of bridging the gap between the two."[167] Because "a number of other religious bodies had already endorsed the boycott," continued the archbishop, "they were rendered useless so far as making any contact between the growers and the workers."[168] Therefore, Donohoe and Manning concluded, it fell upon the Catholic Church to become the "bridge between both groups"[169]

Manning and Donohoe persuaded their colleagues, and the hierarchy rejected the proposed proboycott resolution. Instead, Cardinal Dearden approved Donohoe's idea and ordered the establishment of a five-bishop Committee on Farm Labor to "determine whether or not there was anything that could be done to mediate the dispute" in California.[170] Dearden charged the group with "investigating the California grape dispute with the hope of persuading the two parties to resume the negotiations."[171] Importantly, the USCC/NCCB president empowered the committee "to take such action as it deemed appropriate in the light of its investigation of the facts," and to make statements, if necessary, "in the name of the entire American Hierarchy."[172] The committee enjoyed the full confidence of the USCC/NCCB, and had carte blanche to act, and react, to the situation as it deemed appropriate.[173]

Chairman Dearden tapped Bishops Manning and Donohoe, Bishop Joseph Donnelly of Hartford, Connecticut, Bishop Humberto Medeiros of Brownsville, Texas, and Bishop Walter Curtis of Bridgeport, Connecticut, to staff the five bishop positions on the seven-member Ad Hoc Committee.[174] Lower ranking clergy would fill the two remaining positions—consultant and secretary to the committee.

Experience and geographic considerations dominated the selection process.[175] Donnelly was a veteran of labor disputes; Medeiros had considerable experience with Mexican Americans and farmworkers; and Bishop Curtis served as a member of the USCC/NCCB's Social Action Committee. Additionally, three of the five bishops were from California and Texas—states with large populations of agricultural workers.

The Ad Hoc Committee's members picked Bishop Donnelly to chair the group. Geographically isolated in Connecticut, the bishops felt he would likely be perceived as more objective than his California counterparts.[176] Donnelly, who had once worked as chairman of the state mediation board in Connecticut, valued Higgins's experience in labor affairs and asked his acquaintance of many years to serve as consultant to the committee.[177] Pleased to play an active role again in farmworker issues, Higgins accepted.

Monsignor Roger Mahony was selected to serve as secretary, and he quickly became one of the group's most valuable contributors.[178] Although seven people staffed the Bishops' Committee, only three, Higgins, Donnelly, and Mahony, performed almost all the work.[179] Of the committee's members, Mahony had the greatest reputation for objectivity. Bishop Donnelly commented that Mahony's "unique value rests in the fact that he has the full confidence of both the growers and the Union."[180] Certainly Mahony did have a bias; his writings and actions indicate that he favored Chávez and the farmworkers. Nonetheless, Mahony did not reveal his own pro-UFW sentiment as blatantly as Higgins did his or as openly as Donnelly later would, nor did Mahony appear to side with the growers to the extent of Donohoe and Manning.

By reading between the lines of an April 1969 memorandum to Bishops Manning and Donohoe, we can infer the future cardinal's profarmworker bias. In the memo, Mahony indicated an underlying sympathy for Chávez's use of the boycott. "While it is my opinion that the U.S.

Catholic Bishops should not endorse the boycott of California non-union table grapes at this time," Mahony remarked, "I believe that reference should be made to the *validity of employing those strategies* [emphasis added] needed to attract the nation's conscience to injustices."[181] Presciently, Mahony also suggested "the U.S. Catholic Bishops offer their offices to bring both sides together . . . [and] serve as the catalyst of reconciliation."[182] Less than eight months after Mahony penned his confidential memo, he would have an opportunity to become a major player in the solution he envisioned.

After the November meeting adjourned, Higgins approached Donohoe and Manning to express his disappointment over the bishops' decision not to endorse Chávez's boycott. After speaking his peace, Higgins reassured his interlocutors that, although he disagreed with them, he would go along with their strategy.[183] Ironically, Higgins later admitted that Donohoe and Manning had more accurately assessed the situation, and that they had presented the best solution to resolve the conflict. "It was providential, very providential that Manning and Donohoe won the argument and that I lost," reflected the Labor Priest. If the bishops had "issued a strong statement in support of the boycott," continued Higgins, "it would have meant inevitably that their usefulness as an outside conciliation or mediation service . . . would have been destroyed."[184]

Five factors contributed to the hierarchy's 1969 decision to finally confront the intrafaith conflict in California's vineyards. First, by the end of the decade it had become clear to the hierarchy that the Delano Grape Strike would not resolve itself. Second, neither the U.S. government nor the state of California possessed institutions to mediate the dispute. Third, a large number of religious organizations had already staked a position in favor of Chávez, and therefore, were unable to act as neutral mediators. Fourth, because the majority of participants in the dispute were at least nominally Catholic, it made sense for the Church to act as conciliator. Finally, due to Chávez's national grape boycott campaign and his fasts and marches, public awareness of the situation had grown to such a proportion that *not* to act after two formal requests by Chávez would have been a public relations blunder of colossal proportions. Church leaders would have appeared as moral cowards—unwilling to broker peace between the struggling factions of its faithful.

The flock guided the shepherd. A grassroots movement compelled the hierarchy to act. Faced with a conflict among its faithful, the Church leadership made a pragmatic decision to mediate. Created at the behest of conservative, progrower bishops in reaction to popular pressure, the Bishops' Ad Hoc Committee on Farm Labor, ironically, became the American Catholic hierarchy's greatest contribution to the cause of social justice during the final half of the twentieth century.

1970: Triumph and Defeat

Because Donohoe and Manning clamored for mediation rather than advocacy, the committee decided that the bishops from California should initiate the dialogue with growers in their home state.[185] Although eager to embrace arbitration as an alternative to endorsing the grape boycott, Manning and Donohoe did not possess the same enthusiasm when tasked with launching the committee's efforts at conciliation. In January 1970, Bishop Donnelly approached Monsignor Higgins to inquire as to what, if anything, Donohoe and Manning had accomplished since November. The Labor Priest paused for a moment to think.[186] "In all honesty . . . nothing," replied Higgins.[187]

"Well, that's all I need to know," Donnelly, retorted. "I didn't want to move in unless these two California bishops weren't going to do anything."[188]

Shortly after this frank encounter, Donnelly convoked a Bishops' Committee meeting in Fresno from February 8 to 12 to set the group in motion. After the gathering, the committee began to set up meetings with growers to offer assistance if negotiations broke down.[189] Over the course of the next four months, the Bishops' Committee met with roughly sixty growers.[190] Many agriculturalists invited the committee to observe the negotiations, and, in several instances, participate. The clergy strictly adhered to their policy of only entering talks at the request of both parties and took pains to ensure that the scope of their participation adhered to the role delineated by the principals.[191]

Higgins described the committee's initial encounters with growers as "hesitant-friendly, no blood, but no action either."[192] In a typical encounter, Higgins would tell the farmers that the committee was "interested in bringing the parties together," but he took pains to clarify that the bishops believed "in trade unionism and . . . collective bargaining," and were "not neutral in that sense."[193] For the most part, the growers appeared receptive and listened to what the bishops offered.[194] Through gentle persistence, the Bishops' Committee played a crucial role in accomplishing something once considered impossible: bringing the UFWOC and the growers to the bargaining table.[195]

As more growers accepted the bishops' invitations, Mahony noted "it was the first real breakthrough in five years . . . the first time the parties had ever gotten together across the table."[196] The bishops' strategy worked. Donnelly observed that the Ad Hoc Committee began to serve as a bridge between the warring factions; for example, during one encounter in Fresno, the growers "welcomed [the committee's] interest, stated that the intervention of the Church was the first hopeful sign in this dispute, asked that [the committee] arrange another meeting, and promised to bring in other Growers."[197]

As the committee made its rounds, scant communication between fellow growers and total lack of communications between growers and the UFWOC shocked the bishops.[198] Donnelly claimed very few growers had "ever met Caesar Chávez, or even seen him. During almost five years of the strike, growers in the city of Delano, where the Union headquarters is, have never met Chávez."[199]

Monsignors Higgins and Mahony spent much of March 1970 traveling up and down the San Joaquin Valley, visiting growers, workers, and the union members. Higgins and Mahony's least encouraging meeting involved eleven fathers and sons who ran large ranches in the Bakersfield area. Despite the two priests' best efforts to encourage conciliation, "there was no disposition to do anything that would in any way recognize the existence of the Union." Bishop Donnelly also reported an unpleasant encounter with six or seven growers and a banker from the Delano area. Donnelly commented that he "expected them to be hostile," and was "not disappointed"; they aggressively told the committee how "happy their workers were and how they did not want a Union."[200]

Monsignor Mahony attributed hostility among growers to the fact that they "had to completely switch their relationships. They're not used to sitting down and talking with their workers; for decades," Mahony continued, "they've just been telling them this is the way it's going to be. They're not used to dealing with workers on an equal plane."[201] The *New York Times* drew the conclusion that some of this "animosity has rubbed off on the Catholic Church, which helped arrange the settlements."[202] Despite such occasional setbacks, overall, the growers reacted positively to the bishops' overtures, and felt the Ad Hoc Committee instrumental in the negotiations.[203]

The effectiveness of the UFWOC's national/international grape boycott became the principal reason growers expressed a willingness to accept the bishops' offer of mediation.[204] The first tangible evidence that the boycott had hurt the growers came in July 1969, when agriculturalists filed a seventy-five million dollar suit against the UFWOC claiming

¡Huelga! (Strike!): Monsignor Higgins (left center) and Bishop Joseph Donnelly (right center) march with farmworkers in California.

triple damages due to the boycott.[205] Chávez's boycott proved so effective that demand (and sales) for union-picked grapes actually outstripped sales figures (or lack thereof) for nonunion grapes.[206] Growers were harvesting grapes for which they had no market.[207] By 1970, table grape sales had reportedly been slashed an estimated 30 percent to 35 percent.[208] This devastating economic impact, coupled with the bishops' offers of mediation, is what ultimately brought the growers to the bargaining table.

In addition to skidding sales of nonunion grapes, the Ad Hoc Committee's professional demeanor made the growers receptive to the bishops' peace overtures. The growers were businessmen, and they simply could not tolerate the UFWOC's negotiations, which they characterized as a "circus."[209] Ironically, Chávez, who exercised autocratic control of his union, permitted such lax negotiating sessions that twenty to thirty farmworkers would casually mill about the bargaining table shouting out their opinions.[210] Worse, the UFW reportedly "did not negotiate—it made demands."[211] Desperate for any semblance of traditional professionalism, growers often agreed to negotiate only with the Bishops' Committee's present.[212]

Despite the UFWOC's apparent lack of coherence during negotiations, Chávez did possess an overarching strategy to defeat the growers. In a revealing February 4, 1970, memorandum to Bishop Donnelly, John Cosgrove described the centrality of the boycott to Chávez's design. According to Cosgrove, Chávez fought his battle "on three fronts: 1) Strike, 2) Legal, and 3) Boycott." Although technically the strike continued throughout the five-year conflict, it had become severely crippled, according to Cosgrove's letter, "by the importation in the form of wetbacks and green carders." The legal front was equally discouraging, as state and federal courts issued injunctions, and "local governments were anti-union." Accordingly, the boycott became "the only hope for the union."[213]

The boycott, accentuated by Chávez's high-profile fasts and marches and La Causa's extensive media coverage, rallied public opinion to the farmworkers' side and left the growers fatigued and ready to negotiate. An excellent case in point was a tough-talking, cigar-chomping farmer named Hollis Roberts.[214] Roberts owned a company that farmed almost fifty thousand acres of land in California, which included "more walnuts, almonds, persimmons and cling peaches than any other farm in the world."[215]

But life was not perfect for Roberts. There was Chávez. Roberts disliked Chávez. He firmly believed that Chávez and his associates were communists "out to take over American agriculture."[216] Roberts's attitude softened when La Causa began to threaten his crop in 1970.[217]

Manuel Chávez, César Chávez's cousin, led a strike against Roberts.[218] As usual, Roberts tried to hire strikebreakers. But this time he could not find enough takers.[219] In desperation, Roberts turned to the Ad Hoc Committee.[220]

The bishops agreed to help out, and they successfully facilitated negotiations between Chávez and Roberts. As Roberts prepared to sign with the UFWOC, Higgins asked the grower what had changed his mind. How could he be sitting there signing a contract with his archnemesis?[221]

"Well, I'll tell you reverend," Roberts explained, "I learned I was wrong. I learned that César Chávez is not a Communist, that he is a God-fearing, Christian gentleman. . . . And besides . . . I can't get anyone to pick my goddam peaches and prunes."[222]

In early April 1970, the Ad Hoc Committee's investments began to pay dividends.[223] Three ranches in the Coachella Valley signed with

Hollis Roberts signs with the UFW. César Chávez reviews a contract as Hollis Roberts (center) speaks with Ad Hoc Committee chairman Bishop Joseph Donnelly.

Chávez "marking the first real breakthrough."[224] The following month also brought major resolutions. Higgins wrote Bernardin and detailed how in mid-May he and Donnelly had "to return to Fresno . . . for a series of meetings with some of the more influential growers" to jumpstart stalled negotiations.[225] Chávez, among others, felt that "intervention by the Bishops' Committee may be [the] only hope of getting the parties back on the track."[226]

Donnelly and Higgins arrived in Fresno on May 18 and began meeting with César Chávez, Dolores Huerta, Jerry Cohen, and other UFWOC officials.[227] The union accused the growers of stalling and not bargaining in good faith.[228] Mahony reported such tension built up during prior negotiations that "César . . . agreed to come only upon invitation of the Bishops' Committee."[229] Without the bishops, talks would go nowhere.

The Ad Hoc Committee finished with the UFWOC officials and then met with the growers. "The union was not interested in signing a contract," insisted the growers. Emotions ran high; neither side trusted the other. Undeterred, the committee shuttled between the parties hoping to move talks forward.[230]

The next day a tense exchange led to a deadlock. The committee spent the rest of the day arguing over wages—a political rather than economic issue because the "growers did not want to become the ones to raise the wages all over the Coachella Valley, and bear the ire of fellow growers."[231] Perhaps simply exhausted after yet another stressful day, participants decided to spend the evening relaxing with a good meal. As supper ended, Bishop Donnelly and Monsignors Higgins and Mahony met with some of the growers for an informal drink and discussion. This particular gathering proved valuable, and it resulted in greatly improved relations between the growers and the committee.[232]

By the end of the week, on May 21, 1970, the Bianco Fruit Company and the Bruno Dispoto Company had settled with the UFWOC.[233] Once these two sizeable growers capitulated, resistance began to crumble and smaller growers signed with Chávez's union.[234] At a press conference celebrating this significant event, Bishop Donnelly expressed his satisfaction that "once again, representatives of the Bishops' Committee were privileged to take part, as observers and informal mediators, in the last round of negotiations leading up to these two major break-through agreements."[235] Donnelly ended his speech on a warranted note of optimism by expressing hope that "within the not too distant future, the bitter dispute in the table grape industry . . . will be resolved . . . to the mutual benefit of the parties and of the agricultural industry as a whole."[236] Donnelly would soon have his wish.

After the May victories, the Bishops' Committee continued to build momentum throughout June. Early in the month, Higgins wrote Bernardin a sanguine note that indicated the possibility of a major break-through in the near future, one that could put the Delano situation "over [the] hump."[237] Higgins's optimistic instincts were correct; agriculture giants June Roberts Farms, the S. A. Camp Company, and Tenneco, all signed contracts with the union after requesting and receiving the committee's mediation services. As the major growers signed with the UFWOC, a large number of other growers began to settle on their own.[238]

Although the Bishops' Committee enjoyed several victories, not all the bishops' efforts in June met with success. Some Imperial Valley growers apparently were not enchanted with the committee's presence. For example, Monsignor Mahony recalled a visit in the summer of 1970 to one particular packing shed during which members of the Ad Hoc Committee received such a chilly reception that the owner's sister (the owner reportedly "was not in, and . . . was most likely not going to be in the rest of the day") told the priests to get off the property and that none of the area growers wanted to talk with the committee.[239]

During that same trip, Mahony, Donnelly, and Higgins drove to Mexicali to meet with the AFL-CIO's Bill Kircher. While walking about town, Mahony decided to mingle with the farmworkers and engage them on the subject of unionization. The future cardinal comfortably milled about and talked with several groups of melon workers who were returning home after work. Mahony asked about their opinion of the union, and found that "no Mexican worker had any adverse comment to make about the union effort." Mahony's dialogue with the melon workers proved valuable, for the next day a UFW opponent asked Mahony why the committee did not talk to Mexican workers across the border. Mahony calmly reassured his interlocutor that he "had done just that the previous day," and the gentleman "rapidly changed the subject."[240]

The Delano Grape Strike ended on July 29, 1970, when the twenty-six growers who were the UFWOC's original targets signed contracts with Chávez's union. This final push for peace proved difficult because the UFWOC saw this particular group of growers as central to its difficulties during the five-year struggle.[241] Because of their extreme antipathy for these growers, Chávez and his lieutenants became intransigent and refused to compromise.[242] The growers claimed that they had "acceded to nearly every request . . . [but] that there have been few concessions" in return.[243] The Ad Hoc Committee offered to arbitrate this nightmarish situation, and both sides readily welcomed the bishops' participation.[244]

The UFWOC-grower negotiations began on July 17 and were conducted in utmost secrecy.[245] Starting in Bakersfield and moving to Delano, talks were highly volatile, the issues being resolved slowly and painfully.[246] The bishops did an excellent job of "keeping things glued together," but decided to remove themselves during the final stretch of negotiations so that growers and the union could resolve their differences face-to-face.[247]

The bishops' strategy worked. The two parties signed at 11:10 a.m. on July 29, 1970, at the UFWOC's headquarters in Delano with the Ad Hoc Committee playing the key mediation role.[248] The UFWOC's contracts with the twenty-six ranch owners covered roughly half of California's table grape production.[249] Combined with Chávez's earlier victories, the UFWOC had approximately 80 percent of the state's table grape crop under union contract.[250] Over the next two months, the rest of the growers agreed to contracts and the UFWOC officially terminated the grape boycott.[251] By the end of September 1970, Chávez's union had agreements that covered 150 agricultural operations and represented twenty thousand jobs and more than ten thousand members.[252]

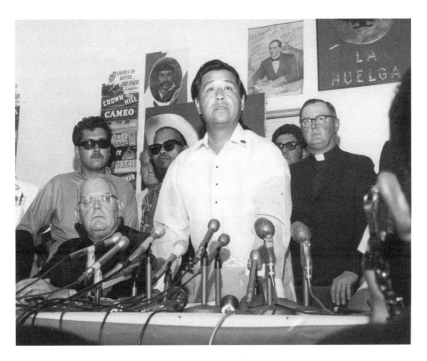

César Chávez holds a press conference as Bishop Joseph Donnelly (left) and Monsignor George Higgins (right, background) look on.

To celebrate the peace, Chávez convoked a press conference on July 29, 1970, and asked Bishop Donnelly to preside.[253] Donnelly made a statement congratulating both sides, reiterated that the Bishops' Committee mediated only at the request of both parties, and said that the Catholic Church desired social justice for grower and worker.[254] The growers' spokesman said he was "overjoyed at the peace that will come to this valley."[255] Donnelly admitted that he was surprised at the Ad Hoc Committee's significant and rapid contributions to the agreement.[256] "To tell the truth," confessed Donnelly, "we didn't expect it would happen this year."[257]

Unfortunately, peace did not even last a day. July 29, 1970, marked both the end of the Delano conflict and the beginning of the Battle of the Salad Bowl. Almost immediately after the twenty-six major grape growers in Delano signed with UFWOC, terrible news ripped through the farmworkers' celebration: the Western Conference of Teamsters and thirty lettuce growers in the Salinas Valley signed contracts covering almost five thousand farmworkers.[258] Chávez would have to embark on yet another struggle for his union's survival. Upon receiving news of the Teamster raids, Chávez immediately turned to the bishops and requested their continued assistance. The committee readily obliged.[259]

Although the Teamsters had traditionally stayed away from organizing field workers, the union shifted its policy once it appeared that Chávez would emerge victorious in Delano. There were two principal reasons for the change. First, the lettuce growers recognized Chávez's impending victory and did not want to negotiate with his union. To avoid bargaining with the UFWOC juggernaut rolling up California valleys, the Salinas Valley lettuce growers cut sweetheart deals with the Teamsters.[260] Second, the Teamsters got involved, according to Monsignor Higgins, to destroy Chávez and the UFWOC. Higgins felt that the Teamsters "saw Chávez winning his long fight with the Delano grape growers and figured that this man might be . . . on his way to taking over the whole industry." For Higgins, that was "the only logical explanation," because otherwise, "it didn't make any sense for the Teamsters to be so worried; . . . they must have felt that they had to organize the whole industry or else their people were going to get hurt."[261]

As the Teamsters Union descended upon California's lettuce fields, the Labor Priest unveiled his pro-Chávez bias. He called the Teamsters' action "obscene" during a "shouting match" with Teamsters president Frank "Fitz" Fitzsimmons.[262] The Battle of the Salad Bowl slowly stripped away the Ad Hoc Committee's veneer of neutrality, and the Catholic hierarchy became less of a mediator and more of an advocate for La Causa.[263]

3 HASTA LA VICTORIA, ONWARD TO VICTORY

1970–1971: The Teamsters' Betrayal

The Battle of the Salad Bowl was considerably more complex than the conflict in Delano. The Grape Strike encompassed two adversaries with a mutual interest in achieving reconciliation. This time, the UFWOC had to battle growers, the Teamsters, and at times, state and local government agencies. Moreover, the Teamsters did not want conciliation; instead, they "were boorishly honest about their intentions" to destroy La Causa.[1] Despite the clear signal, Chávez and the Ad Hoc Committee repeatedly mistook the Teamsters' periodic offer of an olive branch as sincere, especially during the initial stages of the conflict. As the Teamsters feigned peace, Chávez and the bishops dropped their guard, and the Teamsters and growers attacked.

The Teamsters, a far larger, wealthier, and politically well-connected union, did not intimidate Chávez. The farmworkers had "been wiped out before," Chávez explained, "wiped out every day . . . by the short hoe, by the work of the day and the exhaustion of the night."[2] "The Teamsters can't wipe us out," Chávez continued, "we will win."[3]

Oddsmakers disagreed. The "betting in Las Vegas was three to one against" Chávez.[4] The battle was on.

The Teamsters' 1970 raid on California's lettuce fields surprised the UFWOC.[5] Chávez had made a major miscalculation: he trusted the Teamsters. He believed that the Teamsters would honor the two unions' July 21, 1967, accord, in which the Teamsters agreed to cede jurisdiction over the fields to the UFWOC, in return for the UFWOC's acknowledgment of the Teamsters' right to organize the canneries, creameries, frozen food processing plants, dehydrating plants, producers markets and warehouses.[6] One notable exception to this pact was Bud Antle, a major Salinas Valley lettuce grower who had farmworkers under Teamsters' contracts since 1961.[7] Antle's willingness to allow farmworker unionization made him a pariah among his colleagues, and the largest organization of growers in the Salinas Valley, the Grower-Shipper Vegetable Association (GSVA), expelled Antle for contracting with the Teamsters.[8]

The 1967 UFWOC-Teamster treaty began to disintegrate as Chávez's victory in Delano became evident. In early 1970, Chávez traveled extensively throughout the Salad Bowl to prepare the farmworkers for the UFWOC's arrival. Chávez exhorted the workers to hold off striking until the grape dispute was settled.[9] As victory in Delano appeared imminent, Chávez sent letters to Salinas Valley lettuce growers requesting that their field employees be recognized as members of the farm workers union.[10]

The growers did not formally reply. Instead, they sent a message: the UFWOC was not wanted. Painfully aware of the economic havoc Chávez had bought to Delano's agriculturalists, GSVA scampered away from La Causa and sought refuge with the Teamsters. On July 23, 1970, the twenty-nine member GSVA and the Teamsters commenced talks, and just one day later every member of the association signed recognition agreements with the union.[11]

Events continued to move at a breakneck pace. On July 28, GSVA announced its contracts with the Teamsters. Growers in the Imperial Valley and Santa Maria area took note, scrambled away from the UFWOC, and anxiously pounded on the Teamsters' door to escape the Chávez juggernaut marching in the Central Valley.[12] Outraged at what AFL-CIO President George Meany termed the "the most despicable strikebreaking, union-busting activity I have ever seen in my lifetime in the trade union movement,"[13] Chávez declared all-out war on the Teamsters and vowed that La Causa would again "strike, boycott, march, sacrifice and struggle for as many years as it takes to win."[14]

The sweetheart contracts covered the lettuce workers. But apparently, no one consulted the farmworkers.[15] No one asked the farmworkers' opinion of the five-year collective bargaining agreements that stipulated the Teamsters would be the workers' exclusive bargaining agent. No one inquired if the farmworkers felt it acceptable that they would be compelled to join the Teamsters within ten days of hire. And no one solicited the farmworkers' opinion on the contracts' clause allowing the Teamsters to deduct dues directly from their paychecks.[16] Since no one conferred with the farmworkers, they were, as expected, surprised when the growers informed them of the contracts' stipulations.[17]

The Teamster agreements provided farmworkers $1.85 per hour during the harvest season and $1.75 per hour throughout the rest of the year. The contracts proscribed hiring halls—a preferred institution of the UFWOC.[18] The pacts neither gave farmworkers "protection against pesticides beyond what already existed through legislation, nor . . . protected [them] against replacement by mechanization."[19] The NLRA would normally prohibit such absurd sweetheart deals, but the Wagner Act did not cover agricultural workers.[20]

William Grami reportedly masterminded the Teamsters' effort to organize farmworkers in the Salinas Valley in an effort to expand his power base in the West and perhaps to replace Einar Mohn, the Teamsters' vice president.[21] On August 9, Grami's superiors, who privately chaffed at his ambition, ordered him to make peace with the UFWOC.[22] Grami complied, and immediately arranged to meet with Chávez.

The Ad Hoc Committee reprised its role as mediator and brokered the Teamster-UFWOC meeting.[23] Mahony called Higgins, who was witnessing a wedding in Cedar Rapids, Iowa, and told the Labor Priest that Donnelly wanted him "to proceed immediately to the Salinas Valley" to partake in the meeting between Chávez and the Teamsters.[24] Teeming with unwarranted optimism, Higgins remarked that he was "almost certain" that this "meeting . . . will lead to an armistice between UFWOC and the Teamsters."[25] Monsignor Mahony agreed with Higgins, and opined that "the jurisdictional dispute between the UFWOC and the Teamsters is close to settlement."[26]

The negotiations went smoothly. Perhaps too smoothly. On August 11, the Teamsters and the UFWOC signed an agreement reiterating their vows to honor the 1967 jurisdictional agreement.[27] The next day, Higgins made a formal statement on behalf of the Bishops' Committee that reflected, in retrospect, the group's far too optimistic appraisal of the situation. Higgins proclaimed that during UFWOC-Teamster negotiations, the bishops urged the rival unions to draft a positive accord "calculated not so much to defend or protect their separate interests as to promote their mutual interests and the general interest of the entire agricultural industry."[28] Clearly misjudging the Teamsters' sincerity, Higgins added: "we think they have done just this and have done it very well."[29]

The bishops were wrong. Chávez was wrong. They had taken the Teamsters at their word. Less than two weeks after Chávez and Grami renewed their unions' pledges, the GSVA president announced that the growers had signed with the Teamsters, and that both parties intended to honor the contracts.[30] In response, the UFWOC called for a massive strike on August 24, with an estimated 6,000 workers walking off almost 150 farms.[31]

Fields emptied in Salinas, Oxnard, and Santa Maria.[32] Pandemonium erupted.[33] In a flashback to the 1930s, "local patriotic organizations" assaulted labor agitators.[34] "Teamster goons roamed the streets and highways."[35] They carried shotguns, chains, and in a despicable act of violence, savagely beat the UFWOC's lawyer, Jerry Cohen, so severely that he had to spend four days in the hospital.[36] A bomb struck the UFWOC's Watsonville headquarters, and an avalanche of terror descended upon the La Causa.[37]

Chávez faced his most difficult battle to date. Fortunately for the UFWOC, the Ad Hoc Committee began to take a more proactive role on behalf of La Causa. In mid-November 1970, Bishop Donnelly asked Monsignor Mahony to do some detective work on the Citizens Committee for Agriculture—a progrower interest group that had been creating difficulties for the UFWOC and the Bishops' Committee. After some digging, Mahony discovered that the Citizens Committee sought "to save agriculture from 'radicals and militants.'" "Translated," Mahony reported to Donnelly, "this seems to mean to keep UFWOC, and any other Mexican American organization, from the farm labor organizational effort." The Citizens Committee, a decidedly right-wing organization, also aimed to bring "right to work" legislation to the Golden State.[38]

Mahony's investigation took an intriguing twist when he discovered that the Citizens Committee had a close relationship with Father Michael Cross of the Sacred Heart Church in Salinas. Mahony approached the Citizens Committee for Agriculture as "merely . . . an interested citizen calling," and, unaware of Mahony's position in the hierarchy, "Committee leaders shared . . . that they [were] in 'constant contact with Father Cross . . . and that they assisted him with volunteer help in many ways," including financial support.[39] Perhaps due to the group's connection with the Ad Hoc Committee's nemesis, Father Cross, Mahony surmised that the Citizens Committee was totally misinformed about the Bishops' Committee's role, and concluded that the bishops should not be alarmed by the Citizens Committee.[40] By actively investigating Chávez's adversaries, the Ad Hoc Committee began to drop its cloak of neutrality and make its transition from mediation to advocacy.

While the Ad Hoc Committee gradually redefined its mandate, growers acquired greater sophistication in pursuing their goal of destroying Chávez's union. Agriculturalists began to shift their anti-UFWOC strategy to the political realm.[41] The growers engaged in deft legal maneuvering to incapacitate the UFWOC—a move that ultimately became more successful than brute force.[42] For example, a progrower Monterey judge invoked the California Jurisdictional Strike Act to proscribe the UFWOC's use of strikes or boycotts.[43] The local magistrate did not perceive the Teamsters' raiding as union busting, but rather as a "jurisdictional dispute between two unions."[44]

The UFWOC successfully fought this decision, but the legal battle took over two years and led all the way to the California Supreme Court. California's highest court ruled that "the growers displayed 'the . . . ultimate form of favoritism' in selecting the Teamsters and made no attempts to ascertain the preferences of field workers."[45] In the court's opinion, "the majority of the workers desired to be represented by the UFWOC rather than the Teamsters."[46]

Because of the boycott's absolute centrality to La Causa, Chávez openly defied the Monterey judge's prohibition and continued to promote his union's boycott of iceberg lettuce.[47] Sympathetic to agribusiness, the judicial system in Monterey County had little tolerance for Chávez's recalcitrance. Executing the court's threat to enforce the prohibition against boycotts, a local magistrate ordered Chávez's incarceration from December 4 to 24, 1970.[48]

Soon after his release from jail, Chávez addressed a conference on migrant ministry in Atlanta. Higgins attended the January 6–7 meeting, and after listening to Chávez's oratory, fired off two confidential letters that criticized the speech. In his communications, Higgins explained that, although he wanted the letters kept "strictly confidential," he had "no hesitation in repeating the contents . . . to César . . . the next time I get together with . . . [him] in California, but, for obvious reasons, I wouldn't want . . . [him] to get my reaction . . . secondhand."[49]

In a letter to John Cosgrove, Higgins explained that Chávez's speech left the audience with the impression "that anything less than all-out unquestioning support of UFWOC on the part of religious leaders could only be interpreted as another proof that religion in this country is decadent, etc., etc." "Confidentially I was very disappointed in César Chávez' opening speech," reported Higgins. Chávez's authoritarian tone ruffled Higgins. "He made it abundantly clear," lamented the Labor Priest, "that what he wants is a national organization of religious leaders who will support UFWOC 1000 per cent . . . without asking any questions or offering any advice." Chávez "even went so far as to threaten [religious leaders] with the enmity of the poor (meaning, in this case, farm workers) if the religious community fails to measure up to his expectations." Disgusted, Higgins called Chávez's address "a miserable performance."[50]

Higgins's second letter, addressed to A. Garnett Day Jr., went further in criticizing Chávez's speech, and characterized it as threatening, dictatorial, and demanding of blind and unquestioning support. Higgins told Day that he "simply . . . [didn't] cotton to the idea of being threatened—even, or especially, by such a dear personal friend as César Chávez—and . . . strongly object[ed] to being told that the only way . . . to demonstrate . . . concern for farm workers is to support one particular organization blindly and without question." Disappointed in his friend's delivery, Higgins found Chávez's "approach to the question under discussion . . . so crude as to be almost insulting to the group."[51]

Despite his criticism of Chávez, Higgins still loyally supported the man, and he continued seeking opportunities to champion La Causa. Always mindful of the competition, Monsignor Higgins attended the February 10, 1971, annual convention of the United Fresh Fruit and Vegetable Association to gain a sharper understanding of the opposition. Not surprisingly, an ambience of sarcasm against the UFWOC suffused the gathering.[52]

Father Cletus Healy, of *Twin Circle* fame, kicked off the event. The executive vice president of the United Fresh Fruit and Vegetable Association introduced Healy "as an 'enlightened' Catholic priest"—something that "put Healy in a distinct minority in the ranks of the clergy."[53] Higgins reported to Donnelly that "Healy was dumb enough to fall for the Chairman's flattery." Moreover, Healy added "that he could think of only two other priests who are 'enlightened' on the subject of farm labor."[54] Presumably, Higgins was not one of the two.

Higgins blasted the Jesuit's speech as "from the beginning to end, one of the worst performances I have ever sat through." After "a rambling introduction, Healy said . . . that in his experience there is no serious injustice in the area of wages" and that "the farm labor wage system in California is commendable." Unbelievably, Healy "further stated that he was really amazed at the high quality of housing provided for farm workers." All in all, Higgins characterized "Healy's talk [as] a disaster and [his] . . . answers to the few questions addressed to him at the end of the panel were even more disastrous."[55]

In spite of Higgins's assessment, Healy did make a valid point. The Jesuit argued "that the majority of the Bishops . . . are too busy to keep up on farm labor developments and consequently must rely on the judgment of the members of the Bishops Committee who . . . take a one-sided view of the farm labor developments." Healy singled out Monsignor Higgins, and alleged that the Labor Priest had a long pro-Chávez record.[56] Healy was right. Donnelly, Higgins, and Mahony dominated the Ad Hoc Committee, and all three, especially Higgins, had a profarmworker bias.

One of the next speakers, Herbert Fleming, a spokesman for the major Salinas growers, knew Monsignors Higgins and Mahony from meetings during the summer of 1970 in connection with the lettuce dispute. Fleming's presentation criticized the UFWOC, "certain 'priests and do-gooders' who took the side of UFWOC during the lettuce strike last summer," wrote Higgins, and took a "sarcastic slap" at Chávez by insinuating that he was a "man who thinks he has a divine mission to speak for the farm workers."[57]

After delivering his remarks, Fleming approached Higgins and jokingly told the Labor Priest that he hoped that he "wasn't hurt or insulted by anything that had been said about [him] or the Bishops Committee." According to Higgins, he reassured Fleming "that it would take someone much more intelligent than Father Healy to insult me or to hurt my feelings." Like an old friend, Higgins then told Fleming that he would visit him the next time he got out to California, and Fleming encouraged this idea. A colleague of Fleming's then jumped into the conversation and expressed hope that Higgins's next visit to Salinas would not be in relation with his work as a member of the Bishops' Committee. The Labor Priest laughed at that and responded that he was sure the Bishops' Committee would return to Salinas "at the invitation of the growers." According to Higgins, Fleming and his colleague "said they rather doubted that and . . . parted, still in a very friendly mood."[58]

Higgins slowly became Chávez's ambassador of goodwill. Growers and Teamsters knew, despite Higgins's tenuous claims of neutrality, that he sided with La Causa; nonetheless, the Labor Priest earned the growers' respect and he could often act as a bridge between the competing factions. A portion of Higgins's service to La Causa entailed raising Chávez's profile within the Catholic Church and throughout the nation. Continually seeking such opportunities, the Labor Priest wrote to the Reverend Theodore Hesburgh, president of Notre Dame University, to suggest "that the Laetare Medal nominating committee seriously consider the possibility of conferring this year's medal on César Chávez."[59]

Notre Dame had established the Laetare (Latin for "rejoice") Medal in 1883 to recognize Catholics "whose genius has ennobled the arts and sciences, illustrated the ideals of the Church and enriched the heritage of humanity."[60] Higgins felt that Chávez fit this description, and informed Hesburgh that he and "all of the members of the [Ad Hoc] Committee—and notably the Chairman . . . [shared his] . . . high regard for Chávez."[61]

Recognizing Hispanics' vital role in the present and future of the Catholic Church, Higgins emphasized that "honoring Chávez . . . at this particular time . . . would give a great lift to the non-violent majority in the Mexican-American community in the United States, which . . . is at long last coming into its own and is hungering for a little recognition from the Church."[62] Higgins reasoned that the award would not only provide affirmation of the Catholic Church's support for Chávez, but also by extension, show its backing for the cause of the farmworkers and the Latino faithful. Unfortunately, the university did not select Chávez.[63] Thirty years later, however, Notre Dame bestowed the medal on Monsignor Higgins "for following Jesus, a carpenter's son, and heeding a vocation to serve his Lord in the workers of the world."[64]

In March 1971 the Teamsters made another peace overture directed toward Chávez, so the UFWOC and the Teamsters gathered again to renew their jurisdictional vows.[65] As he approached the bargaining table, Chávez lowered his defenses and suspended the lettuce boycott.[66] The Teamsters duped Chávez. Again. After five months of inconclusive quibbling, it became clear the UFWOC was tricked into rescinding its boycott so that the harvest season might conclude without serious disruptions.[67] The Teamster-grower collaboration appeared to be working splendidly.

Through their partnership with the lettuce growers, the Teamsters grew in economic potency as they obtained vertical integration of their union operations. Both found this arrangement financially advantageous, which bolstered the predominantly conservative ideology that the growers and the Teamsters shared.[68] Much like the grape growers, lettuce farmers disdained Chávez's unconventional negotiating style and his union's unique demands, which encompassed policies toward mechanized harvesting and restrictions on pesticide use.[69]

Mechanized harvesting became a thorny issue for growers because the UFWOC's contracts stipulated that the union could deny the introduction of equipment for the sake of preserving jobs.[70] Additionally, agriculturalists felt that the UFWOC's demands to protect the health of their workers were unreasonable. Growers resented Chávez's insistence that farmers cease the use of certain pesticides such as DDT and Endrin, and that his union have an opportunity to approve the use of any new chemicals. Moreover, Chávez wanted the right to determine how soon workers could safely enter a field after it had been sprayed with pesticides.[71]

In sharp contrast to the progressive UFWOC, the Teamsters Union struck the growers as a conservative, traditional, and businesslike organization. Their contract negotiators dressed like businessmen. UFWOC officials wore jeans and plaid shirts. The Teamsters' representatives looked professional, "prosperous, congenial, mostly Anglo, and not overtly religious on weekdays."[72] Unlike the UFWOC, the Teamsters' negotiating sessions were not perceived as "circuses," and Teamster negotiators did not "raise new issues late in the bargaining process."[73]

The Teamsters and growers quickly discovered their ideological and financial interests intersected; this cohesion insulated the Teamster-grower alliance from attempts at division. Unable to drive a wedge between the two, Chávez discovered that, in fact, the Teamsters and growers' mutual antipathy toward the UFWOC gave them common cause and strengthened their resolve. Chávez became the common enemy that united his foes. This combination of factors likely contributed to the Battle of the Salad Bowl's exceptionally lengthy duration.

Planning for a protracted conflict, Monsignor Higgins drafted talking points for responding to criticism of the Ad Hoc Committee's role in the Salad Bowl. Higgins's April 1971 guidance, intended for the USCC/ NCCB's top leadership, noted that the majority of farmworkers "are . . . very good Catholics," and that the record of the Catholic Church "in supporting the right of farm workers to organize has been . . . worthy of the highest commendation." However, if the Church was indeed "guided by Catholic social teaching," insisted Higgins, then it "really . . . [had] no choice in the matter" but to support the farmworkers.[74] The confidential communication from Higgins to Bernardin clearly revealed the Labor Priest's pro-Chávez bias. Higgins claimed that Chávez's "arrival . . . on the scene in 1965 was really providential," and felt Chávez to be not only "a man of great personal integrity and extraordinary ability," but also a "devout and loyal Catholic."[75]

In his letter, which delineated the Church's policy on the La Causa, Higgins touched upon the purveyors of anti-Chávez propaganda, namely, the Labor Priest's intellectual sparring partners, Fathers Lyons and Healy. In a pointed reference to the *Twin Circle*, the Labor Priest noted he was "painfully aware of the fact that a handful of Catholic periodicals . . . [had] been carrying on a relentless, not to say unscrupulous, campaign against Chávez and, to their great shame, have done everything within their power, by fair means or foul, to destroy his reputation." By way of example, Higgins observed that such critics "have repeatedly charged (or slyly suggested) that . . . [Chávez] is a religious 'phony,' that he is totally insincere in his espousal of the philosophy of non-violence, that he is secretly Marxist-oriented in his thinking, [and] that he is getting rich off the workers."[76]

Higgins emphatically felt that "the *Twin Circle* crowd . . . are doing a disastrous disservice to the cause of the Mexican-American Catholics of this country by continuing to undermine Chávez's reputation and by doing so in a totally irresponsible manner." Higgins further chastened such critics by pointing out that, in most cases, they did not personally know Chávez and were "simply repeating irresponsible gossip and misinformation handed on to them by a small minority of California growers . . . who, in turn, have never met Chávez (or have only rarely met him) and seem to be determined, at almost any cost, to destroy his reputation simply because they are opposed to unions in the field of agricultural labor." The Labor Priest made clear that "the members of the Bishops Committee on Farm Labor unanimously reject the anti-Chávez and anti-UFWOC propaganda being circulated by these people and would no doubt be delighted to say so publicly and on the record if they were called upon to do so."[77]

Higgins's letter also addressed the Ad Hoc Committee's impact on farm labor since its inception in November of 1969, and the degree of acceptance the Bishops' Committee enjoyed within the Church. Higgins explained that "the Bishops Committee . . . [had] been extremely helpful in bringing the parties together," and that the "Secretary of the Committee, Monsignor Roger Mahony, [was] one of the best informed priests in California on the subject of farm labor, [and] is available for consultation with the parties on a permanent day-to-day and almost hour-to-hour basis." Tellingly, Higgins also commented that "it is my impression, incidentally, that the overwhelming *majority* [emphasis added] of the Bishops are extremely proud of what the Committee has accomplished during its short term of office and are fully prepared to give the Committee their complete support."[78] By using the word *majority* and not *unanimity*, Higgins appeared to indicate that Cardinal Manning, who seemed to favor the growers over the farmworkers, might have been less than enthusiastic about the committee's mission.

Although the Ad Hoc Committee possessed a pro-UFW bias, the members went through considerable efforts to deny, at least in official/public statements, that such pro-Chávez sympathies existed. The Labor

Priest emphatically derided allegations that Chávez used the committee as a tool of the UFW, describing them as "a demonstrably false and . . . malicious rumor," and lamented "the misguided efforts of woefully uninformed and, for the most part, ultra conservative clerics and laymen to undermine the Bishops Committee." Despite such critics, Higgins believed the work of the Ad Hoc Committee was "more important and more effective than anything that any other committee has done in the field of social action during . . . [his] 26 years at the Conference," and that the "Committee has made a tremendous contribution to the cause of social justice."[79]

Because of the committee's overwhelming efforts to benefit the lives of the poor and implement Catholic social teachings, Higgins advised Bernardin that the NCCB had an obligation to defend the work of the Ad Hoc Committee against critics. Higgins felt strongly about this matter because, according to his perceptions, "most of the Committee's critics (be they misguided clerics from the staff of *Twin Circle* or misguided growers) [were] almost completely uninformed about the work of the Committee and even more woefully uninformed about Chávez as an individual and UFWOC as an organization."[80]

Although neither naïve nor gullible, both Higgins and Mahony continued to consistently overestimate the Teamsters' sincerity throughout the first two years of the Salad Bowl conflict. Mahony opined in his May 1971 report that, although he had no clear indication that "a definite settlement is forthcoming or that negotiations between the growers and UFWOC [are] imminent," he felt "it would be safe to say that all of the signs look promising at this point." Completely misjudging the situation, Mahony maintained that the Teamsters appeared "to be making it . . . clear to the growers that they are definitely pulling out of the farm labor organization effort and that the growers' best route would be to recognize and to negotiate with UFWOC."[81]

Mahony continued his efforts to bring reconciliation, and in June 1971 the future cardinal visited a UFW hiring hall, where he met with growers. During these meetings, the growers raised concerns about past union dues and claimed that the UFW's stipulation that all past dues be paid before a worker is sent out caused major worker shortage problems in the Coachella and Southern Kern County areas. In one case, the UFW held a farmworker back for two dollars in arrears.[82]

As the most unbiased member of the Ad Hoc Committee, Mahony emphasized the growers' concerns over the union dues issue. Mahony asked Chávez "consider this issue in the context of [its] continued efforts to improve the total working conditions of the farm worker."[83] From Mahony's June 11 report to the Ad Hoc Committee, it appears that Chávez took Mahony's advice seriously and began working to rectify the situation. Chávez's solution included providing loans to workers who had dues in arrears and keeping the UFW's monthly dues low ($3.50).[84]

Although the Bishops' Committee on the whole harbored a pro-UFW bias, the group succeeded remarkably in its efforts to bridge the gap between growers and the UFWOC. In a June 1971 letter to Bernardin, Higgins recounted the Ad Hoc Committee's role in successful mediation of the UFWOC's dispute with Heublein, a large U.S. distributor of wine under UFW boycott. According to Higgins, the Ad Hoc Committee agreed to broker the disagreement between Heublein and the UFWOC at the urgent request of Heublein's vice president, Joseph McGarry. McGarry, a devout Catholic, told Higgins that the company would not enter into negotiations with Chávez "unless the Bishops Committee was also invited to attend in an observer capacity." Clearly sensitive to charges of a pro-Chávez bias, Higgins stressed that "the presence of the Bishops Committee at the meeting . . . [was] the absolute *sine qua non* so far as the company . . . [was] concerned," and that it was worth emphasizing "the foregoing point for the obvious reason that . . . the Bishops Committee has been falsely accused from time to time of being prejudiced in favor of the UFWOC and of being unsympathetic to the position of the growers." Higgins felt "that the Heublein company's insistence on . . . [the Ad Hoc Committee's] sitting in on their negotiations with UFWOC . . . is proof positive that this charge against the Committee is completely unfounded."[85] Of course, if the charge was completely unfounded, why did it keep coming up? Because it was true.

Roughly two weeks after Higgins's letter to Bernardin, Mahony reported to the committee on the Heublein situation. In essence, Chávez wanted Heublein to bring some of the grape growers to the bargaining table, and also to agree not to crush grapes from growers under strike.[86] Heublein countered that it could not do anything to persuade grape growers to negotiate with the UFW.[87] As Higgins indicated in an August 2 letter to Bernardin, the Heublein-UFWOC talks had not gone as smoothly as initially expected; nonetheless, the committee pressed forward and kept both parties at the negotiating table.[88]

The renewed efforts at mediation worked. The UFWOC and Heublein settled on August 17, 1971. Terms of the settlement included a provision that the UFWOC take immediate steps to stop the boycott against Heublein and subsidiary products.[89] In return, Heublein agreed to recognize the UFWOC as the collective bargaining agent for all agricultural workers that it or any of its subsidiaries employed.[90] The Heublein-UFWOC settlement also had a special stipulation that benefited growers. Dubbed the Farm Services Agency, the organization would supply labor to growers that used Heublein's crushing plants.[91] Although the agency's workers would all be members of the UFW, the individual grower would not be obligated to sign a contract with the union. Because this system saved growers "a lot of labor problems and headaches," reported Mahony, roughly thirty "chose to proceed with this Agency."[92]

Acknowledging the committee's success in mediating the UFWOC-Heublein dispute, Bishop Donohoe wrote Donnelly to commend the Ad Hoc Committee's work. Once again, financial concerns appeared to weigh heavily on Donohoe's thoughts. The bishop of Fresno made reference to the significance of the UFWOC-Heublein resolution for the charitable work of the Church, an indication that Donohoe continued to be disturbed by the financial pressures exerted by wealthy Catholic growers in his diocese. "[T]he settlement of this particular dispute comes at a critical time here in the Diocese of Fresno," he wrote, "as we are setting out on a Diocesan Development program. . . . It would have been much more difficult to approach our people with this type of program had the level of tension perdured [sic] because of this particular dispute."[93]

Bishop Donohoe had to engage in a daily balancing act between grower and farmworker interests. Although Donohoe clearly did not enjoy challenging the agriculturalists, he nonetheless issued spirited statements defending the Ad Hoc Committee's role in the farm labor conflict. In a June 25, 1971, letter to Allen Grant, president of the pro-grower California Farm Bureau Federation, Donohoe countered the common charge that the clergy had no business meddling in temporal matters by asserting that "there is no human situation in which the Church and all Christians do not have a very proper place." In the case of the farm labor dispute, "there was simply no way a solution could be found without an impartial, third-party entering the dispute." Therefore, Donohoe told Grant that the Ad Hoc Committee had a right to participate "to the extent specifically requested by both sides, and never to serve the interests of either." "Until we have decent national legislation to guide employer/employee relationships," concluded Donohoe, the Ad Hoc Committee would have to function as "a stop-gap mediation group until such time as necessary legislation is passed."[94]

Donohoe's letter to Grant is important because it mentioned "necessary legislation." In 1975, the state of California implemented that legislation through a law called the California Agricultural Labor Relations Act (CALRA). Essentially, CALRA gave the Golden State's farmworkers protections similar to those under the National Labor Relations Act. Soon after the state enacted the CALRA, the Ad Hoc Committee began to disengage from La Causa. The bishops contended that because the legislation protected farmworker rights, the Church's services were no longer needed. However, Donohoe's letter appeared to indicate that, at least in 1971, the committee planned to stand as mediators until *national* legislation protected the farmworkers. Juxtaposing Donohoe's 1971 letter to Grant with the Ad Hoc Committee's 1975 justification for disengagement with La Causa, we are left with the impression that the Church became fatigued, and thus settled for a legislative victory at the state, rather than the national, level.

In 1971, Donohoe, already ailing from the stress brought on by the farm labor dispute, suffered another setback when the *California Farmer* magazine published an article alleging that the Catholic Church poured "thousands of dollars into the efforts of César Chávez." The article, in the magazine's June edition, singled out the Campaign for Human Development grants as a source of funding for Chávez.[95]

Bishop Donohoe wrote to Jack Pickett, editor of the *California Farmer*, to address the allegations.[96] In his rebuttal, Donohoe explained that local parishes had collected $8.5 million for the Campaign for Human Development, and had then remitted the funds to the campaign's national office, which "announced that organizations and groups —Catholic, non-Catholic, and non-sectarian—could apply for a grant from these funds." The Farm Workers Service Center, which provided social services and health care programs, had applied for and received a $55,000 grant. Before the campaign provided the funding, continued Donohoe, "the Farm Workers Service Center, Inc. had to furnish proof that it was a non-profit charitable corporation under California law, that it qualified as a tax exempt organization under the Internal Revenue Code . . . and that it was tax exempt under the California Franchise Tax Board regulations."[97]

In an effort to clear the air, Donohoe offered to open the Diocese of Fresno's financial books and he commented that it would be inconceivable for the Church to jeopardize its nonprofit status by donating to organizations such as unions, which were clearly outside the nonprofit classification. In his statement, Donohoe also countered allegations that the Farm Workers Service Center was "simply a 'front organization' for the United Farm Workers Organizing Committee, AFL-CIO," maintain-

ing that he had "investigated the programs and services of the Farm
Workers Service Center . . . and . . . found them to be both legitimate and
beneficial to any farm worker requesting them." Indeed, the bishop
added, he "would be very pleased to see a joint venture by both growers
and farm workers to establish more health clinics and social service
centers in . . . small, rural areas."[98] Donohoe's explanation served to
clarify the matter at hand, but additional, and greater, pressures awaited
the bishop of Fresno.

1972: The Politics of La Causa

In February 1972, Chávez's organization was transformed from an organizing committee into a full-fledged union. Marking the shift, the United
Farm Workers Organizing Committee changed its name to the United
Farm Workers of America, AFL-CIO—better known as the UFW.[99] With
the new moniker came greater responsibility. As an organizing committee, La Causa had received ten thousand dollars each month in contributions from the AFL-CIO. Now, as a union, the AFL-CIO expected the
UFW to remit funds in exchange for the charter's endowment of "jurisdiction and prestige."[100]

Along with its name, the nature of Chávez's union also began to
change. Chávez became increasingly engaged in political battles within
buildings rather than strikes in fields.[101] Again, César sought the Church's
backing. For example, when the general counsel of the National Labor
Relations Board, Peter Nash, sought an injunction against secondary
boycotts by the farm workers, John Cosgrove wrote Higgins to "recom-
mend a statement . . . jointly condemning this inequity and calling for an
even-handed policy."[102]

Cosgrove found it absurd that "on the one hand the farm workers do
not have the benefit of coverage of the National Labor Relations Act . . .
but on the other hand they are to be subjected to the restrictive provisions of the Act."[103] Higgins readily agreed, and four USCC/NCCB officials, including Higgins and Cosgrove, sent President Nixon a letter.

The communication blasted the U.S. government for not extending
the protections and benefits of the NLRA to farmworkers. Moreover, the
writers argued that seeking an injunction against secondary boycotts by
the farmworkers "clearly lacks the even-handed approach one has a
right to expect from the agencies of our federal government."[104] The
letter closed by urging Nixon "to intervene to halt this wholly unfair
action of the National Labor Relations Board's General Counsel."[105]

Unfortunately for Chávez, President Nixon did not sympathize with La Causa. Under his administration, the Department of Defense purchased lettuce to neutralize the UFW's boycott. Chávez, in a letter to Republican senator Bob Dole, protested "the use of the Department of Defense (DoD) by the Republican Administration to break . . . [the UFW's] strike and boycott of lettuce." According to Chávez, DoD officials, including the chief of the department's Fruit and Vegetable Branch, had crossed UFW picket lines to "to meet secretly with . . . Salinas Valley lettuce growers . . . to break . . . [the UFW's] international boycott of lettuce." The Nixon administration, at U.S. taxpayer expense, claimed Chávez, had generously "guaranteed . . . these Salinas Valley growers a market for their non-union lettuce."[106]

In his letter to Dole, Chávez drew a parallel between the farmworkers and U.S. soldiers conscripted to fight in Vietnam. Chávez remarked that "growers refuse to grant their migrant farm workers even the most basic human rights of dignity and freedom, . . . [whereas] citizens of our country who serve in the Armed Forces are young men and women themselves from the poor and minority groups." Making the connection that farmworkers and U.S. troops fighting in Southeast Asia often shared similar socioeconomic backgrounds, Chávez argued that soldiers "do not want to feast on lettuce or even see it in their mess halls when they know that thousands of farm workers and their families are prevented by rich growers from receiving a just wage and decent working conditions."[107]

While the Nixon administration worked to break the UFW's lettuce embargo, the USCC/NCCB's Committee on Social Development (CSD) adopted a statement that endorsed and supported the UFW's boycott.[108] Monsignor Higgins, John Cosgrove, and Paul Sedillo, director of the Division for Spanish-Speaking, all strongly supported the statement.[109] Donnelly, also a member of the Committee on Social Development, "completely" agreed with the statement, but "in his capacity as chairman of the Ad Hoc Committee . . . chose to abstain from voting in order to keep open the possibility of negotiating."[110] Clearly Donnelly had a pro-UFW bias, and given his rank and influence in shaping the Catholic Church's policies in the farm labor dispute, we can, by extension, claim that the Catholic Church favored the farmworkers over the growers.

Despite this underlying bias, Donnelly struggled to preserve some semblance of neutrality until 1973. Although the USCC CSD supported the boycott, the statement reflected only the support of the members of the CSD and did not pretend to speak for the USCC or the National Conference of Catholic Bishops.[111] The CSD's statement contended that the farm labor dispute presented "a fundamental issue of social justice." "To bring about collective bargaining and a just settlement of the dispute," the CSD recommended "that only lettuce clearly marked with the official United Farm Workers' label, the black Aztec eagle, be purchased."[112]

In addition to the CSD's public endorsement of the boycott, Bishop Raymond J. Gallagher, chairman of the USCC Committee on Social Development and bishop of Lafayette, Indiana, also sent a request to all U.S. bishops "asking them, if possible, to encourage some expression of public support for the farm workers' cause" at Labor Day masses.[113] Always mindful of important details, Higgins suggested to Chávez that he send a personal note of thanks to Gallagher.[114]

Indicating Higgins's concern for Chávez, the Labor Priest made a habit of constantly reminding Chávez to send thank-you notes. Taking his cue from Higgins, Chávez wrote to Cosgrove in gratitude, offering the opinion that the "*Lettuce Boycott* statement by the Committee on Social Development is going to be very helpful . . . [because] we need again the strength of institutional moral support."

The partnership between the Catholic hierarchy and César Chávez was fast approaching its apogee. Reflecting the euphoria of this period, Chávez closed his correspondence to Cosgrove with an uplifting phrase that captured the essence of Chávez's unrelenting optimism and his firm belief that if he persisted in presenting the righteousness of the farmworkers' cause, the UFW would ultimately succeed.

"*Hasta La Victoria*," wrote Chávez—onward to victory.[115]

Soon after the CSD's endorsement of the boycott, Higgins spoke at a clerical conference in Arizona. He remarked that the Ad Hoc Committee's "role, contrary to certain statements made by critics of the Committee, was not an [adversarial] role" and that the bishops "did not go into California to beat the drums for César Chávez and the farm workers, nor did we go there in any way to oppose the growers." Instead, Higgins suggested that the Ad Hoc Committee simply offered its "assistance to help the parties to come together around the negotiating table and hammer out contracts."[116] After denying the committee's pro-Chávez bias, the Labor Priest opened up to the audience and publicly admitted his farmworker bias by clarifying that the committee was not completely neutral. Higgins said that he had "tried . . . to be extremely sympathetic and open-minded with regard to the problems faced by growers," but he would not respond to growers' concerns "at the expense of the workers."[117]

The Ad Hoc Committee's activism had brought financial havoc upon the Diocese of Fresno. As the mid-1970s approached, evidence of Teamsters-grower collusion to destroy the UFW became so obvious that such influential members of the Catholic hierarchy as Higgins and Donnelly, and later USCC/NCCB general secretary Bishop James Rausch, began to abandon any veneer of neutrality and admitted profarmworker sympathies. Tired of the bishops' activism during the Delano Grape Strike, and then during the Battle of the Salad Bowl, wealthy Catholic growers in the Central Valley protested the Church's meddling by abandoning any vestiges of financial support.

The July 1972 closure of the Diocese of Fresno's newspaper, the *Central California Register,* highlighted the extent of the growers' economic influence over the diocese and their dissatisfaction with the Catholic Church's increasingly candid pro-Chávez bias.[118] Roger Mahony provided an exceedingly restrained assessment of the growers' role in the closure of the forty-three year old publication. The future cardinal commented that "the overriding reason to terminate the paper was *not* [emphasis added] the farm labor dispute."[119] Instead, Mahony merely made an oblique reference to the influence of agribusiness in his report: "various factors of that dispute have made the continuation of the paper quite difficult."[120]

Gerald E. Sherry, managing editor of the *Central California Register,* placed far greater emphasis on the growers' role in the paper's demise.[121] According to Sherry, "the beginning of the end came in 1968 when he printed a photo of . . . César Chávez at a mass with Sen. Robert Kennedy."[122] Sherry's highly controversial decision to run, in a Catholic publication, a photo presenting two prominent and devout Catholics sharing communion during a Catholic mass while struggling to implement Catholic social teaching understandably sparked a firestorm of controversy among the Diocese of Fresno's Catholic parishioners.

"Two Catholic women—one of them from a prominent agribusiness family in the San Joaquin Valley" wasted little time in responding to the highly charged picture, recalled Sherry. The concerned parishioners "warned [him] that he was wrong to give 'publicity' to Chávez and the unionization struggle." According to Sherry, the women "mentioned 'economic pressure,' and soon advertising cancellations were reaching the *Register.*" Central Valley growers began to send letters to advertisers, urging them to drop their ads. Sherry continued: noncompliant businesses "were picketed for 'backing' the Catholic newspaper and were warned to stop 'supporting' the *Register* if they wanted to keep growers' families as customers."[123]

Sherry recalled that "growers said we backed the grape boycott, which we never did," and he claimed that the *Register* "bent over backward to be fair and objective to both sides." The growers' main complaint, claimed Sherry, "was that we gave recognition to the fact that Chávez existed and had a cause." According to Sherry, the growers were not interested in objective reporting; instead, they wanted propaganda—"only their viewpoint and no one else's." "The Catholic pastors in the valley were also pressured," he continued, "with many of them afraid to support the paper from the pulpit or even mention the *Register* at risk of losing parish financial support."[124]

The numbers corroborate Sherry's account. Circulation for the *Register* dropped from twenty thousand in 1968 to eleven thousand for its last issue. Both Sherry and Donohoe knew that the paper was doomed and that the growers aimed, in the words of Sherry, to "choke off . . . support and advertising because the *Register* would not confine its coverage of the farm labor issue to their side only." Grower dissatisfaction with the Church's involvement in the farm labor dispute was directly related to the diocese's dwindling coffers. Wrote Sherry: "the fullness of collection plates in many parishes of the Fresno diocese depend[ed] on the generosity of grower families and people employed in agribusiness."

Although the *Register* and the California hierarchy took the relatively moderate stand that "workers did indeed have the right to organize for their own economic betterment and that both sides should negotiate their grievances," Catholic growers clearly resented such socially conscious promulgations from their spiritual leaders and punished such transgressions accordingly. Sherry, who left Fresno to run the San Francisco archdiocesan paper, claimed that the *Register* met its demise carrying "the Christian social message" because "the affluent in our society seem unwilling to carry the virtue of charity to its ultimate conclusion."[125]

As Sherry's account indicates, César Chávez and the issue of farm labor divided the Central Valley's Catholic flock along ideological and socioeconomic lines. Wealthy, powerful, and conservative Catholic growers tended to oppose La Causa; liberal Vatican II enthusiasts, working-class Catholics, and the politically and economically marginalized segments of the faithful by and large supported Chávez and the farmworkers.

The fall of 1972 brought a much-needed morale boost for Bishop Donohoe. After seven years of relentless pressure from irate growers and the bankruptcy of his diocese's newspaper, he received praise from the pope. In a letter celebrating the twenty-fifth anniversary of

Donahoe's consecration as bishop, Pope Paul VI lauded his "defense of the rights of farm workers in the San Joaquin Valley," commended his "evangelical justice" and "vigorous and uncompromising efforts to protect the rights of farm workers," and "zealously encourage[d]" the bishop to continue his work.[126]

Both the press and Pope Paul VI alluded to Donahoe's profarmworker bias, but the bishop continued to deny charges that he favored Chávez.[127] His continual enthusiastic support, even in the face of unrelenting criticism, for the farmworkers' right to organize indicated he might have sympathized with the UFW. Yet his repeated attempts to avoid endorsement of Chávez's boycott and the dispute's negative effect on his emotional health provide convincing evidence to the contrary. If Donohoe did not favor the growers, at the very least he feared their economic potency and considerable influence over the financial health of his diocese.

As the growers set upon the Diocese of Fresno's newspaper, Teamster president Frank Fitzsimmons sealed a political alliance with the White House. Needing a major union endorsement for his 1972 reelection bid, President Nixon courted Fitzsimmons and showered him with attention, visits, and gifts. Fitzsimmons responded to Nixon's overtures by providing the president of the United States with his only major union endorsement. However, it appeared that more than gifts were at stake. Reportedly, the U.S. Justice Department dropped charges against Fitzsimmons's son, Richard, who faced allegations of fraud, and former Teamster president Jimmy Hoffa received a presidential pardon.[128]

Higgins observed Fitzsimmons and Nixon's minuet with amazement. On December 12, 1972, the Farm Bureau invited Fitzsimmons to address one of its gatherings, and perhaps due in part to his relationship with Nixon, the Teamsters' president, according to Higgins, was "naïve enough to think that he was the number one labor leader in the country." The Labor Priest felt otherwise. Before Fitzsimmons's address at the Farm Bureau event, Higgins approached him—the president of a union that had a reputation for placing adversaries in hospitals—and said: "You're idiotic, Fitz."[129]

Fitzsimmons "more or less good-naturedly" shot back, "Well, why don't you mind your business, and I'll mind mine."[130]

Although Fitzsimmons and Higgins enjoyed some repartee, the Teamster president's speech was not so lighthearted. Fitzsimmons's discourse invited a coalition among the Teamsters Union, the American Farm Bureau, the California growers, and the Nixon administration in order to take on what he saw as Chávez's "revolutionary movement, . . . [which was] perpetrating a fraud on the American public."[131]

The Farm Bureau took Fitzsimmons's suggestion to heart and promptly drafted Proposition 22 for consideration in California's November 1972 general election.[132] The bureau reportedly backed the initiative with a million dollar public relations campaign.[133] Fatigued by losing millions of dollars because of the farm union's worldwide boycott of grapes and lettuce, the growers decided to fight back by granting the farmworkers the right to unionize.[134] Of course, the growers' version of the right to unionize outlawed boycotts and sharply limited strikes.[135]

Given the initiative's source, it came as little surprise that Chávez characterized it as "repressive legislation," and "antiunion."[136] The Teamsters also detested the bill, and felt that the regulations would hamstring their effort to organize farmworkers.[137] The proposition made primary boycotts difficult to commence, proscribed secondary boycotts, required a ten-day strike notice, and provided for a sixty-day cooling-off period.[138] If passed, the initiative would destroy the UFW because it removed the only nonviolent instrument the farmworkers had—the boycott.[139] Defeating Proposition 22 became Chávez's top priority.

Jerry Brown, the son of former California governor Pat Brown, California's secretary of state, future governor of California himself, and a benefactor of La Causa, boosted Chávez's efforts when he filed suit to remove the proposition from the ballot.[140] Brown's action found its root in a *Los Angeles Times* article that detailed procedures used in gathering signatures for the proposal.[141] Brown asked District Attorney Joseph Busch to investigate the allegations, and Busch reported evidence of widespread fraud.[142]

The Council of California Growers denied knowledge of any alleged wrongdoing.[143] "The only people making this unproven charge," stated a grower partisan, "seem to be liberal politicians running for office."[144] Governor Ronald Reagan, who supported the initiative, agreed. "I think [Brown's] politically motivated in most areas," said Reagan, "he's come up with some pretty good routines."[145] The courts eventually rejected Brown's action, but his efforts raised the initiative's profile with voters.[146]

In September 1972, the entire Catholic hierarchy in California, led by Archbishop Timothy Manning, issued a statement delineating Proposition 22's unjust restrictions and urged voters to reject the initiative.[147] As the farm labor dispute continued into the 1970s, the Catholic hierarchy met critics of the bishops' activism with increasing intransigence. Despite the financial repercussions stemming from the Church's deepening involvement in the farm labor controversy, the bishops again defied California's potent agribusiness sector by publicly opposing Proposition 22.[148]

The California hierarchy issued a public statement charging that the Farm Bureau initiative "would unjustly limit the rights of farm workers, ... outlaw the boycott, ... restrict farm labor strikes," and allow "growers who sign union contracts to subcontract his entire farm labor requirements to non-union workers, thus displacing all of his union employees." The bishops claimed that Proposition 22 strayed "so widely from a just and equitable approach to settling agricultural labor problems that, if adopted, it would undoubtedly create far more serious tensions and difficulties than it attempts to solve."

From the hierarchy's perspective, Proposition 22 robbed unions of the "right to communicate with the workers on company property and at their homes," and effectively denied "the vast majority of farm workers the right to vote" because of convoluted definitions of eligibility. Furthermore, the bishops felt that Proposition 22 provided growers "rights which make it virtually impossible for the farm workers to negotiate many issues affecting their basic working conditions." Finally, the proposal completely disarmed farmworkers of their "basic right . . . to strike."[149] The Catholic bishops' bold and forceful attack on Proposition 22 exacerbated the Church-grower polarization, and brought the hierarchy increasingly closer to outright partisanship with La Causa.

Chávez, Jerry Brown, and the Catholic bishops took the farmworkers' case to the court of public opinion and won. Voters soundly defeated Proposition 22 by a 58 to 42 percent margin.[150] In 1972, Chávez was still a rising star on the national political stage. The public listened to him. The electorate took action. A mere four years later, this would not be the case.

1973: "Biased" at Last

On January 16, 1973, Bill Grami declared that the Teamsters had successfully renegotiated their original 1970 contracts with lettuce growers.[151] Shamelessly, the Teamsters signed the new agreements in spite of their 1971 jurisdictional pact with the UFW.[152] The 1971 treaty meant little to the growers, and after the resounding defeat of Proposition 22 in November 1972, agribusiness once again had reason to fear Chávez.[153]

The 1973 Teamster contracts granted the farmworkers an immediate pay raise and annual increases thereafter.[154] Additionally, the Teamsters agreed to drop their contracts' mandate for farmworkers to join the union within ten days of hire, and to stop charging initiation dues.[155] Expediency, rather than kindness, motivated the Teamsters' decision. The union had to give the farmworkers some breaks because if labor decided to walk out rather than agree to join the Teamsters, it would be yet another major public relations blunder. Worse yet, the growers would be shorthanded, and of course, very displeased with their choice of union.[156]

The first month of 1973 also brought changes to the Ad Hoc Committee. Bishop Walter Curtis submitted his resignation, citing lack of time due to his recent election to the chairmanship of the NCCB Committee on the Liturgy.[157] According to Monsignor Higgins, Bishop Curtis's resignation "had nothing to do with the pros and cons of the farm labor controversy."[158] Bishop Edward O'Rourke of Peoria indicated his interest in serving on the committee, and because of his knowledge of rural problems and his concern for small growers both USCC/NCCB general secretary James Rausch and Bishop Donnelly recommended his appointment to USCC/NCCB chairman Cardinal Krol. The cardinal approved the request and gave the committee its first change in staffing.[159]

The following month, Chávez peppered Higgins with complimentary letters. Chávez told the Labor Priest that his "willingness to help the farm workers is so evident, and we are always grateful to you."[160] In a separate communication, Chávez praised the Catholic Church's contribution to La Causa by noting "this is truly a time when we are seeing the Church in leadership for justice."[161] Later in the month, Chávez again wrote Higgins to express his deep appreciation "for the tremendous job you are doing for the farm workers."[162]

But Higgins had several partners in his mission to champion the farmworkers. La Causa's highest profile convert, George Meany, conducted a lively press conference in February 1973. When asked if he still supported Chávez and the farmworkers, Meany replied, "very much," adding that the Teamsters strikebreaking in California was "absolutely disgraceful."[163] After Meany's verbal assault on the Teamsters, Higgins fired off a memo to Bishop Rausch from Miami, where he was attending the annual winter meeting of the AFL-CIO Executive Council. According to Higgins, his "recent ['Yardstick'] columns on this subject [the UFW-Teamster dispute] were in part responsible for Meany's blast at the Teamsters."[164]

While Higgins and Meany vigorously defended the UFW by attacking the Teamsters, Jimmy Hoffa, paroled by Nixon in December 1971 after serving fifty-eight months on a jury-tampering conviction, took the offensive against the UFW. In a speech to a less-than-receptive audience at Stanford University, Hoffa claimed, "the César Chávez-led United Farm Workers Union will 'go out of business' once its jurisdictional dispute with the Teamsters Union over organizing lettuce field workers is settled." The crowd of 150 frequently booed Hoffa as he stridently declared that the Teamsters would not "give up to another union what [*sic*] is under . . . [the Teamsters'] jurisdiction," and that his union would "fight Chávez just like we fight employers—until we win."[165]

Hoffa was serious. So was his union. By April 1973, the Teamsters had descended upon Coachella Valley's grape vineyards in an effort to capture the soon-to-expire 1970 contracts that growers had signed with the UFW.[166] On April 15, the Teamsters emerged victorious; they concluded sweetheart contracts with thirty grape growers who had previously signed with the UFW to end the Delano Grape Strike.

Once again, the Teamsters failed even to meet with the workers they purported to represent, and the growers rejoiced in dodging Chávez's union.[167] Monsignor Higgins characterized the Teamsters' action as "one of the darkest and most shameful days in American labor history."[168] Chávez responded to the Teamsters' hostility by calling a strike and renewing the boycott of table grapes.[169]

Organized labor quickly threw its support behind La Causa. The AFL-CIO and the United Auto Workers raised funds for the UFW and provided enough financing for Chávez to increase the UFW's strike benefits from twenty-five dollars to seventy-five dollars per week.[170] Despite organized labor's assistance, La Causa rapidly deteriorated. The UFW's 1970 contracts with Delano growers terminated in late July 1973, and by August 9 the grape growers had signed four-year contracts with the Teamsters covering eight thousand workers, which left the UFW with only two table grape contracts.[171]

The Teamsters conquered Delano—the heart of La Causa. They took the grape contracts from Chávez. They delivered a humiliating defeat and a clear message: The Teamsters aimed to vanquish the UFW.[172] By signing the Delano contracts, the Teamsters unraveled Chávez's five years of marching, striking, fasting, and negotiating, leaving his union with a mere sixty-five hundred farmworkers under contract.[173] By comparison, the Teamsters' fieldworker membership had expanded to thirty-five thousand.[174]

In 1973, the Bishops' Ad Hoc Committee, and by extension the U.S.

During his tenure as USCC/NCCB general secretary, Bishop James Rausch (left) ensured that César Chávez had support from the highest levels of the American Catholic hierarchy. Rausch, who shared Monsignor Higgins's enthusiasm for La Causa, eventually succeeded Bishop Donnelly as chairman of the Ad Hoc Committee. Monsignor Higgins is at the right.

Catholic Church, finally relinquished its veneer of neutrality in the farm labor dispute. The Church came out in public support of La Causa in 1973 because the right people held positions of responsibility. These people were Bishop Joseph Donnelly, USCC/NCCB general secretary Bishop James Rausch, Monsignor George Higgins, and Monsignor Roger Mahony. By 1973, Rausch, a strong partisan of Chávez, commanded the USCC/NCCB's operations as general secretary. Donnelly, Higgins, and Mahony controlled the Ad Hoc Committee, which had carte blanche to make USCC/NCCB policy on farmworker issues. The vast majority of bishops did not have time to devote to the California farmworker conflict, and deferred to the Ad Hoc Committee's judgment; therefore, Donnelly, Higgins, and Mahony, as the most proactive in the group, controlled the policy.

If luck is when preparation meets opportunity, then Rausch, Donnelly, Higgins, and Mahony provided the preparation, but the timing was also right. The 1960s and 1970s were ideal decades for liberal causes—especially liberal Catholic causes. Vatican II had revolutionized the Church. The Civil Rights movement, the termination of the bracero program, a growing public interest in social causes, and rise of politicians interested in advancing farmworker rights (for example, Jerry Brown in California) provided momentum necessary to shift the Catholic Church from neutral mediator to outright partisan of La Causa.

Father James Vizzard, a Jesuit priest who worked with the National Catholic Rural Life Conference and later with the UFW as a legislative representative in Washington, penned an important article published in a 1973 edition of *America*. Titled "Chávez and the Teamsters: David vs. Goliath," the article captured the hierarchy's mood and circulated widely among the bishops. The article made a strong case for the U.S. Catholic Church to declare all-out war against the Teamsters, and importantly, it found a receptive audience.

Vizzard's account derided Frank Fitzsimmons and the "scandal ridden" Teamsters. Fitzsimmons, according to Vizzard, claimed that "farm workers should not be treated as chattel," but then worked to "conceal the Teamsters' sordid history and current practice of consistently doing just that." The article charged that an alliance of Teamsters and "big growers" had "but one purpose: to destroy . . . the upstart United Farm Workers, AFL-CIO, which dares to assert that farm workers are not slaves or chattel, that they have dignity and rights for which the union is willing to fight." Taking pains to substantiate the Teamsters' nefarious intentions, Vizzard highlighted the California State Supreme Court's December 1972 statement that asserted "neither the growers nor the Teamsters ever contemplated allowing the workers any kind of election to determine their desires" during the signing of the Battle of the Salad Bowl's sweetheart contracts.[175] For Vizzard, the Teamsters were the enemy, and the Catholic Church had an obligation to protect La Causa from destruction.

The Church's intellectual progression toward full endorsement of the UFW took a major step forward on April 6, 1973. Higgins wrote Gerald Costello an important letter that chronicled the turn of events, perhaps one of the most meaningful communications in the history of the Catholic Church's involvement with the UFW. In the letter, Higgins admitted that he was "afraid that 'the American Church' (read: The Bishops Committee on Farm Labor) . . . [was] no longer thought of as being a neutral third party in the lettuce dispute and, for this reason . . . [was] not likely to be called upon to mediate the dispute."[176]

The Labor Priest admitted that "to some extent," this perception was "undoubtedly . . . [his] own fault." Higgins had the "impression that [he], . . . Bishop Donnelly, [and] Msgr. Mahony had . . . fallen out of favor with the Teamsters." Not surprising, considering that "Bishop Donnelly [had] . . . sent a copy of Father Vizzard's anti Teamster article . . . to all of the bishops," along with a cover "letter endorsing Vizzard's point of view."[177]

Higgins also expressed concerns regarding the magnitude of the struggle the Catholic Church faced. The Labor Priest wrote that neither he nor Bishop Donnelly "relished the idea of tangling with the Teamsters," but they "felt that it had to be done, even at the risk of jeopardizing [the Ad Hoc Committee's] reputation . . . of being a neutral third party in the lettuce dispute." However, Donnelly and Higgins felt "that there comes a time when neutrality can easily be interpreted as a cop-out," and that it would be "difficult if not impossible to be neutral in a dispute between the biggest and wealthiest union in the world . . . and the poorest and most disadvantaged union."[178]

Higgins concluded his letter to Costello with a statement that forged the bond between Higgins and Chávez—between the Catholic Church and La Causa. Higgins and Donnelly made a decision that, viewed from a perspective thirty years later, seems so natural that one would only *expect* the Catholic Church to take such a stand. However, in 1973 choosing outright partisanship with César Chávez and the farmworkers would have certainly envoked a firestorm of criticism. Higgins told Costello that "only time will tell whether or not Bishop Donnelly and I have made the right decision," but "for my own part," Higgins continued, "I am convinced that we have landed on the side of the angels."[179]

Although the Teamsters had effectively duped Mahony and Higgins during the initial years of the Battle of the Salad Bowl, the two monsignors were now fully cognizant of the Teamsters' true intentions, and Higgins used his column, the "Yardstick," to relentlessly expose the union's treachery. Higgins declared the Teamsters' "pious talk about the sacred right of farm workers to belong to a union of their own choosing . . . somewhat less than sincere." Higgins continued defiantly: "if the Teamsters are determined to have a fight to the finish, that's precisely what they are going to get"; moreover, Higgins felt "confident that they will eventually lose the war" because "time and public opinion are on the side of the [UFW]."[180]

Although Monsignor Higgins traditionally refused to take sides in the internal politics of unions, he made an exception in the case of the Battle of the Salad Bowl due to the Teamsters' dishonesty and the "moral rightness of [the UFWOC's] cause."[181] Pulling no punches, Higgins said that he "tapped whatever good will . . . [he] had in the labor movement . . . and seized every opportunity to oppose the Teamsters. . . . [I]t was strictly open warfare."[182] From Higgins's perspective, it made "no sense . . . for the biggest and probably the wealthiest union in the world to engage in a life and death struggle with a union that can speak for, at most, no more than 50,000 farm workers, the most exploited workers in the American labor market."[183] The Labor Priest felt he had no choice but to take a stand. He did.

Frank Fitzsimmons, president of the Teamsters Union, had an odd relationship with Monsignor Higgins. Because Fitzsimmons served as head of the Teamsters and because he was Higgins's arch-nemesis, the two continually engaged in heated personal exchanges. Nonetheless, Higgins and Fitzsimmons shared an Irish heritage, a fondness for cigars, and a drink or two of scotch on the rocks. Perhaps because of this commonality, Higgins and Fitzsimmons punctuated their skirmishes with humorous banter and occasional overtures of friendship.[184] In one tense situation, Higgins even invoked Fitzsimmons's name to save himself from a beating at the hands of a Teamster thug.

While in Salinas, Monsignor Higgins frequented a restaurant where a Teamster named Speedy also enjoyed his meals. Higgins often dined alone, read the paper, and quietly minded his business. With his gang, Speedy sat across the room watching, his eyes fixed on the Labor Priest.

On a couple of occasions, after a few drinks Speedy would shout: "we're going to get the clergy, too.

"We're sick and tired of the Catholic Church.

"I'll cut off your water."

Higgins usually ignored Speedy's taunts, but one day Speedy crossed the line. He made a scene, and he shouted "very loud."

Higgins asked the waiter, " 'Would you ask that gentleman to come over here?' "

Speedy obliged.

"Look Speedy," said Higgins, "we'd better have an understanding. For all I know you've got a gun, and maybe your people have got guns or blackjacks. But in any event, I'm in no position to fight you physically."

Speedy listened.

"I can't . . . throw you out of the restaurant," Higgins trenchantly

observed, "but if you do that once more, I'll get on the phone immediately and call Fitzsimmons in Washington."

Speedy ears perked up. Higgins wasn't finished.

"And I'll give it to the newspapers," Higgins continued.

" . . . and I'll demand that Fitzsimmons withdraw you . . .

" . . . and take away your charter . . .

" . . . and destroy you."

Higgins had Speedy's attention. Speedy was apologetic.

"Very apologetic." [185]

Although Higgins, on occasion, would invoke Fitzsimmons's name
for protection, the two had a major point of disagreement: César E.
Chávez. Whereas Higgins admired and befriended Chávez, Fitzsimmons despised him. In Fitzsimmons's mind, Chávez "was not a real trade
unionist."[186]

But Fitzsimmons's antipathy toward Chávez went deeper. Both Fitzsimmons and the union he represented had a public relations problem,
whereas Chávez and the UFW did not. The mass media adored Chávez;
the same could not be said of Fitzsimmons or the Teamsters.[187] Jimmy
Hoffa did jail time, Teamster goons became fixtures at UFWOC strikes,
and the union proved so crooked that the AFL-CIO expelled the Teamsters in 1957 "for failing to eliminate corruption."[188]

In contrast to Fitzsimmons and the Teamsters, Chávez ran the UFW
"like a monastic cooperative," where union officers and volunteers
alike existed in poverty.[189] Whereas Chávez earned an annual salary of
$5,144—including a $5 paycheck each week (the same as all other UFW
officers and appointed staffers), $960 for rent, $1,440 for food, and $1,904
for medical bills resulting from fasting, Fitzsimmons enjoyed a base
salary of $125,000, plus a private jet (courtesy of the Teamsters), and an
unlimited expense account.[190]

Journalists did not have to write the story; the story wrote itself:
David vs. Goliath. The biggest and probably wealthiest union in the
world assaulting a group of, at most, fifty thousand humble farmworkers.[191] Higgins noted that, despite the Teamsters' overwhelming superi-
ority in terms of "money and muscle," they ultimately couldn't beat "the
poverty-stricken but inspired and selfless members and officers of the
farm workers."[192]

The Labor Priest took a hard line against the Teamsters and wrote
about Fitzsimmons's union in hard-hitting terms.[193] Although Higgins
described Fitzsimmons as "an old friend," business and friendship were
two different things.[194] The Labor Priest swore that he and his fellow

priests would "do everything in . . . [their] power (even if it means an all-out struggle with another union) to make sure that . . . [the] poor exploited farm workers get the right to economic self-determination."[195]

La Causa's detractors claimed that the Teamsters were a bigger union and could represent the farmworkers better than the UFW. Higgins disagreed. "The argument . . . that some other union with more muscle, more money, more power, more political influence . . . could do more for these people economically than the UFW . . . [is] a phony argument," wrote the Labor Priest. "Clearly aside from the fact that Chávez's contracts are better than the Teamsters' contracts," Higgins continued, "no self-respecting trade unionist has ever judged the value of a union purely in economic terms."[196]

Higgins's "old friend" Fitzsimmons did not appreciate the Church's increasingly hostile stance toward the Teamsters. The Teamsters' president upbraided the Labor Priest in a harsh April 1973 letter that insulted Higgins's understanding of collective bargaining. Fitzsimmons accused Higgins of having "the interest of the United Farm Workers' Union first in mind, and only secondly the interest of the workers themselves." As an example, he cited Higgins's (now public) support for the UFW boycott, and argued that "while UFWU officials boycott, disrupt, and create confusion, the farm workers go without paychecks." Fitzsimmons summed up his sentiments by telling Higgins that "in my meetings with you I have not found you very receptive to logic, or the cold, hard knowledge of what it takes in the practical give and take of collective bargaining to make things work for members."[197]

The Labor Priest wasted little time launching his counteroffensive. Higgins countered that "George Meany, Leonard Woodcock, and a number of other prominent labor leaders . . . completely disagree with the Teamsters," and that he had "yet to meet a single labor leader anywhere in the United States (outside of . . . [the Teamsters]) who agreed with" Fitzsimmons's assessment of the farm labor situation. Higgins went on to note that "the overwhelming majority of labor reporters, labor economists, and clergymen (of all faiths) who have had any contact with the farm labor problem in recent years" also disagreed with the Teamsters, and that "the Supreme Court of California is persuaded . . . [that the Teamsters'] intervention in the lettuce industry, following the Delano grape settlement, was a pretty phony operation."[198]

Despite the jousting, Higgins did not want to close on a bitter note. The Labor Priest admitted that although his tone "may sound a little belligerent," he "really didn't mean it to sound that way." Playing upon their common ethnicity, Higgins told Fitzsimmons that he "simply felt that, like a good Irishman," he should "be as frank as possible." Clearly looking to keep the disagreement professional, and not personal, Higgins reassured Fitzsimmons that he had "great respect for the Teamsters and no desire whatsoever to tangle with them on this or any other issue. . . . [T]o the contrary, I would much prefer to be able to cooperate with them in a joint effort to advance the cause of social justice in the United States." But, unfortunately for Fitzsimmons and the Teamsters, business was business, and Higgins would not compromise the farmworkers' welfare.[199]

Later in the year, Fitzsimmons and Higgins exchanged other correspondence. Higgins's previous overture of peace apparently fell on deaf ears as Fitzsimmons's letter sternly impugned Higgins for allegedly placing Chávez's interests over that of the farmworkers. Fitzsimmons charged that Higgins's "prejudice against the Teamsters . . . [was] much stronger than . . . [his] desire to see economic justice done for farm workers," because under the Teamsters, farmworkers enjoyed "better wages and working conditions than ever before." The Labor Priest's "silence on . . . protests of farm workers against Chávez's hiring hall abuses, payment of dues in advance, fines for shopping Safeway . . . and acts of violence against the workers," led Fitzsimmons to openly question whether Higgins's "long-standing prejudice against the . . . Teamsters, and [his] over-committed writings on the subject . . . [precluded him] from a frank reevaluation of the facts." Fitzsimmons suggested to Higgins that he "retreat for a moment and examine . . . [his] conscience," because what "the Teamsters have done for farm workers—the workers, not César Chávez—far outweighs [the Teamsters'] image as conceived by myopic eyes such as [Higgins's]."[200]

In a highly charged closing, Fitzsimmons accused the Labor Priest of perpetuating the dispute and precluding its settlement through writings in his "Yardstick" columns. He challenged Higgins to ask himself: "Had I never written a word on the farm worker controversy, would the situation be any different? Or in fact, have I really added any reason to the argument, or have I fanned the flames and prolonged the dispute?"[201]

Higgins's reply indicated that he was somewhat taken aback by Fitzsimmons's abrasive tone. In his response, the Labor Priest again attempted to assuage Fitzsimmons's anger by complimenting his "willingness to lay it right on the line." After the gracious opening, Higgins questioned Fitzsimmons's contention that the Labor Priest had a long-standing prejudice against the Teamsters. Higgins told Fitzsimmons that he had checked his files and discovered that he had written only six articles about the Teamsters during the past twenty-five years. Given the Labor Priest's dearth of extensive writings on the union, he flatly denied Fitzsimmons's "unsupported charge."

Higgins conjectured that certain members of the Teamsters' Washington staff were circulating the charge that he had something against the Teamsters because he had never attended a Teamster convention and seldom visited its headquarters in Washington, D.C. Higgins continued that he seldom went where he was not invited, but that if Fitzsimmons had invited him, he would have accepted.[202]

Higgins's letter acknowledged Fitzsimmons's anger that so many clergymen were supporting the UFW. Nonetheless, the Labor Priest counseled the Teamsters' president that he should be more concerned "that the entire AFL-CIO is publicly supporting the UFW and publicly opposing the Teamsters in the current farm labor dispute." Higgins told Fitzsimmons that he could "write off the clergy . . . [as] a bunch of do-gooders who don't know what they are talking about in the area of collective bargaining and labor-management relations," but that he could not ignore "George Meany . . . the members of the AFL-CIO Executive Council," and Leonard Woodcock's support for Chávez and the farm-workers. Higgins concluded by offering another olive branch to Fitzsimmons and suggested that they get together for lunch or dinner. For Higgins, it simply didn't "make sense for two Irishmen to be carrying on a dialogue of this kind by means of correspondence."[203]

Higgins and the Ad Hoc Committee had tried to mediate the Battle of the Salad Bowl, but by 1973, as Higgins's correspondence with Fitzsimmons indicates, the parties found little common ground. As the year wore on, Higgins began to push even harder for the hierarchy's public endorsement of Chávez's boycott, and by extension, La Causa. He wanted the bishops to issue a statement supporting Chávez's grape and lettuce boycotts at the hierarchy's November meeting. Momentum, timing, and personalities were on Higgins's side. They were on Chávez's side, on the side of the farmworkers and La Causa.

On May 23, 1973, the Committee on Social Development at the USCC made progress toward Higgins's goal. The committee issued a resolution that excoriated the Teamsters and reiterated the Committee on Social Development's endorsement of the lettuce boycott. The resolution asserted that the signing of sweetheart contracts between California's table grape growers and the Teamsters violated "all canons of trade union ethics." Importantly, the committee emphasized its endorsement of "the boycott of table grapes and iceberg (head) lettuce" and urged "the purchase of table grapes and lettuce only if they clearly carry the Aztec black eagle label of the United Farm Workers Union, AFL-CIO."[204]

On July 3, Higgins wrote Bishop Rausch to inform him that both he and Bishop Donnelly wanted to publicly support the UFW over the Teamsters. Higgins reminded Rausch that in the committee's original mandate, "it was made a matter of official record that if the Committee's efforts to persuade the parties to negotiate were unsuccessful, the NCCB . . . might at the appropriate time come out in favor of the boycott." In Delano, continued Higgins, the committee "scrupulously avoided taking sides between the parties," but "made it perfectly clear . . . that it favored the organization of farm workers into a union."

Higgins's letter indicated that he had already publicly broken his guise of neutrality, and that neither he nor Donnelly could "in good faith continue to be neutral in this life and death struggle between the Teamsters and the Farm Workers," especially since the dispute was in "clear violation of trade union ethics." Higgins told Rausch that "at this stage of the game, to be neutral means to favor the Teamsters," and that was "a risk that the Committee simply [couldn't] afford to take."[205]

Compellingly, the Labor Priest argued that the time had arrived "for the Committee to come out forthrightly and explicitly in favor of the UFW, . . . [and] it would be appropriate for the NCCB to follow suit in this regard." After all, Higgins concluded, there were clear indications that the Teamsters "were determined, in collusion with the growers, to destroy the UFW."[206]

Soon after Higgins's message to Rausch, Donnelly drafted a statement delineating the Ad Hoc Committee's policy shift. The proposed declaration adopted language from Higgins's letter almost word for word. In fact, Donnelly's version strengthened Higgins's rendering by adding that "a great injustice is being done and I do not think that we can be neutral in the face of this injustice."[207]

Despite Donnelly and Higgins's enthusiasm for the committee's revaluation of its neutrality, not all of its members embraced the proposed shift with zeal. In particular, Archbishop Timothy Manning took issue with Donnelly and Higgins's assessment of the situation. In a confidential memo to the USCC/NCCB president, Cardinal Krol, Manning undercut his colleagues by expressing concern about "the current agitation in the farm labor controversy."[208]

The archbishop of Los Angeles reminded Krol that "when the Ad Hoc Committee of Bishops was created it was the mind of the Conference that the Committee would serve as a bridge between the workers and the growers, and take no active sides with one party or the other." Unfortunately, from Manning's perspective, "Bishop Donnelly . . . [had] been out . . . in California repeatedly and [had] taken an active part in the strike demonstrations in favor of the farm workers union." Because Donnelly was "pledged to neutrality as a member of the Ad Hoc Committee," Manning continued, he "fear[ed] that . . . [Donnelly's] actions have emasculated the strength of the Committee and that it cannot now act as an effective medium of peace." "The Committee is discredited," lamented Manning.[209]

In his interim reply to Manning, Krol indicated that he felt the archbishop of Los Angeles had a valid point. Krol noted that he did "not question the sincerity of Bishop Donnelly's convictions, . . . [but] the fact remains that he has identified himself with one of the parties and thereby reduced the effectiveness of the Ad Hoc Committee to serve as a bridge between the workers and the growers." The USCC/NCCB chairman took the liberty of sharing Manning's letter with Bishop Rausch in case he wished to raise the issue with Higgins, "who seemingly has also identified himself with one of the parties." But Rausch, like Higgins, had also identified with the UFW and became one of La Causa's strongest supporters in the U.S. Catholic hierarchy. Krol closed by empathizing with Manning, and commented that he would seek "some delicate way in which to convey your concern, which I share, to Bishop Donnelly and Monsignor Higgins."[210]

Rausch's reaction to Manning's note reflected his strong pro-Chávez bias. It came as little surprise when the general secretary, who would later become chairman of the Bishops' Ad Hoc Committee, asserted that "the Committee was given a rather free hand in responding to specific situations as they developed. . . . [I]t is . . . within the Committee's mandate to take a position on an issue when circumstances warrant." Supporting the work of the committee's leadership, Rausch continued that he did "not think that Bishop Donnelly . . . [had been] acting beyond the mandate given to the Committee when it was established." Slightly hedging his support of Donnelly and Higgins, Rausch noted that he was "in no position to judge the merits of their present activity" because he was "not aware of all the specific circumstances which have motivated Bishop Donnelly and Monsignor Higgins to become progressively more involved in the present situation."[211]

One day later, perhaps feeling a bit guilty for including the disclaimer on "specific circumstances which have motivated" Donnelly and Higgins, Rausch again wrote Krol, and he offered his complete support for the committee's chairman and consultant. At that point, it became clear that the highest levels of the U.S. Catholic Church had begun to favor outright support of Chávez and the farmworkers. Rauch wrote Krol: "I realize the committee and, indirectly, the Conference is taking sides in this dispute," but "to do less would be harmful to the Church's credibility among the farm laborers."[212]

In July 1973, Higgins came across Teamster propaganda claiming that Chávez was losing Catholic support. Nothing could have been further from the truth. After discovering the disinformation pamphlets, Higgins quickly fired off a letter alerting Donnelly "to the fact that the Teamsters are becoming completely irresponsible in their ill-advised attempt to destroy the [UFW]." "Chávez is not losing the support of the Catholics," wrote Higgins, in fact, Chávez "is currently receiving more Catholic support than at any previous time in the history of his movement."[213]

The years 1973 through 1976 marked the pinnacle of the hierarchy's support for Chávez. Rausch, Donnelly, and Higgins were all at the height of their influence, and they shaped the bishops' policy on farm labor. Moreover, many local parish priests and nuns continued to come out in large numbers to work with the UFW. This partnership between *los curas* (the priests) and La Causa became a highlight of the Church's involvement in late twentieth-century progressive causes, and, in the words of Higgins, helped the Church make "a tremendous contribution to the cause of social justice."[214]

Chávez gushed with appreciation for the Catholic Church's backing. He characterized the bishops' "strong and continuing support" as "deeply appreciated and vitally needed."[215] In a letter to Donnelly, Chávez said that he found "it hard to express my gratitude for your commitment and dedication to our efforts."[216] Chávez also sent Higgins a note thanking him "sincerely for [his] strong support of the [UFW's] current struggle against the illegal injunctions that have been invoked by local authorities," and recognizing that the Labor Priest's "continued support will win victory in the fields and dignity for farmworkers everywhere."[217]

Bishop Rausch, especially in his capacity as general secretary of the USCC/NCCB, proved to be one of La Causa's most influential supporters. Monsignor John Egan, chairman of the Catholic Committee on Urban Ministry, complimented Rausch's "unfailing support" for "the UFW over the last difficult years, and in particular, for the encouragement you have given to Msgr. Higgins." Egan strongly, and correctly, believed that without Higgins's "influence and that of Bishop Donnelly, the UFW as an organization might well have disappeared by this time."[218]

In responding to Egan's letter, Rausch assured him "that Monsignor Higgins, Bishop Donnelly and his committee will continue to have my wholehearted support in their efforts to assist in the achievement of justice for farm workers," and that the USCC/NCCB was "fortunate indeed to have their kind of tireless dedication to this cause."[219] Again, the Church's support for Chávez and La Causa appeared as a result of both the times and the forceful personalities that staffed the decision-making positions at the highest reaches of the U.S. Catholic Church.

Just prior to the hierarchy's November meeting, Chávez wrote Donnelly requesting that the bishops formally endorse the UFW's grape and lettuce boycotts. In his letter, Chávez characterized his petition as a "hard request," but went on to note that "these are very hard times . . . and we desperately need the unqualified and specific support of our bishops." Chávez also appeared fatigued by the Teamsters "characteristically" breaking "their word and . . . [betraying] not only the farm workers, but the consumer, distributers [sic] and growers." Chávez closed his letter noting that, unlike the Teamsters, the UFW "best . . . [represented] the workers culturally" because the UFW respected the "religious and cultural values of the workers."[220]

Bishop Donnelly agreed with Chávez. In a November 13 report, Donnelly remarked that when the Teamsters agreed on September 28 to a third jurisdictional agreement with the UFW, "it was generally thought that this pact, unlike the earlier Teamster-UFW agreements, would stick and that it would prepare the way for an orderly and peaceful settlement of the farm labor dispute."[221] Characteristically, the Teamsters Union broke its word.

In light of the Teamsters' treachery, the UFW had little choice but to intensify its national consumer boycott of head lettuce and table grapes. Donnelly argued that "the very existence of the UFW is at stake in this struggle, . . . that the cause represented by César Chávez and the United Farm Workers Union is a just cause, [and] that the UFW represents the best interests of the nation's agricultural workers." As such, Donnelly felt it only natural that Chávez "deserves our wholehearted support in [his union's] struggle to protect the legitimate economic rights of one of the most disadvantaged groups of workers in the American economy."[222]

In November 1973, the U.S. Catholic Church made the break from its traditional position of neutrality. The bishops adopted a policy supporting Chávez's boycotts and, by extension, Chávez. Higgins had done it.

He had finally succeeded in obtaining the hierarchy's outright endorsement of La Causa.

The bishops' endorsement of the grape and lettuce boycotts declared that "the NCCB go[es] on record in support of the right of the field workers . . . to free secret ballot elections which will determine whether or not they want Union representation and which Union they want to represent them." The hierarchy also called upon the growers and Teamsters to accede to this demand "without further delay," and stated that the Catholic Church officially "endorses and supports the UFW's consumer boycott of table grapes and head lettuce until such time as free secret ballot elections are held."[223]

The resolution did not pass unanimously.[224] Cardinal Manning and Bishop Donohoe, as in 1968 and 1969, did not support the NCCB's endorsement of the UFW's boycott. In 1973, however, their dissatisfaction was of little consequence. The hierarchy adopted the resolution without dissent. Cardinal Manning did not speak against the declaration, and Bishop Donohoe was absent from the November meeting.[225] Both Manning and Donohoe agreed that, despite their displeasure, "neither would publicly speak against the proposal."[226]

How times had changed. Just five years earlier the concerns of two conservative bishops from California had dominated the hierarchy's fall gathering. By 1973, however, Manning and Donohoe were silent, and the agenda of more liberal clergy carried the day.

The American hierarchy's involvement in the Battle of the Salad Bowl had created such a stir that the Vatican's secretary of state, the Most Reverend Giovanni Benelli, wrote Bishop Rausch a confidential memo in November 1973 to inquire about the hostilities. Benelli remarked that "the complicated situation of the Farm Labor problem in the United States has more than once been brought to the attention of the Holy See." The Vatican's secretary of state then told Rausch that he sought to "request confidentially . . . a judgment on the complex question [of the farm labor dispute], and . . . [Rausch's] opinion as to the attitude to be assumed by the Holy See in this regard."[227]

In his response to Benelli, Rausch explained "there exists here a clear case of social justice which is being violated separately and jointly by the growers and the Teamsters Union," and that "the American Hierarchy . . . recommends action which will assist in resolving the injustices suffered by the field workers in this dispute." Furthermore, Rausch expressed his desire to have the Holy See "adopt an attitude in accord with that of the Bishops' Conference and, if a suitable occasion should

present itself . . . express itself in such a way as to aid the large minority of Spanish-speaking Catholics in the United States in their justice claim."[228] Rausch, Higgins, and Donnelly took charge—at the right
time—and shaped the American hierarchy's pro-Chávez position. Ultimately, their influence reached the highest level of the Catholic Church.

After the bishops' November 1973 endorsement, Chávez wrote Krol
to express his appreciation for the NCCB's long-awaited backing of the
UFW boycotts. Chávez reassured Krol that the Church's support would
give La Causa "added strength and hope to continue the long, difficult
struggle ahead."[229]

While Chávez euphorically wrote letters of appreciation, Fitzsimmons fumed. The Teamsters president prepared a lengthy letter to Cardinal Krol protesting the hierarchy's endorsement of the boycott. Fitzsimmons began by assuring Krol "that each and every contract that we
negotiated and signed with the growers is superior to any contracts the
farm workers' union ever negotiated." In addition to better contracts,
Fitzsimmons insisted that the Teamsters were honest and reliable, and
that Chávez, not the Teamsters, had difficulty keeping his word. Fitzsimmons called upon Krol "to rescind the action that you have taken in
supporting boycotts," because the embargos create "unrest and deprive
the American public of the opportunity to buy goods in the market place,
which every citizen of the United States is entitled to do."[230]

After reviewing Fitzsimmons's letter to Krol, Donnelly opined that
Fitzsimmons's take on the facts was "a bit dreamy," and proceeded
to take Fitzsimmons's arguments apart. In a letter to the NCCB, Donnelly observed that "the Teamsters have consistently resisted UFWA
request[s] for free elections." Donnelly remarked that the UFW's boycott is neither illegal nor immoral, but was rather necessary to "make the
protest effective . . . until free elections are held." He exhorted his
colleagues that "personally, in private and in public, we should support
the boycott by our practice," and that "institutions under the jurisdiction
of the Bishop should be advised of the boycott and asked to support it."
Donnelly closed his memo noting that "the action of the Bishops in this
matter . . . is a noble instance of protest against injustice and support of
the poorest of workers," and that the Catholic Church's support of Chávez marked a "proud day for religion in America."[231]

After reading a copy of Fitzsimmons's November 20 telegram to Krol,
George Meany agreed with Donnelly's assessment. He felt that although
the letter contained "a number of misrepresentations and misstate-

ments," the principal issue was that "the Teamsters raided the Farm Workers Union in an effort to destroy it and to take over its membership and its contracts."[232] Deploring the Teamsters' incursion, Meany commented that "thousands of farm workers . . . have been forced to have the Teamsters represent them through a series of secret deals made by Teamster officials."[233] In light of such challenges to the UFW, Meany reaffirmed the AFL-CIO's pledge to continue its consistent support for the farmworkers and Chávez's union.[234]

In addition to Fitzsimmons's protests, the Catholic hierarchy received a parade of letters from UFW opponents criticizing the Church's decision to endorse Chávez's boycotts. For example, William J. Kuhfuss, president of the American Farm Bureau Federation, strongly rebuked the hierarchy's action. Much like Fitzsimmons, Kuhfuss accused the NCCB of not listening to both sides, and claimed that his organization was "stunned at the call of [the] National Conference of Catholic Bishops for nationwide boycotts of lettuce and table grapes as a stated means to induce elections for farm workers." To the contrary, argued Kuhfuss, "boycotts are designed to compel farmers to sign over their workers to the United Farm Workers organization without elections of any kind."[235]

Kuhfuss profoundly regretted the bishop's "failure to hear from both sides before arriving at . . . [a] decision which can only inflame rather than conciliate the issues of farm labor organization." In heated rhetoric, the president of the American Farm Bureau Federation closed by noting that the hierarchy's "action places in jeopardy the incomes of thousands of farmers and farm workers."[236]

Letters of appreciation from Chávez continued to counter such unsympathetic correspondence. Writing Higgins in late November, Chávez complimented the Labor Priest's "beautiful work . . . during the meeting of the National Conference of Catholic Bishops," in helping push for official Church endorsement of the grape and lettuce boycotts. Chávez praised Higgins for "once again . . . [speaking] out strongly and clearly in favor of the course . . . the Church must take, and . . . [helping the UFW] to win a real victory." Chávez also reassured Higgins that "the resolutions which the Conference passed have already begun to take effect . . . and this is going to add real strength to the boycott." Closing his letter on a personal note, and accentuating the close bond the two had developed, Chávez told Higgins that their "friendship means a great deal."[237]

The Catholic Church's support for Chávez in 1973 was indeed a "proud day for religion in America" and a proud day for the Catholic

Church.[238] By supporting La Causa, the hierarchy moved Catholic social teachings "beyond the dusty pages of unread documents to the dusty fields where workers sought dignity and justice."[239]

1974: Chávez and the Pope

Throughout 1974, the Catholic Church continued to increase its support for La Causa. The Church developed a new leave policy that facilitated the movement of priests and nuns into UFW staff positions. More than seven hundred religious brothers and sisters eagerly responded to the opportunity, and by the summer of 1974 the UFW's full-time staff had almost doubled. The clergy's presence bolstered the union's resources and, importantly, lent credibility to the boycotts.[240]

As the Catholic Church sought new ways to assist Chávez, Fitzsimmons continued to seek the UFW's demise. In a statement to the presidents of all international unions affiliated with the AFL-CIO, the Teamsters' president declared, "if you are not with us, you must be against us." Nobody misunderstood Fitzsimmons. He publicly threatened all AFL-CIO affiliates. If they supported "a boycott of Teamster products . . . in any way . . . [they] would naturally [be] . . . taking a definite position against the International Brotherhood of Teamsters." Fitzsimmons continued, "I would be remiss if I did not say to you that in the future our cooperation with your organization will be judged accordingly. . . . We do not propose to support unions that are fighting us."[241]

Higgins often appeared to relish his intellectual sparring with the Teamsters' president, but this time the Labor Priest felt that Fitzsimmons went overboard. In a letter to Joseph Keenan, secretary of the International Brotherhood of Electrical Workers, the Labor Priest wrote, "much as I like good old Fitz, I am afraid he has gone a bit off his rocker in this particular area." Higgins felt "it would be a monumental mistake for the American labor movement to let the Teamsters get by with their avowed plan to destroy the UFW," and expressed his "hope that all of the affiliates of the AFL-CIO will do everything within their power to support the UFW and to put the Teamsters in their place."[242]

"Off his rocker" or not, "old Fitz" invested considerable resources in an effort to rally support for the Teamsters in the nation's capital. William Baum, archbishop of Washington, agreed to meet with Fitzsimmons regarding the Teamsters-UFW dispute, and reported on the encounter in a letter to Bishop Rausch. In the meeting, "Fitzsimmons . . . expressed concern . . . that the Teamsters had not been treated fairly by the Bishops." Fitzsimmons claimed that although "both Bishop Donnelly and Monsignor Higgins had visited him . . . he interpreted their visits as representing the interests of the United Farm Workers." Baum listened patiently and promised Fitzsimmons that he would "convey these concerns . . . to . . . the General Secretary for whatever action . . . [Rausch] would judge proper."[243]

Rausch told Baum that "Mr. Fitzsimmons knows . . . that I am available for an appointment with him at any time that is mutually convenient," but that, at this juncture, there was "no reason for the Conference to reevaluate its position on the farm labor question."[244]

In mid-April 1974, Donnelly made an official statement on the status of the farm labor dispute. Donnelly's briefing clarified an important distinction between the AFL-CIO's and the USCC/NCCB's boycott endorsements. Whereas the AFL-CIO announced its support of the boycott until the UFW had contracts, the NCCB threw its weight behind the boycott "until the field workers are given the opportunity to indicate their choice of unions by free, secret ballot elections."[245] The bishops felt that "secret ballot election, not the boycott . . . should be the principal concern" in the dispute because the desire of the farmworker, *not* the union, was the ultimate concern.[246] Monsignor Mahony echoed these sentiments: "My main concern is for the Farm Workers and not for either of the unions. In the meantime we will try very hard to encourage the passage of good legislation to safeguard the rights of farm workers to a secret ballot election."[247]

Despite the AFL-CIO and NCCB's endorsements of the grape and lettuce boycotts, the Teamsters Union announced early in 1974 that it would "begin organizing very extensively among other crops in the State of California which until this time have not been the target of union organization.[248] As the Teamsters ratcheted up the pressure on La Causa, Chávez again turned to his staunchest ally, Monsignor Higgins. In a letter of gratitude for Higgins's liaison work with UFW partisans, Chávez noted that the UFW appreciated "so much your continued presence with us, and want you to know that your work on our behalf does not go unnoticed."[249]

Higgins tirelessly continued his labor of love for La Causa. In May 1974, the Labor Priest prepared talking points for the bishops. UFW critics charged that Chávez's union did not adequately represent the interests of the farmworkers, and that the Teamsters possessed better contracts. Higgins countered that although the "economic provisions" of the Teamsters' contracts "roughly" matched those of the UFW, Chávez's agreements were "far superior to the Teamster contracts in several other respects." As an example, Higgins cited the UFW contracts' "provision requiring the growers to observe the seniority principle by recruiting their workers through a hiring hall," as opposed to the Teamster contracts, which allowed "the growers to continue to recruit their workers through labor contractors." Additionally, the UFW had "far superior . . . contracts on the matter of controlling the use of dangerous pesticides" because the Teamsters' pacts merely "settled for the enforcement (such as it is) of state and federal regulations in this area, which . . . are less than adequate."[250]

In addition to providing intellectual services to La Causa, Higgins continued to network in support of Chávez. After participating in a Clergy and Religious Breakfast that honored Chávez, Susan Sachen of the UFW praised Higgins's "generosity and good will . . . and tremendous support . . . in the cause of justice for farm workers."[251] Higgins also wrote to the Reverend Monsignor F. J. Smyth of St. Francis Xavier University to praise Chávez's personal integrity and commitment to the Catholic faith.[252] After discovering that the university had been "considering the possibility of conferring an honorary degree on César Chávez," Higgins informed Smyth that he "had the privilege of working very closely with Chávez during the past five years . . . [and could] honestly say that . . . he is a man of great personal integrity and a near genius when it comes to organizing disadvantaged farm workers into a viable union."[253] Higgins continued his flattering assessment by noting that Chávez was "by all odds, one of the most influential social reformers to have appeared on the American scene in recent generations . . . [and] thoroughly committed to Catholic social principles."[254]

Given Higgins's high regard for Chávez, it comes as no surprise that in 1974 he played the key role in orchestrating what Chávez termed "one of the highlights of my life," Chávez's personal audience with Pope Paul VI. The leader of La Causa described the experience as "a small miracle," and remarked that "getting . . . [Pope Paul VI's] blessing was especially significant . . . a tremendous joy, [and] something that . . . [he] never thought would happen."[255]

Chávez's encounter with the pontiff demonstrated both the strong friendship that he and Higgins shared and the important role of the Catholic faith in Chávez's life. Bishop Donnelly and Monsignor Higgins laid the groundwork for Chávez's papal audience.[256] Higgins drafted a letter for Bishop Rausch's signature that asked the Apostolic Delegate to request a private audience with Pope Paul VI on September 26.[257] Citing three of Chávez's staunchest supporters in the hierarchy, Higgins told Chávez, "Bishop Donnelly, Bishop Rausch and I will keep after this matter and will do everything we possibly can to secure an audience for you," but "because of the Holy Father's advanced age and declining health . . . it is becoming increasingly difficult for anyone to get a private audience." There was "simply no way that anyone, including the Apostolic Delegate . . . [could] either guarantee an audience in advance or guarantee that the audience will take place on schedule."[258] Nonetheless, Higgins felt optimistic about the situation because Archbishop Benelli, the pope's top assistant, knew "all about the UFW and the work of [the] Bishops Committee on Farm Labor" and was "an enthusiastic supporter of the cause."[259] Of course, Rausch's communications with the Benelli undoubtedly influenced his zeal for La Causa.

Clearly excited about Chávez's upcoming meeting, Higgins sent Chávez a brief update, noting that he had talked to Monsignor Joseph Gremillion and planned to "urge him as a personal favor to endorse and support your request for a private audience on September 26." Higgins told Chávez that he couldn't "think of a better man in the entire world to arrange such a" visit because "Gremillion knows Rome like the palm of his hand . . . [and] is an enthusiastic supporter of UFW."[260] Higgins placed such importance on the success of Chávez's trip to Rome that he even took care to remind Chávez of details such as applying "for your passports in plenty of time."[261]

Chávez expressed his gratitude to Higgins for "the preparations and good work being done to enlist support for an audience for the Holy Father," and told Higgins that he looked "forward to this great experience."[262] Additionally, Chávez took a moment to thank Higgins "for the many, many good deeds you have done for us, over all these many years."[263]

Despite meticulous planning, the audience almost never took place. Originally, the meeting was scheduled to occur on September 26, 1974. But on September 24 at 4:30 p.m., Higgins placed an urgent call to the U.S. embassy in Stockholm, where Chávez had stopped en route to Rome, to contact Chávez and inform him that he had to be in Rome by 10 a.m. the next day if he wanted to meet the Holy Father.[264] Chávez wasted no time and began searching for an expedient way to Rome. Regrettably, there were no flights from Stockholm to Rome that would get him to see the pope on time.[265]

Undaunted, Chávez calmly said, "We'll make it."[266] A resourceful embassy employee found Chávez a British flight that left Stockholm at 6:55 p.m. and arrived in London with sufficient time for him to catch a Nigerian aircraft bound for Italy's capital.[267] Chávez arrived in Rome after 1:00 in the morning. Once again demonstrating his commitment to La Causa, Monsignor Higgins stood waiting for Chávez as he disembarked the plane.[268]

As scheduled, the next day Chávez met His Holiness.[269] The pope gave Chávez an enthusiastic salutation and praised him for his "sustained effort to apply the principles of Christian social teaching."[270] Reflecting on Chávez's meeting with the pontiff, Higgins wrote: "Chávez got to Rome in time for his audience with Pope Paul VI and ... in general, his visit to Rome was eminently successful from every point of view."[271] When recalling, years later, his personal involvement in arranging Chávez's meeting with the pope, Higgins minimized the extent of his role in arranging the meeting, and omitted entirely the fact that he waited at the Rome airport until after 1 a.m. to meet Chávez.[272] But that was Higgins. Always a good soldier, the Labor Priest consistently subordinated himself to the greater mission.

After the visit, Higgins presented Chávez with a list of people in Rome to thank.[273] Higgins advised Chávez that "When you write to Archbishop Benelli, be sure to ask him to extend your personal thanks to His Holiness Pope Paul VI for his extraordinary kindness in granting us a personal audience, etc."[274] In a separate letter, Higgins further counseled Chávez to "send a personal note of thanks to Bishop Rausch for his kindness in requesting your audience with Pope Paul."[275]

As evidence of Higgins's concern for Chávez, and highlighting his unofficial role as the Catholic Church's ambassador to the UFW, the Labor Priest constantly reminded Chávez to send notes of appreciation or congratulations to his allies in the Catholic Church. For example, after Chávez's "good friend" Archbishop Bernardin commenced his three-year term as president of the NCCB, Higgins suggested that Chávez send him a note of congratulations.[276] Chávez appeared to appreciate Higgins's reminders, and four days after Higgins penned this letter, Chávez wrote the Labor Priest that La Causa counted on his "continued support in our struggle to build a union."[277]

By 1974, the actions of Higgins, Mahony, Donnelly, and Rausch clearly demonstrated that the U.S. Catholic Church had become a full participant in La Causa. Acknowledging and expressing appreciation for this shift, Chávez wrote to Rausch on Halloween 1974, conveying his gratitude for past support, apprising the general secretary of current events, and seeking continued assurances of the Church's support.[278]

Responding to Chávez's Halloween letter, Rausch reassured Chávez that he and the Catholic Church stood firmly behind him. "[M]y support for your work, which is an expression of your deep faith in God and your fellow man, will continue," promised Rausch.[279] In his correspondence, Rausch also highlighted Higgins's critical role as chief liaison between *los curas* and La Causa, noting that "Msgr. George Higgins is the one . . . I . . . rely upon . . . in order to be kept up-to-date on the most recent developments in your efforts."[280]

With the Catholic Church and the AFL-CIO firmly behind Chávez by the mid-1970s, the farmworkers required one additional ally to propel La Causa to its political apogee: a friend in the California governor's office. In 1975, the year of the UFW's political zenith, the voters of California elected Jerry Brown to the governorship, and the former Jesuit seminarian brought to bear his full political clout to support Chávez and the farmworkers.

1975: Jerry Brown, the CALRA, and the UFW

Monsignor Higgins launched 1975 with a spirited defense of the U.S. Catholic Church's involvement in the farm labor controversy. After reading a January 11 editorial on the farm labor situation in the *Catholic Register*, a Toronto-based publication, Higgins felt the author did not have a sufficient understanding of either the California dispute or the Catholic Church's role in the conflict.[281] Always willing to educate, Higgins wrote the magazine's editor to clarify the issue.

The Labor Priest criticized the author for misrepresenting the bishops' position by claiming "that the National Conference of Catholic Bishops (U.S.), which had endorsed the boycott in 1973, has become 'disenchanted with this approach.'" "To the contrary," Higgins countered, "the official minutes of the November, 1974, meeting of the National Conference of Catholic Bishops will show that any such inference is completely unwarranted."[282]

The Labor Priest seriously disagreed with other parts of the editorial, as well. For example, Higgins told the editor that he "was appalled by [the] statement . . . that California farm workers are free to 'go home or move on to other jobs' if they are not satisfied with . . . wages and conditions." Higgins quickly pointed out that farmworkers' " 'home,' in the majority of cases, is right here in the United States." Higgins also took considerable umbrage at the author's assertion that "the California farm labor dispute has become 'strictly an interunion struggle,'" and called this assessment "woefully simplistic."[283]

Higgins explained that "the national AFL-CIO, representing the overwhelming majority of American unions, has characterized the California dispute not as an inter-union struggle, but rather as a case of union busting pure and simple."[284] Higgins condemned the author's analysis of the boycott's accomplishments as "obviously based on the most primitive kind of anti-UFW propaganda," and closed his letter pointedly: "I get the impression that your present knowledge of the problem is very inadequate."[285]

At times, even Chávez was not safe from Higgins's pen-lashings; however, the Labor Priest as a rule treaded lightly when criticizing Chávez. In a "personal and confidential letter" to Chávez, Higgins remarked that he had "recently . . . came across a number of local UFW leaflets and handbills which clearly . . . create the impression that the Gallo boycott has been officially endorsed by the National Conference of Catholic Bishops." Because such "misleading material is not going to be helpful to the UFW's cause," Higgins suggested to Chávez that he "look for an opportunity to instruct the local boycott offices to be completely honest and objective in their references to the position of the National Conference of Catholic Bishops concerning the boycott issue." Higgins reminded Chávez that "the 1973 NCCB resolution . . . [referred] only to the table grape and lettuce boycott and . . . [made] no mention whatsoever of the Gallo boycott"; additionally, he cautioned Chávez that "any carelessness on the part of the local boycott offices in their treatment of this matter is very likely to boomerang against [the] UFW."[286]

Although Higgins would gently chastise Chávez in private, he unfailingly defended the UFW leader in public. His excellent sense of discretion is one reason the Labor Priest curried favor with so many powerful people—from cabinet-level officials, to labor and civil rights leaders, to bishops and cardinals—throughout his career. Higgins could be trusted to provide honest and intellectually sound advice while keeping private disagreements confidential—all qualities in high demand but short supply.

By 1975, the Teamsters had finally begun to weaken. In a confidential report to the Ad Hoc Committee, Monsignor Mahony mentioned that "the Teamsters were in serious trouble because the UFW . . . offices were actually helping the Teamster work force." Apparently, a deluge of personal injury, antitrust, and conspiracy lawsuits against the Teamsters began to place legal pressure on the organization. Importantly, Mahony noted that "the AFL-CIO was going to work . . . with newly elected Governor Brown to get a decent farm labor bill passed."[287] With the Teamsters weakening and the governor of California eager to pass protective legislation for farmworkers, La Causa's *victoria* had finally arrived.

Riding La Causa's wave of prosperity, Chávez's secretary-treasurer, Gilbert Padilla, sent Bishop Rausch a letter announcing the UFW's new film *Fighting for Our Lives*, and asked the USCC/NCCB's general secretary to sponsor the movie's Washington, D.C., premier showing.[288] Torn between his deep personal loyalty to Chávez and an awareness of conference rules on sponsorship, Rausch deferred the decision to his resident expert on farm labor, George Higgins.

Higgins advised Rausch that if he agreed to sponsor the UFW film he could "legitimately rationalize and defend . . . [his] decision by citing the fact that the USCC Advisory Council . . . again supported UFW's boycott of lettuce and grapes." However, if Rausch decided to decline Padilla's invitation, the Labor Priest suggested that Rausch tell the UFW that as general secretary "it [is] a policy not to sponsor outside events," but that Higgins could "sponsor the film in . . . [his] own name."[289]

Although clearly sympathetic to La Causa, Rausch selected the second option. The general secretary explained to Padilla that, although he had "a deep personal commitment to the cause of the United Farm Workers and [had] stated [his] position publicly on a number of occasions," he felt it best to adhere to conference policy on sponsorship, which obliged him to decline. The general secretary noted that it had "been a practice of the Conference not to sponsor any program or event in which it did not participate from the planning stage onward," and that because of his rank, he was bound by that practice. Rausch closed by suggesting to Chávez that Higgins would be willing and able to attend the premier on behalf of the Church.[290]

Higgins attended the opening and promoted the film. The Labor Priest's efforts on behalf of La Causa, yet again, garnered praise. Chávez thanked Higgins for his "active involvement in the premiere showing of *Fighting for Our Lives*," and went on to comment that because of Higgins's support, La Causa had "been able to touch so many . . . people."[291]

Although Higgins had the confidence and support of the NCCB's leadership, not all high-ranking members in the U.S. Catholic hierarchy appreciated Higgins's work. In a strictly confidential section of his letter to the Reverend Martin Farrell of St. Mary's Church in Des Plaines,

Illinois, Higgins advised Farrell that the archbishop of Chicago, Cardinal John Patrick Cody, was "unhappy about some of the things" the Labor Priest had said and done "in connection with the farm labor dispute." According to Higgins, Cody "had a couple of meetings with the Teamsters, at which . . . my name, as you might expect, was taken in vain, not by John Patrick, of course, but by the Teamsters themselves."[292]

Higgins advised Farrell that he provided "this information in confidence so that you can be guided accordingly in any conversations you might have with the Cardinal concerning the farm labor problem." Presciently, Higgins also mentioned to Farrell the UFW's Achilles heel—its weak administrative structure. The "UFW ought to organize and pay for a staff of professionally trained organizers and administrators," remarked Higgins, because "sooner or later this will undoubtedly have to be done."[293] Higgins also shared this insight with Chávez, who ignored the Labor Priest's advice. Chávez's inattention toward creating a viable administrative apparatus weakened the UFW, and ultimately contributed to the union's decline and fall.

As 1975 progressed and the California Agricultural Labor Relations Act (CALRA) became a reality, rumors abounded concerning the NCCB's policy of endorsing the UFW's boycott of grapes and lettuce. In a March 20 letter to the Reverend Brad Massman, Bishop Donohoe set the record straight by noting that "there has been no official repudiation of the boycott of grapes and lettuce on the part of the body of Bishops of the United States," and that "the resolution of 1973 is still maintained and the boycott is scheduled to be upheld until satisfactory legislation is written."[294] Donohoe then shifted gears and commented that he personally "felt that the very word boycott was a red flag that served to nullify any efforts on our part to bring farm workers and growers together."[295] Even in 1975, after having witnessed the boycotts' efficacy in softening the growers' resistance, Donohoe still did not feel at ease with the Church's support for Chávez's boycott.

Accenting the high level of interest and confusion regarding the U.S. Catholic hierarchy's official policy on the boycotts, the Most Reverend G. Emmett Carter, bishop of London, wrote General Secretary Rausch for clarification on the matter. In a personal and confidential reply, Rausch delineated some of the more contentious issues in the U.S. hierarchy's decision to endorse the boycott.[296]

Rausch's letter to Carter implied that the wealthy growers did indeed exert significant political pressure on the bishops in California's Central Valley. Specifically, Rausch commented that a "complicating factor is that the boycott is difficult for the California bishops, but is well supported by other bishops of the country." Despite the complications, Rausch assured Emmett that the "California bishops have not asked the Conference to withdraw their support" of the boycott. Additionally, Rausch identified the now-familiar tale of Maxwell's letter to the Reverend Gajda as a major factor in the widespread misperceptions with regard to the conference's policy on the UFW's boycotts, but emphasized that "the U.S. Bishops' Conference continues to support fully the boycott endorsed in 1973."[297]

During the hierarchy's November 1975 meeting, the bishops decided not to renew their support of the boycott because California enacted "satisfactory legislation," that is, the CALRA, to protect the farmworkers. The CALRA and the election of the man who made it happen, Governor Jerry "Moonbeam" Brown, brought victory to Chávez and La Causa.

Jerry Brown, who ascended to the governorship of the Golden State in 1975, became one of Chávez's most powerful political allies. Brown passionately sought farmworker justice and played *the* central role in enacting the CALRA. One of the most socially progressive governors in California's history, Jerry Brown appeared to be a product of the times, and his selection to lead California mirrored the mood of state's electorate.

Author Robert Pack has remarked that Jerry Brown "marches to the beat of a different drummer . . . [and] is totally his own kind of politician."[298] When he assumed duties as governor on January 6, 1975, at the age of thirty-six, Brown became the youngest person to hold the Golden State's highest office in more than one hundred years.[299] His partisans noted that he masterfully harmonized genuine concern for the downtrodden with strict fiscal discipline during his 1975–83 stewardship of California.[300]

Since the late 1970s, much has been made of Jerry Brown's unofficial moniker, "Governor Moonbeam." Conceived by the late *Chicago Tribune* columnist Mike Royko as a mocking reference "to Brown's interest in Zen Buddhism, his talk about exploring outer space and other unconventional (for a politician) topics," the term has been unjustly employed by critics to dismiss Brown as an eccentric with a tenuous grasp on reality.[301] Incidentally, Royko himself subsequently renounced his oft-quoted description of Brown, and in 1991 described him as "a serious man and every bit as normal as the next candidate, if not more so. . . . There's nothing strange about him, unless you consider it strange to recognize that Washington is filled with career hustlers who live from one campaign bundle to another.... So enough of this 'Moonbeam' stuff. As the creator of this monster, I declare it null, void and deceased."[302]

Brown is a paradox. On the one hand, he is an idealist who cares deeply about people.[303] Yet, Robert Pack's biography on Brown also describes him as "fairly awkward at meeting people" and "somewhat of a loner."[304] In many respects, Brown became the antithesis of his father, Governor Edmund Gerald (Pat) Brown. Whereas Pat Brown had a reputation for being an establishment politician who consistently worked to accommodate agricultural interests, Jerry Brown, ironically, became known as an independent thinker and champion of the farmworkers.[305]

As with Chávez, the Catholic Church influenced much of Brown's young life, and perhaps created a spiritual bond between the governor and the leader of La Causa. Brown attended Catholic school from fourth grade through high school, and during these formative years he decided to dedicate his life to the priesthood.[306] At age eighteen, Brown enrolled at the Sacred Heart Novitiate in Los Gatos, California, to begin his studies with the Society of Jesus (the Jesuits).[307] Although he left the seminary after almost three years, Brown retained the character traits and interests that first led him to seek a religious vocation.[308] Specifically, his "Jesuit training helped reinforce the intellectual aloofness that people note about Jerry."[309]

Brown's style has prompted labels of "antipolitician" and "an ascetic figure."[310] He has low tolerance for frivolity, and abhors unnecessary meetings.[311] Brown established his liberal credentials as California's secretary of state from 1970 to 1974. During his tenure, he helped Chávez defeat the Farm Bureau–backed Proposition 22.[312] Brown also marched with Chávez in Calexico and became a widely recognized friend of the farmworkers.[313] Chávez, felt Brown, achieved "more for agricultural workers than anyone else has been able to accomplish in the last fifty years."[314]

César Chávez and Jerry Brown's alliance deepened as Brown's political fortunes waxed. The two became codependent because the UFW needed someone like Brown to represent its interests on the political level, whereas Brown sought La Causa's political support and legitimacy.[315] In fact, claims Pack, the "closest thing Brown [had] to his own constituency [was] the UFW."[316]

During Brown's 1976 bid for the Democratic presidential nomination, Chávez and the UFW endorsed him and worked hard, though unsuccessfully, for his selection.[317] The grand irony of Chávez and Brown's collaboration is that Pat Brown, as governor of California during Chávez's 1966 march from Delano to Sacramento, avoided Chávez when he reached the state's capital.[318] The younger Brown didn't avoid Chávez—he embraced him.

J. D. Lorenz, a former research assistant to Jerry Brown, has provided a less-than-flattering account of the former governor in his book *Jerry Brown: The Man on the White Horse.* Lorenz is hostile to Brown, but upfront about his bias. Although Brown refused to live in the governor's mansion that his predecessor, Ronald Reagan, had built, and drove an old Plymouth instead of using the state's chauffeur-driven limousine, Lorenz nonetheless took exception to the opinion that Jerry was an antipolitician.[319]

Lorenz remarks that Chávez concerned Jerry Brown because in dealing with the UFW, the governor "couldn't resort to symbolic politics the way he liked to do with the other groups." For example, if Brown "indulg[ed] in ostentatious austerity the way he did with the university bureaucrats, . . . César would point out that Jerry earned more in a year than six farmworker families" combined. Disinterested in sinecures, Chávez couldn't be bought by an appointment to a regulatory commission because he "was only interested in higher wages and better working conditions for his farmworkers."[320]

Neither could Brown "mystify César with late-night séances," because "better than anybody else, César could expose Jerry as a hype artist." Lorenz emphasizes that whereas Brown "spoke of austerity, . . . César practiced it." Whereas "Jerry dropped references to Gandhi, . . . [Chávez] fasted for forty days." If "César's world was set up against the artificiality of Jerry's, it would become apparent how up in the air Jerry really was. Jerry knew it. César knew it . . . [and] Jerry knew César knew."[321]

Lorenz believes that Brown embraced Chávez solely out of political expediency; as "the last remaining charismatic leader from the 1960s," Chávez could bring Jerry the liberal vote.[322] Whatever Brown's alleged motivations for partnering with La Causa, the UFW lauded the governor "for not yielding to agribusiness pressure."[323] Without Brown, CALRA might not have become a reality.

For Chávez and the farmworkers, a Moonbeam lit the way.

Immediately upon assuming the governorship in January 1975, Brown relentlessly pushed for the CALRA's passage. If enacted, the law would give migrant workers the right to chose what, if any, union they wanted to represent them via secret ballot elections.[324] Additionally, the

CALRA established the California Agricultural Labor Relations Board (CALRB) to supervise union elections and provide a mechanism to resolve conflicts between unions and growers.[325]

In his inaugural address, Brown highlighted the proposed legislation's importance by asserting that it was "time to extend the rule of law to the agriculture sector and establish the right of secret ballot elections for farm workers."[326] To make the CALRA a reality, Brown assembled a team that included Rose Bird, California's secretary of agriculture and services; Paul Halvonik, assistant to the governor for legislative affairs; LeRoy Chatfield, a former UFW official; Assemblyman Howard Berman; and Stephen Reinhardt, a labor lawyer Brown brought to Sacramento from Los Angeles.[327]

The group began to talk to various sides in the farm labor dispute— the UFW, the Teamsters, and the growers—to see what each wanted.[328] Agribusiness and Teamster officials sought a bill that would outlaw harvest strikes and boycotts and restrict ballots to permanent workers, who were more conservative.[329] Chávez and the farmworkers preferred a version that allowed unrestricted strikes and boycotts, and they wanted elections timed for the harvest peak, when their supporters would control the vote.[330] By 1975, five years of continuous turmoil had fatigued the growers, left the Teamsters weary, and the UFW exhausted. The interested parties were willing to negotiate. Peace had a chance. Jerry Brown could bring it.

To ensure that the legislation would pass, Brown invited all parties with a major stake in the CALRA to the governor's office, but he kept them in separate rooms so that he could move between them "like Henry Kissinger in the Middle East."[331] During these negotiations, the growers yielded more than the UFW.[332] Lettuce growers, just like their grape counterparts in Delano five years earlier, were vulnerable because they were feeling the effects of Chávez's nationwide boycott.[333]

After meeting with the unions and growers, Brown simultaneously presented a draft compromise bill to the Assembly, where the UFW was influential, and the Senate, where Teamsters and growers prevailed.[334] After everyone criticized the draft, Brown convoked another bargaining session.[335] This second round produced a draft that granted growers "protections against boycotts and strikes until after recognition elections," the Teamsters "guarantees on their contracts," and the UFW "the right to strike and boycott after recognition."[336] Brown's revision swept through California's Senate by a 31–7 margin and met the Assembly's approval 64–10. Brown signed the bill in June, and the law went into effect on August 18, 1975.[337]

The Ad Hoc Committee, and by extension the Catholic hierarchy, wholeheartedly supported the CALRA, and they played a role in the law's development. Roger Mahony, who for six years labored diligently as the Ad Hoc Committee's secretary, took the lead for the Catholic Church during the CALRA's development. According to Archbishop Manning, Mahony provided much of the language used in the CALRA.[338] Higgins corroborated Manning's observations, commenting that Mahony represented the California bishops in the negotiations and "played a major role in" the talks.[339]

In May 1975, Bishop Mahony reflected on the "long and difficult struggle" to achieve passage of the CALRA, and he remarked that "the role of the California Bishops has surely been one of great leadership." Mahony felt "that the [CALRA] would not have progressed . . . without the active and diligent involvement of the Church." For Mahony, it became "a source of pride that the Church . . . [had] given such great leadership" in advancing the farmworkers' cause.[340]

Spiritual and temporal authorities alike recognized Mahony's significant contributions toward resolving California's farm labor dispute. In January 1975, Pope Paul VI appointed Mahony to the rank of bishop— just thirteen years after his ordination.[341] A few months later, on July 26, 1975, Governor Jerry Brown tapped Mahony to serve as chairman of the California Agriculture Labor Relations Board.[342] Given his new duties, Mahony, quite rightly, took the position that it would be inappropriate to continue serving on the Ad Hoc Committee, and stepped down.[343]

CALRA's passage greatly pleased, and perhaps relieved, the Catholic hierarchy. With the law's enactment, the bishops finally had an opportunity to withdrawal from their controversial involvement in California's farm labor dispute. The California Conference of Catholic Bishops issued an enthusiastic statement supporting the law, praising Jerry Brown, and calling upon the growers, Teamsters, and UFW to work together to end hostilities.[344]

The bishops' statement was realistic; it recognized that "the mere signing of legislation . . . [would] not guarantee an end to all the anguish and strife that has accompanied this dispute over the years," but rather "only . . . a change of individual attitudes" could accomplish this objective. Apparently weary from almost ten years of conflict in California's fields, the bishops pleaded that both parties *not* wait until late August (when CALRA would become effective) to cease hostilities. Instead, the bishops called "upon the parties to demonstrate their good will" in three "very concrete ways."[345]

First, the hierarchy suggested that growers should "allow . . . the farm workers to [become acquainted] with the benefits of the union movement." Second, growers and Teamsters should "suspend . . . all contract negotiations and contract signings until the Act becomes effective and the workers have had the opportunity to express their wishes through secret ballot elections." Finally, the bishops recommended that if, and only if, "the above can be implemented," the UFW should "suspend at once, boycotts, strikes, slow-downs, and other activities, until the terms of the new legislation become effective."[346]

Apparently eager to end the Church's formal endorsement of the UFW's boycotts, Auxiliary Bishop William Johnson, Archdiocese of Los Angeles, introduced a resolution to rescind the hierarchy's proboycott stance. Johnson aimed to present the proposal at the NCCB Administrative Committee's annual spring meeting. In a letter to Bishop Donnelly, General Secretary Rausch requested the Ad Hoc Committee's opinion on Auxiliary Bishop Johnson's suggestion.[347]

After considering the matter carefully, Donnelly recommended "that the NCCB say nothing," until the bishops' November meeting. Donnelly emphasized that the 1973 NCCB endorsement of the UFW's boycott stated that the bishops supported "the UFW's consumer boycott of table grapes and head lettuce until such time as free secret ballot elections are held." Donnelly took care to highlight the resolution's differentiation between the mere *enactment* of legislation, and the actual successful *implementation* of the law via secret ballot elections. "The distinction between these two alternate wordings is crucial," remarked Donnelly, and "it is quite probable that some growers will resort to . . . delaying tactics to interfere with the prompt and orderly implementation of the law."[348]

Given the Teamsters' poor track record of honoring jurisdictional agreements, Donnelly opined that "it would be totally unrealistic to expect the UFW to unilaterally call off the boycott until elections have been held." Donnelly felt "very strongly that any NCCB resolution calling upon the UFW to unilaterally rescind the boycott before elections have been held would be extremely unrealistic and completely unfair." "Until elections have been held under the terms of the new California law," concluded the Ad Hoc Committee's chairman, "the 1973 NCCB resolution [should] remain in effect."[349]

Roughly two weeks after Donnelly penned his opinion, Donohoe wrote the chairman of the Ad Hoc Committee to share his thoughts on the matter. From the tone of the letter, it appears that Donohoe continued to experience pressure from California growers and that he preferred to terminate the hierarchy's endorsement of the UFW's boycotts at the earliest opportunity.[350]

Donohoe felt that "after two or three bona fide elections in California under the new law, the intent of the 1973 resolution [will have] been fulfilled."[351] Therefore, "the Administrative Committee should be faithful to the intent and language of the 1973 resolution," continued Donohoe, and call "off the consumer boycott as soon as the first free secret ballot election is held." The bishop of Fresno maintained that the "first election should be regarded as the guarantee of further elections to come," and that "it would end considerable confusion across the country if the Administrative Committee would rule in September, 1975, that the . . . [Boycott] Resolution no longer stands." Such action, wrote Donohoe, "would certainly be in harmony with the thinking of all the California Bishops."[352]

According to an August 21 letter from Donnelly to Rausch, it appears that the majority of the Ad Hoc Committee overruled Donohoe's objections.[353] Donnelly commented that "the majority of the [Bishops' Ad Hoc] Committee" recommended that the Administrative Committee "take no action on the 1973 Resolution."[354]

Despite intensive lobbying by Donohoe, Manning, and Johnson, NCCB president Bernardin reported that, at its September meeting, the Administrative Committee decided to let the 1973 boycott resolution stand.[355] Justifying the decision, Bernardin remarked that "even though elections are now being held under the new California law . . . it was premature to make any change in our previous position."[356] The Administrative Committee followed the Ad Hoc Committee's recommendation and reserved final judgment on the boycott resolution until November.

As the bishops' November gathering approached, Chávez sought the Church's continued support for the UFW's boycotts. Apparently, credible reports surfaced of attempts to sabotage the CALRA. The allegations centered on a copy of a one-hundred page UFW white paper titled the "Sabotage and Subversion of the Agricultural Labor Relations Act." In the report, the UFW charged "that the election process under the terms of the . . . [CALRA had] been subverted . . . by various forms of grower intimidation and . . . the General Counsel of . . . [CALRB,] Walter Kintz."[357]

Bishop Mahony lent credence to the allegations, and told Higgins "that he . . . [agreed] with many of Chávez' complaints against Kintz." Unfortunately for the UFW, "there . . . [was] little that [Mahony could] do about this matter, in view of the fact that, under the terms of the new Act, the General Counsel is completely independent of the Board." Mahony did, however, inform Governor Brown that he "disagree[d] with Kintz and consider[d] his performance a serious liability to the orderly administration of the Act."[358]

As the bishops' November meeting drew closer, Chávez continued pressing the hierarchy to uphold the Church's endorsement of the UFW's boycotts. In a November 7 letter to President Bernardin, Chávez expressed his appreciation for the Church's invaluable assistance, and acknowledged that CALRA resulted, in part, because of the boycott's success. Chávez went on to comment that CALRA "is a good law and Governor Brown's Board appointees are decent and sincere men," but "tragically . . . the Board's General Counsel has worked to furiously undermine the Act."[359]

After establishing the boycott's centrality to La Causa and CALRA's precarious situation, Chávez brought his argument to its logical conclusion: he requested that the Church continue to support the UFW's boycott efforts. Chávez felt if the Church didn't renew its endorsement of the boycotts, "the Growers and Teamsters . . . [would] seize upon termination of the boycott resolution to avoid negotiations and claim . . . [the UFW had] lost irreplaceable support in elections." Importantly, Chávez reminded Bernardin of the large and growing segment of Hispanic faithful, closing his correspondence by noting that "farm workers are overwhelmingly Catholic and they would be demoralized by an adverse Conference action."[360]

Apparently Chávez did not convince the bishops. The NCCB held its annual fall assembly from November 17 to 20, 1975, and the bishops "unanimously adopted a resolution saluting the enactment of the California Agricultural Labor Relations Act, congratulating all of those who took part in the process which led up to the passage of this important statute, and calling upon all concerned to cooperate with one another in implementing the spirit as well as the letter of the law."[361] The NCCB's 1975 "Resolution on Farm Labor" celebrated the farmworkers' "right to determine, by secret ballot elections, which union, if any, they want to represent them," and acknowledged the "innovative leadership of Governor Brown who set into motion the process which resulted in the enactment of this long overdue statute by an overwhelming vote of the California legislature."[362]

The 1975 NCCB Resolution on Farm Labor recognized that, with the passage of the CALRA, the farmworkers in California had achieved what the U.S. Catholic hierarchy had defined as its ultimate objective in the farm labor dispute: enabling farmworkers to determine via secret ballot elections which, if any, union they wanted to represent their interests. In 1973, the Church claimed it would "continue to support the boycott until such time as free secret ballot elections have been held."[363] By November 1975, it appeared that CALRB, especially with Mahony as its chairman, would be a step in the right direction toward farmworker justice. The bishops congratulated themselves on a job well done, and began to disengage from La Causa.[364]

1976 and Beyond: The Beginning of the End

And so the end began. With CALRA's enactment, the Ad Hoc Committee began to disengage from the UFW. The once-gushing correspondence between Higgins and Chávez slowed to a trickle.[365] It's doubtful that the hierarchy saw CALRA as a panacea, and it's unlikely the bishops pictured the state fully protecting the farmworkers' interests. CALRA was not the *national* legislation Donohoe had envisioned in 1971, but it did provide the hierarchy with an exit.[366] The Catholic Church could gracefully bow out. The bishops had done their part, and now it was in the hands of the state. But the job was not finished. As soon as Jerry Brown and his team had implemented the protective legislation, agriculturalists and their lawyers sought ways to undermine it.

Mahony, as CALRB chairman, became one of the last vestiges of the Catholic Church's connection with La Causa. Throughout his tenure with the Ad Hoc Committee, Mahony had scrupulously worked to maintain an image of neutrality, but despite Bishop Mahony's best efforts at impartiality, growers were outraged to learn of his nomination to head CALRB. Mahony attempted to counter allegations that he was a farmworker partisan by maintaining "that he had never personally endorsed UFW boycotts."[367] In his California State Senate confirmation hearing, Bishop Mahony tried to deflect accusations of bias by arguing that "the bishops' ad hoc committee did not take sides with any faction, but aimed to win the right of representation and secret ballots for agricultural workers."[368] Of course, the Ad Hoc Committee and the hierarchy did take a position. The Church formally endorsed Chávez's boycotts, and by extension, the UFW.

Jerry Brown's other CALRB nominations—LeRoy Chatfield; Joe C.

Ortega, executive director of a poverty-law agency in Los Angeles; Joseph R. Grodin, a law professor; and Richard Johnsen Jr., executive vice president of the Agricultural Council of California—fueled the controversy over the board's alleged "pro-Chávez/pro-UFW" bias.[369] Growers pointed to Chatfield, Ortega, and Mahony as UFW partisans.[370] Brown countered that his selections were "balanced."[371] The governor envisioned Chatfield and Ortega as sympathetic to the farmworkers, Johnsen Jr., and Grodin, as progrower, and Mahony as "the impartial swing vote."[372]

Instead, Mahony became a lighting rod. Brown later remarked that he "didn't know [Mahony] that well," and didn't anticipate the bishop to be "as much of a polarizing force as he" was.[373] Mahony's "image in the farming community was more pro-UFW" than Brown realized, but regardless, the governor "felt it was important to have a board that all sides would have some confidence in, but particularly the farm workers."[374]

Despite the controversy, the California State Senate confirmed all five of Brown's selections to CALRB, including Mahony as chairman.[375] Although California's legislators granted Bishop Mahony their stamp of approval, the Teamsters did not. In October 1975, one month after his confirmation as CALRB chairman, Teamster thugs threatened and jostled Mahony and vandalized his vehicle after he had presented a talk regarding the charge that CALRB members were biased against the Teamsters.[376]

Mahony may have harbored a personal preference for the farmworkers, but CALRB's records indicate that the bishop maintained his professionalism.[377] The findings of a CALRB study, titled *Setting the Record Straight*, countered the accusation that three of the five board's members were UFW partisans.[378] According to the report, a dissenting opinion occurred in only 7 percent of the Board's decisions, and the dissents did not show a split along partisan lines.[379] Moreover, in only one case did the "members accused of being pro-UFW" vote as a bloc.[380]

During his tenure as CALRB chairman, Mahony faced numerous challenges, none as daunting as CALRB's funding crisis. After just three months of operation, the board exhausted its original endowment of $1.3 million due to a gross underestimate of its workload.[381] The State Department of Finance provided a $1.2 million supplement, but pro-agribusiness lawmakers denied appeals for any additional funding. By February 6, 1976, CALRB was bankrupt.[382]

Mahony took action. He furloughed most of his staff. The bishop sought Higgins's help in getting the Catholic community to put pressure on the California Legislature for approval of the appropriations bill.[383] Wasting no time, the Labor Priest responded and relayed Mahony's request to a number of Catholic organizations.[384]

After speaking with Mahony, Higgins reported to Rausch on the situation. Apparently, a coalition of growers and friends in the California Legislature had blocked CALRB's appropriations bill in an attempt to "blackmail the Governor into supporting some radical changes" to the law.[385] Mahony contended that the proposed changes shifted "the emphasis away from encouraging and protecting the right of farm workers to organize."[386] The growers and the Teamsters opposed CALRB's refunding because they believed the board was biased toward the UFW and thought funding should be granted only after substantial changes were made in the law.[387]

The growers' blackmail enraged Higgins; he deemed their action "completely reprehensible."[388] "The nub of the problem," according to the Labor Priest, was that farmworkers had "voted overwhelmingly in favor of the UFW in the supervised elections conducted thus far." This was not the bargain the growers and Teamsters had hoped for. They had "grossly underestimated the strength" of Chávez's union, and now they had to accept pro-UFW election results.[389]

Dissatisfied with what Higgins called their "serious miscalculation," agriculturalists and Teamsters "decided to go for the jugular" and shut down CALRB.[390] Higgins reported that the growers' actions were so unjust that even Mahony "had radicalized . . . to a remarkable degree."[391] In fact, Mahony became so incensed that Higgins told Donnelly he had "never heard . . . [Mahony] speak so critically about UFW's opponents or so favorably about [the] UFW itself."[392]

By early April 1976, Mahony began to despair. The CALRB crisis had not abated, and the Senate would not provide any additional funding before the beginning of the next fiscal year, which started on July 1.[393] Lacking paychecks and job security, many of the hardest-working and most dedicated CALRB employees resigned, and three of the five board members stepped down.[394]

LeRoy Chatfield left CALRB to work on Jerry Brown's campaign for the Democratic presidential nomination. Joseph Grodin went back to teaching labor law at Hastings College, and Joseph Ortega resigned for personal reasons. Only two of the original five members, Richard Johnsen Jr. and Mahony, agreed to continue serving indefinitely on a voluntary basis. CALRB also lost its general counsel and frequent target of the UFW's criticism, Walter Kintz. Despite his reported disagreements with

Kintz, Mahony did not disparage the departing general counsel; instead, when explaining Kintz's exit, Mahony flatly noted the "uncertainty of the CALRB future made it impossible for him to continue."[395]

In the midst of this crisis, Governor Brown had been focusing on his bid for the 1976 presidential nomination and, therefore, moved slowly to fill the vacancies.[396] Finally, on June 20, 1976, the governor named three new board members. Soon thereafter, the California legislature provided CALRB with $6.8 million for the fiscal year, and the agency staggered back onto its feet.[397]

As CALRB tried to come back up to speed, it had to divert significant precious resources to recruiting and training new employees.[398] This became especially problematic because CALRB faced an overwhelming workload.[399] During CALRB's first year there were 361 elections, and 80 percent were challenged.[400] Accusations of grower and Teamster threats became a major problem throughout the election process, accounting for an estimated 15–20 percent drop in UFW's share of the vote.[401] Although elections were, at least in theory, secret, the reality was that growers and Teamsters could discover how the farmworkers voted and make systematic reprisals—retributions—which included demotions, pay cuts, evictions, tougher assignments, and a variety of physical and mental abuses. [402] Despite these challenges, the majority of the farmworkers voted for UFW representation.[403]

Although CALRB survived the budget crisis, the experience had serious and far-reaching repercussions for La Causa. Chávez characterized CALRB's shutdown as "a day of infamy for the farm worker."[404] To preserve La Causa's gains, Chávez would have to move the CALRA out of the legislative arena—an area where the growers enjoyed a definite home court advantage.[405]

But Chávez had a court of his own: the court of public opinion. Since 1965, Chávez had presented the farmworkers' case to the populace and won. The media, academics, clergy, and students supported La Causa. Chávez figured he could beat the growers and save the CALRA if the electorate had an opportunity to decide the outcome. Chávez created Proposition 14 to raise public awareness of CALRB's budget difficulties and to place the CALRA's future in the voters' hands.[406] Proposition 14 mandated that CALRA could only be changed via ballot initiative.[407] If it passed, growers would have to go through the electorate to change the rules of the game. Chávez believed the people would protect La Causa. Since 1965, they always had.

UFW supporters canvassed the Golden State and gathered roughly

720,000 signatures.[408] Only 360,000 signatures were needed.[409] Proposition 14 easily made the November ballot and appeared poised for success. A Who's Who of Democrats, including Governor Jerry Brown and President Jimmy Carter, endorsed the initiative.[410] Brown publicly supported Proposition 14, but privately felt that Chávez should *not* have put the proposal to the voters. Brown believed that once the threat of Proposition 14 compelled the State Legislature to refund CALRB, Chávez should have accepted victory and withdrawn the initiative.[411] But Chávez did not back down.

Brown conjectured that Chávez pressed on because he felt obligated to maintain his credibility.[412] Despite Brown's better political instincts, he stood by Chávez and campaigned for Proposition 14. Reflecting on his decision, Brown felt that, given his history of supporting Chávez, "there was no legitimate position of neutrality . . . [he] could accept."[413]

Agriculturalists had grown wise to Chávez's tactics and decided to adopt his strategy as their own. Sparing no expense, they hired the brightest lawyers and public relations experts to present the electorate with their side.[414] Proposition 14, argued the growers' media experts, did not protect farmworkers' rights; instead, it violated the sanctity of private property.[415] Grower-funded advertisements inundated the Golden State's airwaves with warnings of UFW organizers potentially running amuck on private land.[416]

The alarmist message resonated well with a post-Watergate electorate suspicious of government and concerned about the protection of private property rights.[417] Voters crushed the initiative 62–38 percent.[418] Chávez had taken his case to the people, to the very public that had supported his marches, fasts, and boycotts. But this time, for the first time since he had risen to national prominence, the public did not hear his plea. Or worse, perhaps they did, but did not care to listen.

Mahony's year as CALRB chairman had been, to say the least, tumultuous. Bishop Mahony informed Brown that he planned to resign effective December 31, 1976, in order to resume his full-time pastoral responsibilities in the Diocese of Fresno.[419] Reflecting on CALRA, Mahony commented that he believed it to be "a good law . . . in complete harmony with all the social encyclicals of the Church."[420] But despite its merits, Mahony admitted that "resistance from the grower community" should be expected because unionized farm labor was "a new concept." The "deep emotional and historical barriers" to change precluded "an instant, overnight transition from one era to another." Mahony estimated that it would "take another two or three years of reconciliation efforts to bring a more widespread peace and stability to California's fields." Nevertheless, Mahony felt confident that "a new, irreversible course has been set to grant farm workers full justice," and that, notably, the U.S. Catholic Church had "played a major role both in proclaiming the rights of farm workers and in working to implement those rights."[421]

Subsequent to Mahony's departure, CALRA went into a spiraling descent. Chávez's political alliances began to crumble as the conservative upheaval of the 1980s shattered the liberal political landscape. By 1983, George Deukmejian had succeeded Jerry Brown as governor of California. Deukmejian, a conservative Republican backed by agricultural interests, stood in stark contrast to Jerry Brown and had little sympathy for La Causa.[422]

During his two terms as governor of California, from 1983 to 1991, Deukmejian transformed CALRA into a law that placed increasing obstacles in the way of agricultural labor unionization.[423] The governor stacked the five-member CALRB with people who were unsympathetic to the UFW, who in turn launched open warfare on the UFW.[424] By 1988, Deukmejian had so radically perverted the original intent of CALRA that the law's existence had become injurious to farm workers. In response, Chávez requested the total eradication of CALRB's budget.[425]

Although CALRA ultimately failed, during the mid-1970s La Causa still had hope. By 1976, it appeared that the UFW had outlasted the Teamsters in the Battle of the Salad Bowl.[426] In June of America's bicentennial, the Teamsters decided to initiate—this time with sincere intentions—exploratory talks with the UFW to renew their jurisdictional vows.[427] After repeated floggings with what could be seen as an olive branch of jurisdictional agreements (in 1967, 1971, and 1973), Chávez amazingly agreed to negotiate.

After six long years of battle, the Teamsters had three reasons to be serious. First, top Teamster officials were tired of being publicly vilified—in addition to their misdeeds against the UFW and the disappearance of Jimmy Hoffa, the Teamsters had been chastised for inappropriate use of pension funds. Second, with Hoffa gone, Fitzsimmons lost a major contender for his job and had less need to appear tough. Finally, the UFW may have agreed to dismiss lawsuits it had against the Teamsters, including one that sought twenty-eight million dollars in damages.[428]

The UFW and the Teamsters reached a general agreement in January 1977, and spent the next two months negotiating specifics.[429] In March 1977, the two parties signed a five-year agreement that incorporated thirteen states and gave the UFW jurisdiction over organizing farmworkers with one exception: the peace treaty allowed the Teamsters to continue their long-running relationship with Salinas Valley lettuce grower Bud Antle.[430] Demonstrating their sincerity, the Teamsters ceased petitioning CALRB for representation elections and asked the board not to certify any of their still-unofficial election victories.[431]

Finally out of the Teamsters' shadow, La Causa could blossom. More than fifteen long years of struggle had brought Chávez's movement to its organizational apogee. In 1978, the UFW claimed more than one hundred thousand members, and Chávez could at last terminate the UFW's long-running grape and lettuce boycotts.[432]

The Bishops' Ad Hoc Committee was noticeably absent from the UFW's victory celebrations. With Mahony's departure from CALRB, *los curas* had left La Causa. In fact, one of the USCC/NCCB's last major defenses of the bishops' role in the farmworker controversy occurred in May 1976, when Alan Grant, president of the American Farm Bureau Federation, denounced Bishop Rausch for allegedly alienating growers in the farm labor dispute. Grant suggested that the Catholic Church had engaged in the "vilification of farm employers as shameless exploiters of human beings," and that such "creation of angels and devils occupying the various sides is not only simplisticly [*sic*] untruthful, but abusive to useful ideas of cooperation and reconciliation."[433]

In an effort to ensure that the Catholic hierarchy fully understood the extent of his displeasure, Grant double-tracked his correspondence to Rausch with a letter to USCC/NCCB chairman Joseph Bernardin. In the communication to Bernardin, Grant complained that the bishop of Brownsville, Texas, had insinuated that growers were slaveholders. Grant then accused Bishop Rausch of being unduly close to a "pro-Chávez faction" at the Conference of Bishops, and of working to build support for the UFW, a "movement . . . that has caused grave dislocation and bankruptcy for small farmers in California, and that has consistently betrayed its public image of a dedication to 'non-violence.'" Grant closed his letter protesting "an almost historic lack of opportunity to present our case to the Conference of Bishops or to have any input whatsoever into its deliberations on farm labor."[434]

Bernardin and Rausch both dispatched succinct rejoinders. Bernardin suggested a face-to-face meeting would be the most appropriate venue to address the serious charges, and reaffirmed the farmworkers' right to secret elections.[435] Rausch followed up Bernardin's communication with a polite but firm reply. As with the USCC/NCCB chairman,

Rausch maintained that such serious differences of opinion would best be reconciled via conversation rather than through correspondence, and accordingly opened the possibility of a meeting to address the numerous points of disagreement.[436]

By 1977, the once white-hot relationship between the Bishops' Committee and Chávez had cooled. The Battle of the Salad Bowl ended in March 1977, but nobody seemed to notice. There were no cheering crowds, no flurry of letters gushing with mutual admiration. There is little germane archival material post-1975, and that speaks volumes.

It appears that the bishops believed, or wanted to believe, that passage of CALRA in 1975 relieved them of their commitment to the farmworkers. In one sense they were correct. The Ad Hoc Committee began to disengage from La Causa in 1975—the year of Chávez's political zenith. La Causa's long slide into political oblivion began the following year with the voters' rejection of Chávez's Proposition 14. Organizationally, however, La Causa was still strong. The UFW hit its apex of one hundred thousand members in 1978–79 on the shoulders of the U.S. Catholic Church's assistance during the Battles of Delano and the Salad Bowl, and the campaign to enact the CALRA. After propelling the UFW to the height of its influence, the hierarchy promptly retreated.

During the summer of 1977, the farmworkers lost a good friend and loyal supporter. On June 30, 1977, Bishop Joseph Donnelly, chairman of the Ad Hoc Committee, passed away. Bernardin appointed Bishop Rausch to succeed Donnelly as the committee's chairman.[437]

In his new capacity as Ad Hoc Committee chairman, Rausch presented a moving address to the Biennial Convention of the UFW in Fresno, California. A masterful amalgamation of sophistication and warmth, Rausch's speech weaved seemingly disparate topics into a hard-hitting conclusion. Rausch commenced his talk by acknowledging a profound respect for his "good friend" Chávez, and paid a heartfelt tribute to Bishop Donnelly, vowing to "keep his memory alive, [and] more importantly, to take up where he left off and to strengthen the bond of friendship which he helped to establish between the Church and the UFW."[438]

Rausch lauded the UFW's "ambassador-at-large," Monsignor George Higgins, as a "good friend and staunch supporter" of the farmworkers, and emphasized that the Labor Priest had spent the greater part of the late 1960s and 1970s promoting the UFW's "interests within the labor movement, not only at AFL-CIO headquarters in Washington, but throughout the nation." The new chairman recalled that Higgins undertook such efforts "because he . . . [felt] strongly that the UFW . . .

[needed] the support of the AFL-CIO and its affiliates and that the labor movement, by the same token . . . [needed] the UFW." Rausch then exhorted the UFW to "spread . . . [its] wings and play a very active and constructive role in the councils of organized labor at the national as well as at the local and regional level."[439]

In the most important section of his address, Rausch castigated the UFW for its administrative deficiencies. The chairman felt that he "would be less than honest if . . . [he] did not . . . take note of the fact that . . . [the UFW] still face[ed] certain internal problems which . . . [it] alone can solve." For example, although the UFW possessed considerable "skill in running strikes, pilgrimages, and boycotts," it "must begin to switch gears psychologically and organizationally and develop the rather unglamorous administrative skills so essential to the day to day operation of an established union."[440] Rausch's admonition to La Causa clearly set forth that Chávez and his colleagues *had* to become a bread-and-butter union in *addition* to being a social movement.[441] Only one year earlier, Higgins had also met with Chávez to deliver the same message.[442] Given the UFW's precipitous decline during the 1980s, it is not apparent that anyone had listened to the clergy's counsel.

Rausch's address also explained why the Church had supported the farmworkers. The chairman maintained that the Church should not take sides, but "whenever the fundamental rights of any particular group and, more especially, when the rights of the poor and the underprivileged are violated or ignored, the Church, at any cost, must come to their defense, even at the risk of being falsely accused of taking sides, in a prejudiced manner." Rausch countered the Church's detractors by asserting that the clergy have "the responsibility, under God, to give prophetic witness in the area of social justice and . . . to exercise progressive leadership in helping people from all walks of life to construct a more humane society."[443] Rausch had a clear sense of mission, and the farmworkers benefited from his support, especially during his tenure in the influential position of USCC/NCCB general secretary.

In spite of Rausch's stirring speech, in which he referred to escalating "the bond of friendship which [Donnelly] helped to establish between the Church and the UFW," there are no archival records at the USCCB, The Catholic University of America, the University of Notre Dame, or Wayne State University of the Ad Hoc Committee's activities under Rausch. Furthermore, the Diocese of Phoenix, where Rausch served as bishop, does not possess any significant documentation germane to Rausch's tenure as chairman of the Ad Hoc Committee. The next noteworthy correspondence on the committee's activities did not appear until Bishop Rausch's passing in 1981.

Upon Rausch's death, the Labor Priest suggested that Bishop Roger M. Mahony be named as chairman, and that "the committee continue in existence against the possibility of new circumstances that might require its reactivation."[444] The Ad Hoc Committee had been inactive for years, but Higgins nonetheless felt it "would be an inappropriate time to dissolve . . . [the] committee, in spite of the fact that it . . . [did] not have any immediate agenda."[445]

Mahony became the natural choice because he had both the experience and the necessary rank (Mahony became auxiliary bishop of Fresno under Bishop Donohoe in 1975; bishop of Stockton in 1980; archbishop of Los Angeles in 1985; and finally, rose to his current rank of cardinal in 1991).[446] In his offer to Mahony, Bishop John Roach, chairman of the NCCB, acknowledged that "while the NCCB Committee on Farm Labor has not been active recently it probably would be premature or misinterpreted if we were to suppress it." Roach felt Mahony was "certainly the most knowledgeable of the bishops in this complex area," and indicated he would be grateful if Mahony could assume the chairmanship.[447] Bishop Mahony concurred that "it might be a wrong signal to disband the Committee at this juncture," and graciously accepted Bishop Roach's offer with the understanding that the Ad Hoc Committee's "present and future activity may not be great."[448]

Although Archbishop Roach designated Mahony to serve as chairman, the group had essentially become a shell—a symbol of days past.[449]

EPILOGUE

La Causa's Self-Destruction

By the end of the 1970s, the UFW appeared poised to become a major force in the AFL-CIO with a membership of more than one hundred thousand farmworkers; instead, the union atrophied over the next decade losing 80 percent of its organizational strength. Both internal and external factors contributed to the UFW's demise. Internally, Chávez failed to prepare his organization for its transition from a social movement/union to a union/social movement; externally, declining national interest in social causes and a corresponding rise of conservatism combined to exacerbate the internal ailments that wracked La Causa.

As the UFW matured, Chávez should have prepared La Causa to make the necessary transition from a social movement/union to a union/social movement—a process that required an efficient administrative apparatus rather than marching or fasting. Despite the fact that Higgins and Rausch had advised Chávez of the need for administrative reform, he did not undertake corrective action. Moreover, it appeared that Chávez did not wish to remedy the situation by becoming a conventional labor union; after observing traditional union officials "at the conventions in their gray pinstripe suits and red ties," Chávez noted with disdain that "they looked like the employers of their workers."[1]

Three principal factors contributed to the UFW's deterioration. First, Chávez reportedly possessed a charismatic yet authoritarian management style that ultimately made his union an unattractive long-term employer. Second, Chávez wanted to staff his organization with true believers and demanded a radical level of commitment (for example, accepting abysmally low pay for exceptionally long hours) that was not sustainable over a normal career span. Finally, Chávez did not establish an administrative structure capable of successfully functioning independent of his charismatic leadership.[2]

The union's deficiencies worsened as La Causa experienced its major victories during the late 1970s. Apparently, the UFW could only find peace in war. The March 1977 jurisdictional agreement with the Teamsters should have ushered in an era of sustained prosperity for the UFW. Instead of parlaying victories into better contracts for the farmworkers, union officials fought bitterly among themselves and La Causa imploded.[3]

Between 1977 and 1981, many of Chávez's most dedicated and competent employees resigned. The torrent of high-profile departures included Marshall Ganz, the fifteen-year UFW veteran and chief organizer; Gilbert Padilla, the UFW's secretary-treasurer and founding member of the NFWA; and perhaps most importantly from an administrative standpoint, Jerry Cohen, chief UFW legal counsel and director of the legal office for seventeen years. Making matters worse, an exodus of almost the entire UFW legal staff followed Cohen's departure.[4]

Jerry Cohen's resignation merits special attention because it indicated the extent of Chávez's inability, or unwillingness, to transform the UFW from a social cause to a conventional union. In 1979, Cohen asked the executive board to consider a proposal "to pay staff salaries rather than in-kind subsistence." Although seemingly a reasonable request—Cohen and his legal team performed a vital function for La Causa and deserved adequate compensation—Chávez opposed the idea and successfully persuaded the board to reject Jerry's proposal.[5] Although Cohen agreed to stay on until March 1981, the loss of legal talent devastated the union.

Monsignor Higgins, ever loyal to La Causa, defended Chávez throughout the UFW's disintegration. Dismissing critics of Chávez's authoritarian behavior, the Labor Priest attributed the union's reversal of fortunes to the overall weakening of labor's potency during the 1980s. Higgins maintained that "the farm workers, . . . like many other labor movements, have fallen on hard times," and "the question of whether the union is overly identified with a single 'charismatic' personality seem[ed] beside the point."[6]

Clearly, a social movement's success requires an appropriate national mood and an opportune political climate, but a suitable leader—Chávez in the UFW's case—must also emerge at the proper time. Therefore, because it is plausible to link the UFW's rise to Chávez, we must also consider it highly probable, despite Higgins's assessment, that Chávez bore at least partial responsibility for La Causa's decline.

Compadrazgo, the Mexican custom of serving as a personal friend and protector for individual workers, pervaded the UFW.[7] Accordingly, workers felt that Chávez should personally address their union-related problems.[8] The obvious flaw with this cult-of-personality approach is that compadrazgo "cannot be transferred to a cadre of administrators."[9] Ideally, Chávez would have used his charisma to launch the movement, and then by the late 1970s, when his union had an estimated one hundred thousand workers, he would have redirected the UFW's emphasis toward formal organizations with written rules and managerial hierarchies, including associating authority with offices instead of personal qualities and extraordinary abilities.[10]

As La Causa atrophied, critics openly assailed Chávez's management style as inflexible and autocratic.[11] Disgruntled UFW employees charged Chávez with centralizing power and mistreating staff members.[12] While the union skidded toward political and organizational oblivion, La Causa's leadership sank into paranoia over the presence of leftists and others who supposedly had their own agenda within the union.[13] Student volunteers, once critical to Chávez's success, were marginalized and not invited to participate in the union's policy decisions.[14] Additionally, allegations emerged that Chávez's union, with his brother, sister-in-law, and son-in-law sitting on the executive board, had essentially become a "family cartel."[15]

Aristeo Zambrano, a one-time union activist until fired by Chávez, remarked that "in the mid-seventies, when I became an activist, Chávez was making every decision in the union." For example, "if a car in Salinas needed a new tire . . . [the UFW staff] had to check with Chávez in La Paz. [Chávez] controlled every detail of union business. And nobody was allowed to say Chávez made a mistake, even when he had." Zambrano also contradicted reports of Chávez's characteristic humility. "[W]hen you talked to him you had to humble yourself," claimed Zambrano, "as if he were a King or the Pope." Apparently, Chávez "was incapable of sharing power," and according to Zambrano, Chávez believed that the "farmworkers were good for boycotting, or walking the picket lines, or paying union dues, but not for leading" the UFW. Finally, Zambrano maintained that "Chávez built the union and then . . . destroyed it. . . . When the Republicans came back in the 1980s and the growers moved against the union, there wasn't any farmworker movement left."[16]

In addition to ineffective management, the UFW's staff endured abysmally low salaries. Joining the UFW meant sacrificing both one's personal life and financial security. La Causa's weekly paychecks of five dollars plus room and board could not attract and retain career-minded professionals.[17] Admirably, Chávez and his top lieutenants shared in the same appalling compensation package; however, Chávez upbraided those who did not share his sense of sacrifice because he felt that they failed to exhibit sufficient dedication.[18] Many such supposedly "uncommitted" officials departed the union after devoting more than a decade to the movement.[19] Ironically, the same UFW employees who labored to bring, among other things, a living wage to the farmworkers did not earn one themselves.

The three internal factors that led to the UFW's decline occurred against the backdrop of a withering national interest in social causes and a flourishing conservative movement. These two external factors exacerbated the UFW's internal ailments and expedited La Causa's demise. Chávez's union thrived as the baby boomer generation came of age in the 1960s and early 1970s, but by 1976, as exemplified by the defeat of Proposition 14, La Causa's once vibrant public following began to fade.

Rarely can idealism be carried past youth. The demands of life—bills, children, and the pursuit of a means to provide for them—compelled the baby boomers to labor in and for the very system they once criticized. The level of commitment, and ensuing poverty, that Chávez demanded could not harmonize with the ethos of a generation that entered professional life during the late 1970s and 1980s.

In a final blow to La Causa, the domestic political climate by the 1980s turned conservative and decimated Chávez's political alliances. Monsignor Higgins acknowledged that during the "material" decade, "the plight of farm workers . . . [was] not uppermost in the minds of people."[20] As the nation's concern for the La Causa diminished, California's electorate lost interest in Chávez's most politically powerful ally, Jerry Brown. Republican (and future California governor) Pete Wilson's defeat of Brown in a 1982 senate race highlighted the UFW's protracted decline, and progrower Republican George Deukmejian's assumption of the governorship simply intensified the problem.

Chávez ascended on the liberal ethos of the 1960s and early 1970s, but stumbled as baby boomers traded their Birkenstocks for wingtips during the 1980s.[21] Because Chávez had not taken the time to develop a solid administrative structure during his years of political bounty, La Causa could not endure the cycle of reaction by vested interests against him that characterized the 1980s.[22] Instead of Jerry Brown, Chávez had to engage Deukmejian and Reagan—neither of whom expressed sympathy for organized labor.[23]

In his address to the UFW's seventh constitutional convention in September 1984, Chávez made clear his enmity for Reagan and Deukmejian by calling them "the enemies of the poor and the working classes" because they "give away millions of dollars in cash money to the richest corporate growers in America for not growing crops, while unemployment benefits for farm workers are cut and while food and medical care for the poor are reduced."[24] Chávez mocked Reagan's invocations of the Almighty, observing that "President Reagan sees a proper role for government and a proper role for God. It's very simple: Reagan's government helps the rich, and God helps the rest of us."[25]

As the 1980s wore on, Chávez repeatedly made serious miscalculations. In one glaring blunder, Chávez continued to place the UFW's emphasis on boycotts and fasts rather than on organizing the farmworkers. Like a fading movie star, Chávez doggedly clung to the formula that brought him success twenty years earlier, but the audience had moved on. His now ineffective boycotts took the best farmworker activists from the fields and placed them in major urban centers—a disastrous misstep from the standpoint of building farmworker membership.[26] By the time of Chávez's death in 1993, the UFW was not primarily a farmworker organization. Instead, it reportedly was "a fundraising operation ... staffed by members of Chávez's extended family and using as its political capital, Chávez's legend, and the warm memories of millions of aging boycotters."[27]

Today the UFW still exists as the largest agricultural labor union in California with contracts that cover 70 percent of the mushroom workers on California's Central Coast and more than 50 percent of rose workers in California's Central Valley. Additionally, the UFW has an agreement with Coastal Berry, the largest U.S. employer of strawberry workers.[28] Under the majority of UFW contracts, farmworkers receive family medical care, job security, paid holidays, and vacations, as well as pensions and a host of other benefits.[29]

The UFW is still devoting considerable resources to activities beyond traditional organizing. For example, the union now has a goal of helping ten million Latinos and working families in ten years by expanding its radio network, building low-income housing, and developing educational programs for underprivileged children.[30] La Causa has also recently made progress on the legislative front. California's mandatory mediation law, SB 1736, took effect in 2002 and forced growers to agree to contracts after farmworkers have voted for union representation. The law favors the UFW and eliminated growers' ability to prolong the contract process indefinitely.[31] The union now represents approximately twenty-seven thousand farmworkers—a respectable improvement from its nadir of twenty thousand laborers, but far below its organization apogee of more than one hundred thousand members.[32]

Did César E. Chávez make a difference? Were the farmworkers better off after Chávez than before? Definitely.

By 1980, the UFW had brought farmworkers improvements in wages, benefits, and job security.[33] For example, between 1964 and 1980 farmworkers' real wages adjusted for inflation increased 70 percent.[34] The UFW built health care facilities for farmworkers, and created service centers where they could receive assistance such as workers' compensation and food stamps.[35] Monsignor Higgins unequivocally stated that the UFW had "significantly improved the lot of its members," and that "UFW workers['] . . . pay rates . . . [ran] well above those of other farm workers."[36]

In addition, Chávez's movement raised awareness of the farmworkers' plight and increased pressure on legislators to bring justice to California's valleys. In part because of Chávez's persistent efforts, lawmakers abolished the hated short-hoe (cortito), heightened regulations on pesticide use, and brought CALRA into force.[37] Farmworkers also experienced long deserved improvements in basic working conditions, which included two scheduled rest periods each day and cool, potable water and individual cups.[38]

One of the UFW's greatest legacies has been its practice of currying political favor to advance farmworker interests. Although this strategy backfired with the rise of conservatism in the 1980s, the union attained its most meaningful achievements, including CALRA, by developing powerful allies throughout the 1960s and 1970s.[39] Because the UFW could successfully apply political pressure, state and national elites did not automatically sided with the growers.[40]

Chávez once said that "it is how we use our lives that determines what kind of people we are."[41] Accordingly, he was, as the late Senator Robert Kennedy noted, "one of the heroic figures of our time."[42]

Six days after Chávez died peacefully in his sleep on April 23, 1993, near Yuma, Arizona, more than fifty thousand people attended his funeral—the largest such gathering for any U.S. labor leader.[43]

In recognition of Chávez's contributions to social justice, President Bill Clinton in August 1994 posthumously awarded Chávez the Presidential Medal of Freedom, America's highest civilian honor. "César Chávez left our world better than he found it," reflected President Clinton, "he was for his own people a Moses figure."[44] Acknowledging this contribution in bringing farmworkers closer to the promised land of fair wages and working conditions, California established March 31 as César Chávez Day—an official state holiday.[45]

César Chávez had led a revolution—a peaceful movement for social change—that, if only for a brief period during the early 1970s, prompted the American Catholic hierarchy to make social justice one of its highest priorities.

Why Los Curas Left La Causa

Given the U.S. Catholic hierarchy's overwhelming success in implementing papal encyclicals on social justice through the work of the Bishops' Ad Hoc Committee, one must ask what happened to the once-vibrant relationship between Chávez and the Church.

Once the California Legislature enacted CALRA, the hierarchy eagerly withdrew from their highly controversial affiliation with César Chávez—a relationship that placed California's bishops in the politically precarious, and financially punitive, position of favoring the Catholic farmworkers over the Central Valley's wealthy Catholic growers. As the Ad Hoc Committee slipped into inactivity, the deluge of correspondence between César Chávez and Monsignor Higgins, who clearly acted as the driving force behind the Catholic Church's support for La Causa, evaporated. It is plausible to assume that the Labor Priest had a finite amount of time, and after having dedicated over half a decade to La Causa, decided that the committee had successfully assisted the UFW through its most critical battles and could now disengage on amicable terms.

Another related explanation is that Higgins, by his own admission, let the headlines determine his work. The Labor Priest "rarely knew what his day's agenda would be until he'd looked at the front pages of the morning's *Washington Post* and *New York Times*." By 1976, Chávez had started to fade from the spotlight, and if Higgins wanted "to be in the thick of contemporary issues," his focus would have needed to drift away from La Causa.[46]

As the USCC/NCCB withdrew, it became evident that Chávez's movement also began losing clerical support at the grassroots level. For example, during an August 1979 UFW march from San Francisco to Salinas, the Catholic presence was thin with only a few clergy visible.[47] Bishop Mahony reportedly attributed the decline of church participation in La Causa to the UFW's efforts to "become more of a union than a social cause," as well as the UFW's desire "to be able to operate successfully without depending on churches and other 'outside' groups."[48] By the late 1970s, the partnership between the U.S. Catholic Church and the La Causa had ended. However, one critical aspect of this story remains untold: the epilogue to the friendship between Chávez and Higgins.

From the late 1960s through the mid-1970s, Higgins and Chávez enjoyed a vibrant relationship based on pursuit of a common goal. However, once the Ad Hoc Committee began to withdraw from La Causa, it appeared that the crisis du jour caused Chávez and Higgins to drift apart. As the 1970s came to a close, serious vocational complications beset both men and distracted their focus.

The Labor Priest's career took a major tumble in 1978. The USCC/NCCB's leadership expressed its appreciation for Higgins's innumerable contributions to the cause of social justice by placing his position on the chopping block and mandating his early retirement. After thirty-four years of tireless service, the conference's Research, Plans, and Programs Committee decided to close Higgins's Office of Research and retire the Labor Priest due to budgetary difficulties.[49] In a one-page letter explaining the NCCB's move to the Reverend Joe O'Brien, chairman of the Association of Chicago Priests (Higgins was a priest of the Archdiocese of Chicago), NCCB/USCC general secretary Thomas Kelly noted that the "termination of Monsignor's services is a disappointment" and that the action was "the result of an inflationary economy, and reflects cutbacks being made in Church organizations at all levels."[50]

A more revealing letter to Joe O'Brien came from Joseph Bernardin. In his communication, Bernardin indicated that because he had "a great deal of respect and affection for George," he "wanted to reply personally" to O'Brien's request for an explanation. After providing the standard "budgetary crunch" response, Bernardin transitioned into an account of his efforts to ensure just compensation for Higgins. "It was certainly the intent of the Committee to give George adequate time to phase out," explained Bernardin, "and also to take care of him as far as compensation and retirement are concerned." Bernardin closed his letter by conveying his personal misgivings about the conference's decision to release Higgins, admitting that he felt "badly about the matter," and acknowledging that "the Committee may not have made a correct decision," even though "at the time it seemed reasonable in light of the facts presented."[51]

Higgins appeared to be at peace with the conference's determination. In his press interviews, the Labor Priest tried to put the decision to retire him in the best possible light, but he acknowledged that his "words . . . [fell] on deaf ears." Higgins reported that "Kelly, Quinn and the other members of the Committee . . . [were] being bombarded with irate letters and phone calls from friends and associates . . . from all over the country," and that, quite frankly, there was nothing more he could "do to save face for the Committee."[52]

The NCCB's decision to retire Higgins might have been motivated in part by a conservative ideological/policy shift at the conference. Although the documents are silent on this issue, it is plausible that the bishops perceived Higgins and his work as a liberal relic of Vatican II, especially in light of the growing conservatism in both the U.S. populace and the hierarchy of the Catholic Church. As the 1970s waned, perhaps the U.S. bishops foresaw the Church's conservative elements reclaiming the Vatican, and wanted to position the U.S. hierarchy to be in alignment with the impending trend.

Regardless of their motivations, the intense public outcry against Higgins's retirement pressured the bishops to reconsider their handling of the matter, and the hierarchy promptly reversed its decision agreeing to continue his services.[53]

Higgins remained at the conference for two additional years, and he retired from the NCCB in 1980.[54] For Higgins, retirement simply entailed changing occupations. He spent the next twenty years at his alma mater, The Catholic University of America, lecturing on labor and social ethics until 1994 and holding the post of professor emeritus until 2000.[55] Monsignor Higgins passed away after an extended illness on May 1, 2002, in his hometown of LaGrange, Illinois, at the age of eighty-six.[56]

At Higgins's 1980 retirement tribute, the Labor Priest's old friend César E. Chávez reappeared at one of the front tables.[57] As he had done before, Chávez acknowledged "all that Higgins meant to the farm labor movement."[58] Their relationship appeared to have grown distant, not out of enmity, but simply due to the turmoil that appeared to envelop both their lives during the late 1970s. In 1981, after almost five years of sporadic contact, the two exchanged a detailed correspondence that irreparably shattered their friendship. The exchange made clear that the once-close friends had not held any meaningful discussions regarding La Causa's declining fortunes.

Higgins began his letter to Chávez noting that "as a friend of the movement," he was "appalled to learn . . . that Jerry Cohen, Gilbert Padilla, Marshall Ganz and other stalwart leaders . . . [had] all left [the] UFW in quick succession." Although the Labor Priest admitted that he had "no way of knowing whether they left on their own initiative or whether they were requested to leave," he did realize "that the movement can ill afford to lose men of their caliber, dedication and experience." Higgins felt "even more appalled by reports . . . to the effect that they are being bad-mouthed by certain UFW staff members and officers and sickened to learn that some of their UFW critics are making public or semi-public anti-Semitic remarks about Cohen and Ganz." "If the latter reports are correct," Higgins continued, "I fear for the future of the movement," and "for obvious reasons . . . could not and would not continue to work with any movement which would permit any of its staffers or officers to indulge in anti-Semitism." Higgins requested that Chávez inform him if such "reports are accurate and, if so, what if anything the UFW plans to do to discipline the guilty parties." Higgins warned Chávez that "even the slightest compromise on the issue of anti-Semitism would seriously endanger the movement and could conceivably destroy it."[59]

In his extensive communication, Higgins also told Chávez that he was "badly shaken to read in the California papers that you had publicly stated at your recent Fresno convention that you 'hate' all the growers." "I can't believe that you really mean this," wrote the Labor Priest, "but whether you do or not, I wonder if you fully realize that such intemperate rhetoric puts me in a very awkward position as the 'impartial' chairman of the [Martin Luther King] Fund." "The growers would have to be completely insane," continued Higgins, "to think that I was really 'impartial' if they got the impression that I agreed with your attack on them at the Fresno convention."[60]

The Labor Priest made "no apologies" for his "extremely frank" letter to Chávez; instead, Higgins told Chávez that he wrote "as one whose credentials as a strong supporter of the movement are in good order," and that one "should never trust a friend who is afraid to tell you the truth, no matter how distasteful the truth may be." The truth, as Higgins saw it, was that the UFW was "in serious trouble and that some of this trouble . . . [was] strictly of its own making."[61]

Higgins closed his letter to Chávez by observing "that unless some of these matters are satisfactorily cleared up, [the] UFW will be playing right into the hands of the Teamsters and some of the more anti-union growers." Given the gravity of his letter, Higgins requested that Chávez "reply . . . without delay, or, in any event, no later than October 12."[62]

Chávez appeared to take serious umbrage at Higgins's accusations, and the Labor Priest's question as to *why* Chávez's top aids departed noticeably went unanswered. Chávez opened his letter with a back-handed compliment "praising" Higgins's record for staying out of "internal union fights." Chávez recognized that although it was not the Labor Priest's "intention to take sides in . . . [the UFW's] current internal struggles . . . a careful re-reading" of Higgins's letter indicated that the Labor Priest had "reached some definite conclusions without having talked to" any UFW officials. Chávez went on to tell Higgins that although his words might have been "carefully qualified," the "words and the tone together convey some firm conclusions about . . . [the UFW's] situation."[63]

Chávez addressed Higgins's concerns over the departures of several UFW lieutenants simply by noting that "they all submitted letters of resignation stating they were leaving for personal reasons; in each case the Executive Board accepted the resignations unanimously and with regrets." Chávez maintained that it should come as no "surprise . . . that there has been no public discussion of these resignations" as the union, as a matter of policy, did not "discuss such matters in public unless . . . responding to inquiries."[64] Apparently, Chávez felt no further explanation necessary.

Chávez told Higgins that he had "heard the same charges you have heard about anti-Semitic remarks by our leaders," but that the UFW has "a long record of friendship and solidarity with the Jewish Community, a record that goes back to my days with the CSO, long before the Union was begun." Clearly upset that Higgins could believe such accusations, Chávez wrote the Labor Priest that he felt it "very hard . . . to understand how you could give credence to these charges without at least talking with me. Isn't it true that you did come to a conclusion without consulting with any of us?" "Please let me know if I am wrong on this," continued Chávez, "and be assured that you have absolutely nothing to fear for the future of the movement on this score."[65]

Chávez conceded that he "*did* [emphasis Chávez's] use very strong language in talking about the growers," but felt no need "apologize for it." Becoming increasingly belligerent toward his (soon to be former) friend, Chávez sarcastically remarked: "regarding your fears about our being in serious trouble of our own making, we are always in trouble. Unless something changes dramatically in the industry and the world, that is the nature of our struggle. Perhaps you know something specific that we don't know. If so, please let me know at your earliest convenience."[66]

Snuffing out the last flicker of their once-radiant friendship, Chávez sent Higgins a clear message when he told the Labor Priest, "thank you for your offer of mediation but we don't think it is necessary at this time."[67]

And so it ended. All the struggles, sacrifice, shared triumphs and setbacks—as if they had never happened. There would be no more effervescent letters gushing with praise. Most likely both Higgins and Chávez felt affronted by their 1981 exchange; Chávez because of Higgins's accusations, and Higgins because of Chávez's brusque reply.

To a minor extent, Chávez and Higgins carried on their correspondence, but the notes in the archives are short and pedestrian—merely tokens of good manners. Although Higgins remained a loyal friend and never publicly denigrated Chávez, the damage had been done. The Labor Priest no longer extended warm overtures to Chávez; instead, he withdrew from the relationship, and their lively association withered into what could euphemistically be characterized as cordial relations.

In 1983, Higgins wrote Chávez to remind him that their "good friend," Bill Kircher, who at the time was in "rather shaky health," might appreciate a ceremony to "honor him at a public UFW gathering for all that he has done for the Union."[68] Two years later, Chávez remembered Higgins's mother's birthday, and the Labor Priest sent Chávez a note expressing appreciation and acknowledging that his mother "was overjoyed" to get Chávez's birthday wishes.[69]

During the early 1970s, the height of Higgins's career, the Labor Priest allotted substantial amounts of his precious time to tirelessly promote La Causa. Evidencing the extent to which their relationship had cooled by the late 1980s, Higgins apparently could not break away from his schedule to attend the UFW's silver anniversary celebration. Higgins politely sent his regrets, noting that it broke his heart that, due to circumstances beyond his control, he could not attend.[70]

Though brief, Higgins's RSVP said much. Almost six years after Chávez's 1981 reply, the Labor Priest still appeared to feel the sting of Chávez's letter. As the years wore on, Higgins commented that "when people ask me how things are going with the farm workers, I have to tell them I really don't know." Although he saw Chávez a few times a year, usually after meetings of the Robert F. Kennedy Memorial Fund, a social welfare fund administered by farmworkers and growers, their conversations rarely, if ever, touched on union business.[71]

Addressing the apparent disconnect, Higgins maintained that he was "not the only one who feels somewhat out of the UFW's loop" as "long-time friends of the movement" had commented "that the UFW . . . seem[ed] distant and removed from those who . . . helped the union along the way." Speaking from experience, Higgins shared that "the union . . . never explain[ed] the problems and differences," and "neither do the departing staffers, who admirably remain loyal to the end."[72]

Less than a year after Chávez's death, top UFW officials presented Higgins with a UFW flag that now hangs in The American Catholic History Research Center and University Archives at The Catholic University of America. On the banner Dolores Huerta wrote, "Msgr.—The farm workers are eternally grateful to you for your tremendous help in getting justice!"[73] Arturo Rodriguez, UFW president, told Monsignor Higgins that his "contributions to the success of the farm workers will always be a part of our history."[74]

And the farmworkers became a part of the Catholic Church's history—a history that reminds us of an era when the Catholic hierarchy reluctantly stepped into a conflict among its faithful only to eventually embrace the cause of the underprivileged in the face of relentless criticism by the prosperous.

"When the history of the California dispute is finally written," Monsignor Higgins once remarked, "the [Ad Hoc] Committee will undoubtedly be credited with having made an indispensable contribution" toward its peaceful resolution.[75]

It was. Upon Higgins's passing, UFW president Arturo Rodriguez echoed Chávez's sentiments regarding the man who spearheaded the Ad Hoc Committee's work with La Causa. "During good times and bad," recalled Rodriguez, "there was no greater champion of César Chávez and the farmworkers' cause than Msgr. Higgins. He was by César's side at the UFW's greatest triumphs and during its darkest days."[76]

NOTES

Introduction

1. George G. Higgins with William Bole, *Organized Labor and the Church: Reflections of a "Labor Priest"* (New York: Paulist Press, 1993), 87.

2. George Higgins to the editor, *Toronto Catholic Register*, January 13, 1975.

3. Tracy Early, "Cesar Chavez Sees 'Hard Times' With Reagan Presidency," National Catholic News Service, November 11, 1980.

Chapter 1. Roots of the Conflict

1. John Gregory Dunne, *Delano* (New York: Farrar, Straus and Giroux, 1971), 34.

2. David G. Gutierrez, *Walls and Mirrors: Mexican Americans, Mexican Immigrants and the Politics of Ethnicity* (Berkeley: University of California Press, 1995), 19.

3. Ibid., 24.

4. Dunne, *Delano*, 34–35.

5. Ibid., 36.

6. Ibid., 37.

7. Valerie J. Matsumoto, *Farming the Home Place: A Japanese American Community in California, 1919–1982* (Ithaca: Cornell University Press, 1993), 24.

8. Dunne, *Delano*, 38.

9. Ibid.

10. Ibid., 38.

11. Matsumoto, *Farming the Home Place*, 21.

12. Dunne, *Delano*, 38.

13. Camille Guerin-Gonzales, *Mexican Workers and American Dreams: Immigration, Repatriation, and California Farm Labor, 1900–1939* (New Brunswick, N.J.: Rutgers University Press, 1996), 20.

14. Matsumoto, *Farming the Home Place*, 22.

15. Ibid., 46.

16. Ibid., 25.

17. Ibid., 48.

18. Ibid., 25.

19. Ibid., 42.

20. George J. Sanchez, *Becoming Mexican American: Ethnicity, Culture and Identity in Chicano Los Angeles, 1900–1945* (Oxford: Oxford University Press, 1993), 132.

21. For a full discussion about the effects of modernization and the Mexican Revolution, see Alan Knight's *The Mexican Revolution: Porfirians, Liberals and Democrats*

(Lincoln: University of Nebraska Press, 1986); and Ramon Eduardo Ruiz's *The Great Rebellion: Mexico 1905–1924* (New York: W. W. Norton, 1980).

22. Sanchez, *Becoming Mexican American*, 132.

23. Douglas Monroy, *Rebirth: Mexican Los Angeles from the Great Migration to the Great Depression* (Berkeley: University of California Press, 1982), 94.

24. Sanchez, *Becoming Mexican American*, 96.

25. Ibid., 39.

26. Ibid., 49.

27. Guerin-Gonzales, *Mexican Workers and American Dreams*, 31.

28. Ibid., 44.

29. Ibid., 44.

30. D. Gutierrez, *Walls and Mirrors*, 52; and Sanchez, *Becoming Mexican American*, 59.

31. Guerin-Gonzales, *Mexican Workers and American Dreams*, 24.

32. Ibid., 45.

33. Ibid., 25.

34. Monroy, *Rebirth*, 119.

35. Ibid., 126.

36. Ibid., 147.

37. Geoffrey Fox, *Hispanic Nation: Culture, Politics, and the Constructing of Identity* (Tucson: University of Arizona Press, 1996), 78.

38. Monroy, *Rebirth*, 111.

39. Guerin-Gonzales, *Mexican Workers and American Dreams*, 77.

40. Ibid., 98.

41. Ibid., 112.

42. Ibid., 124.

43. Ibid., 129.

44. Ibid., 135.

45. Ibid.

46. Daniel Rothenberg, *With These Hands: The Hidden World of Migrant Farmworkers Today* (New York: Harcourt Brace, 1998), 218.

47. Linda Majka and Theo Majka, *Farm Workers, Agribusiness, and the State* (Philadelphia: Temple University Press, 1982), 139.

48. Ibid., 144.

49. Ibid., 145.

50. "The Bracero Program," *Handbook of Texas Online*, University of Texas at Austin, www.tsha.utexas.edu.

51. Ibid.

52. Majka and Majka, *Farm Workers, Agribusiness, and the State*, 142.

53. Patrick Mooney and Theo Majka, *Farmers' and Farm Workers' Movements: Social Protest in American Agriculture* (New York: Twayne, 1995), 151–152.

54. Majka and Majka, *Farm Workers, Agribusiness, and the State*, 136.

55. Rothenberg, *With These Hands*, 249.

56. Mooney and Majka, *Farmers' and Farm Workers' Movements*, 153.

57. Ibid., 153.

58. Ibid., 157.

59. Ibid.

60. Ibid., 149.

61. Rothenberg, *With These Hands*, 249.

62. Majka and Majka, *Farm Workers, Agribusiness, and the State*, 157.

63. Ibid., 157–58.

64. Ibid.

65. Ibid., 158.

66. Ibid.

67. Michael J. Schultheis, Edward P. DeBerri, and Peter J. Henriot, *Our Best Kept Secret: The Rich Heritage of Catholic Social Teaching* (Washington, D.C.: Center of Concern, 1987), 11.

68. Ibid., 27.

69. Ibid., 11, 27.

70. Ibid., 11.

71. Ibid.

72. Ibid., 30.

73. Higgins and Bole, *Organized Labor and the Church*, 87.

74. Sean B. Flanagan, "Catholic Social Principles and Chavez: A Case Study" (Master's thesis, Loyola University of Los Angeles, 1971), 6.

75. Schultheis, DeBerri and Henriot, *Our Best Kept Secret*, 45, 56–57.

76. Ibid., 45, 56–57.

77. Martin Marty, *An Invitation to American Catholic History* (Chicago: Thomas More, 1986), 155.

78. Neil Betten, *Catholic Activism and the Industrial Worker* (Gainesville: University Presses of Florida, 1976), 33.

79. Chester Gillis, *Roman Catholicism in America* (New York: Columbia University Press, 1999), 69–71.

80. Betten, *Catholic Activism and the Industrial Worker*, 34.

81. Marty, *An Invitation to American Catholic History*, 154.

82. Betten, *Catholic Activism and the Industrial Worker*, 35.

83. Ibid.

84. John J. Sweeney, "Reflections on Monsignor George Higgins," *U.S. Catholic Historian* 19, no. 4 (fall 2001): 17, 20.

85. Gillis, *Roman Catholicism in America*, 73.

86. Betten, *Catholic Activism and the Industrial Worker*, 34.

87. David J. O'Brien, *American Catholics and Social Reform: The New Deal Years* (New York: Oxford, 1968), 44.

88. Ibid., 46.

89. Betten, *Catholic Activism and the Industrial Worker*, 34.

90. D. J. O'Brien, *American Catholics and Social Reform*, 47.

91. Betten, *Catholic Activism and the Industrial Worker*, 40–41.

92. Ibid., 46–47.

93. Ibid., 43.

94. Marty, *An Invitation to American Catholic History*, 160.

95. D. J. O'Brien, *American Catholics and Social Reform*, 55.

96. Ibid., 71.

97. Ibid.

98. Betten, *Catholic Activism and the Industrial Worker*, 32.

99. D. J. O'Brien, *American Catholics and Social Reform*, 105.

100. Ibid., 103.

101. Betten, *Catholic Activism and the Industrial Worker*, 36.

102. D. J. O'Brien, *American Catholics and Social Reform*, 99.

103. George G. Higgins with William Bole, *Organized Labor and the Church: Reflections of a "Labor Priest"* (New York: Paulist Press, 1993): 26–34.

104. Steve Rosswurm, *The CIO's Left-Led Unions* (New Brunswick, N.J.: Rutgers University Press, 1992), 120–21.

105. Betten, *Catholic Activism and the Industrial Worker*, 48.

106. Kenneth Heineman, *A Catholic New Deal: Religion and Reform in Depression Pittsburgh* (University Park: Pennsylvania State University Press, 1999), 72.

107. Betten, *Catholic Activism and the Industrial Worker*, 48.

108. Leslie Woodcock Tentler, *Seasons of Grace: A History of the Catholic Archdiocese of Detroit* (Detroit: Wayne State University Press, 1990), 437.

109. Heineman, *A Catholic New Deal*, 72.

110. Ronald Schatz, *The Electrical Workers: A History of Labor at General Electric and Westinghouse, 1923–60* (Chicago: University of Illinois Press, 1983), 181.

111. Douglas Seaton, *Catholics and Radicals: The Association of Catholic Trade Unionists and the American Labor Movement, from Depression to Cold War* (Lewisburg, N.J.: Bucknell University Press, 1981), 23.

112. Ibid.

113. Rosswurm, *The CIO's Left-Led Unions*, 123.

114. Seaton, *Catholics and Radicals*, 94.

115. Schatz, *The Electrical Workers*, 181.

116. Rosswurm, *The CIO's Left-Led Unions*, 125.

117. Tentler, *Seasons of Grace*, 344.

118. Seaton, *Catholics and Radicals*, 243.

119. Tentler, *Seasons of Grace*, 439.

120. John J. O'Brien, *George G. Higgins and the Quest for Worker Justice: The Evolution of Catholic Social Thought in America* (Lanham, Md.: Rowman and Littlefield, 2005), 18.

121. Ibid., 19.

122. Ibid.

123. Ibid., 20.

124. Ibid.

125. Ibid., 21.

126. Ibid., 77.

127. Ibid., 75.

128. Ibid., xiii, xv.

129. Ibid., 141.

130. Sean Segal, "Early Church Involvement in U.S. Farm Labor" (Senior thesis, The Catholic University of America, 2000), 13.

131. Ibid., 18.

132. Ibid.

133. Ibid., 19.

134. Ibid.

135. Ibid.

136. Michael Garvey, "Monsignor George G. Higgins to Receive the 2001 Laetare Medal," March 23, 2001, University of Notre Dame Web site: www.nd.edu/7Ehlrc/MsgrHiggins%20Laetare.htm.

137. John J. O'Brien, "George G. Higgins and the 'Yardstick' Columns," *U.S. Catholic Historian* 19 (fall 2001): 98.

138. Segal, "Early Church Involvement in U.S. Farm Labor," 22.

139. Majka and Majka, *Farm Workers, Agribusiness, and the State*, 160.

140. Segal, "Early Church Involvement in U.S. Farm Labor," 21.

141. Ibid., 23.

142. George Higgins, "Catholic Tests of a Social Order: Why Revive the Old Bracero Program," Box 129/74, folder Mix-Mix, GHC, written as "Yardstick" column, National Catholic News Service, July 9, 1973.

143. Segal, "Early Church Involvement in U.S. Farm Labor," 24.

144. Higgins and Bole, *Organized Labor and the Church,* 85.

145. Ibid., 85.

146. Segal, "Early Church Involvement in U.S. Farm Labor," 24.

147. Ibid., 26.

148. George Higgins, "The Bracero Program," Box 129/74, folder Mix-Mix, GHC, written as "Yardstick" column, National Catholic News Service, March 5, 1973.

149. George G. Higgins, "Catholic Tests of a Social Order: Why Revive the Old Bracero Program."

150. Segal, "Early Church Involvement in U.S. Farm Labor," 27.

151. J. J. O'Brien, *George G. Higgins and the Quest for Worker Justice*, 98.

152. Gillis, *Roman Catholicism in America*, 86–87.

153. Ibid., 88.

154. Ibid., 90.

155. Ibid.

156. Gerald M. Costello, *Without Fear or Favor: George Higgins on the Record* (Mystic, Conn.: Twenty-Third Publications: 1984), 98.

157. Ibid., 98.

158. Higgins and Bole, *Organized Labor and the Church*, 88.

159. Costello, *Without Fear or Favor*, 89.

160. J. J. O'Brien, *George G. Higgins and the Quest for Worker Justice*, 142.

161. Costello, *Without Fear or Favor*, 95.

162. Frederick John Dalton, *The Moral Vision of César Chávez* (New York: Orbis Books, 2003), 46.

163. Costello, *Without Fear or Favor*, 95.

164. Richard Griswold del Castillo and Richard A. Garcia, *César Chávez: A Triumph of Spirit* (Norman: University of Oklahoma Press, 1995), 23.

165. Ibid.

166. Ibid., 47.

167. Ibid., 46.

168. Susan Ferris, Ricardo Sandoval, and Diana Hembree, eds., *The Fight in the Fields: Cesar Chavez and the Farm Workers Movement* (New York: Harcourt Brace, 1997), 46.

169. Flanagan, "Catholic Social Principles and Chavez," 23.

170. John C. Hammerback and Richard Jensen, *The Rhetorical Career of César Chávez* (College Station: Texas A&M University Press), xviii.

171. Ibid., xxii.

172. Dalton, *The Moral Vision of César Chávez*, 98.

173. Griswold del Castillo and Garcia, *César Chávez: A Triumph of Spirit*, 148.

174. Hammerback and Jensen, *The Rhetorical Career of César Chávez*, 73.

175. Ferris, Sandoval, and Hembree, *The Fight in the Fields*, 174.

176. Hammerback and Jensen, *The Rhetorical Career of César Chávez*, 32.

177. Ibid., 85.

178. Juan L. Gonzales Jr., *Mexican and Mexican American Farm Workers: The California Agricultural Industry* (New York: Praeger, 1985), 26.

179. Costello, *Without Fear or Favor*, 97–98.

180. J. Craig Jenkins, *The Politics of Insurgency: The Farm Worker Movement in the 1960s* (New York: Columbia Press, 1985), 167.

181. Dalton, *The Moral Vision of César Chávez*, 153.

182. Jacques E. Levy, *Cesar Chavez: Autobiography of La Causa*, (New York: W. W. Norton, 1975), 282–83.

183. Griswold del Castillo and Garcia, *César Chávez: A Triumph of Spirit*, 85.

184. Ferris, Sandoval, and Hembree, *The Fight in the Fields*, 174.

185. Flanagan, "Catholic Social Principles and Chavez," 10.

186. Majka and Majka, *Farm Workers, Agribusiness, and the State*, 170.

187. Richard J. Jensen and John Hammerback, eds., *The Words of César Chávez* (College Station: Texas A&M University Press, 2002), xxii.

188. Griswold del Castillo and Garcia, *César Chávez: A Triumph of Spirit*, 29.

189. Ibid.

190. Ibid., 30.

191. Majka and Majka, *Farm Workers, Agribusiness, and the State*, 162.

192. Ibid., 162.

193. Ibid.

194. Dalton, *The Moral Vision of César Chávez*, 15.

195. Peter Matthiessen, *Sal Si Puedes: Cesar Chavez and the New American Revolution* (New York: Random House, 1969), 52.

196. Ibid., 52.

197. Ibid., 53.

198. Ibid.

199. Majka and Majka, *Farm Workers, Agribusiness, and the State*, 170.

200. Griswold del Castillo and Garcia, *César Chávez: A Triumph of Spirit*, 59.

201. Rothenberg, *With These Hands*, 241.

202. Griswold del Castillo and Garcia, *César Chávez: A Triumph of Spirit*, 60.

203. Majka and Majka, *Farm Workers, Agribusiness, and the State*, 170.

204. Paul Ortiz, "From Slavery to Cesar Chavez and Beyond: Farmworker Organizing in the United States," in *The Human Cost of Food: Farmworkers' Lives, Labor and Advocacy*, Charles D. Thompson Jr. and Melinda F. Wiggins, eds. (Austin: University of Texas Press, 2002), 256.

205. Jensen and Hammerback, *The Words of César Chávez*, 4.

206. Ibid.

207. Ibid.

208. Ortiz, "From Slavery to Cesar Chavez and Beyond," 258.

209. Ronald Goldfarb, *Migrant Farm Workers: A Caste of Despair* (Ames: Iowa State University Press, 1981), 186.

210. Jensen and Hammerback, *The Words of César Chávez*, 4.

211. Costello, *Without Fear or Favor*, 97.

212. Flanagan, "Catholic Social Principles and Chavez," 9.

213. Majka and Majka, *Farm Workers, Agribusiness, and the State*, 172.

214. Ibid.

215. Griswold del Castillo and Garcia, *César Chávez: A Triumph of Spirit*, 42.

216. Majka and Majka, *Farm Workers, Agribusiness, and the State*, 172.

217. Ortiz, "From Slavery to Cesar Chavez and Beyond," 261.

218. Majka and Majka, *Farm Workers, Agribusiness, and the State*, 172.

219. Dalton, *The Moral Vision of César Chávez*, 16.

220. Hammerback and Jensen, *The Rhetorical Career of César Chávez*, 6–7.

221. Ortiz, "From Slavery to Cesar Chavez and Beyond," 266.

222. Jensen and Hammerback, *The Words of César Chávez*, 3.

223. Ibid., 9.

224. Ibid.

225. Dalton, *The Moral Vision of César Chávez*, 86–88.

226. Ortiz, "From Slavery to Cesar Chavez and Beyond," 264.

227. Jensen and Hammerback, *The Words of César Chávez*, 5.

228. Ortiz, "From Slavery to Cesar Chavez and Beyond," 262.

229. Mooney and Majka, *Farmers' and Farm Workers' Movements*, 162.

230. Ortiz, "From Slavery to Cesar Chavez and Beyond," 262.

231. Ibid., 263.

232. Griswold del Castillo and Garcia, *César Chávez: A Triumph of Spirit*, 76.

233. "History," United Farm Workers Web site: www.ufw.org/ufw.htm.

234. "La Causa: A History of the United Farm Workers of America," Walter P. Reuther Library, Wayne State University, www.reuther.wayne.edu/ufw-article.html.

235. "Cesar Chavez Chronology," Las Culturas.com, www.lasculturas.com/aa/bio/bioCesarChavezChron.htm.

236. Griswold del Castillo and Garcia, *César Chávez: A Triumph of Spirit*, 57.

237. Mooney and Majka, *Farmers' and Farm Workers' Movements*, 161.

238. "Cesar Chavez Chronology."

239. Mooney and Majka, *Farmers' and Farm Workers' Movements*, 161.

240. "La Causa: A History of the United Farm Workers of America."

241. Jim Burns, "Bill Proposed to Name Cesar Chavez 'Hero,'" CNSNews.com, September 25, 2001.

242. Mooney and Majka, *Farmers' and Farm Workers' Movements*, 161.

243. Ortiz, "From Slavery to Cesar Chavez and Beyond," 264.

244. Griswold del Castillo and Garcia, *César Chávez: A Triumph of Spirit*, 92.

245. Ferris, Sandoval, and Hembree, *The Fight in the Fields*, 146.

246. Mooney and Majka, *Farmers' and Farm Workers' Movements*, 162.

247. Ibid.

248. Ibid.

249. Ibid.

250. Costello, *Without Fear or Favor*, 109.

Chapter 2. Chávez and the Bishops' Ad Hoc Committee

1. Interview with Cardinal Roger Mahony in *The Fight in the Fields: Cesar Chavez and the Farmworkers' Struggle*, directed by Ray Telles and Rick Tejada-Flores (New York: Paradigm Productions, Cinema Guild, 1996).

2. Jerry Filteau, "Cesar Chavez Dead at Age 66, Led Farm Labor Struggle," Catholic News Service, April 23, 1993.

3. Ibid.

4. Ibid.

5. "Farm Labor Efforts Earn Papal Praise," *Fresno Bee*, October 3, 1972.

6. Gerald Sherry, "Farm Labor Battle: Church's Involvement Outlined," National Catholic News Service, December 17, 1973.

7. Ibid.

8. Ibid.

9. Jo-Ann Price, "Church Forced into Leadership, Farmworker Says." National Catholic News Service, May 14, 1974.

10. Philip Vera Cruz, "The Farm Workers and the Church," *The Catholic Worker*, September, 1970.

11. Sherry, "Farm Labor Battle."

12. Ibid.

13. Gerald Sherry, "Catholic Editor Recalls Memories of Cesar Chavez," Catholic News Service, April 28, 1993.

14. Ibid.

15. Sherry, "Farm Labor Battle."

16. "Victory for Cesar Chavez," *Newsweek*, August 10, 1970. *Newsweek* noted that the Catholic Church in the Central Valley shifted from progrower in the early 1960s to conciliator in the Delano Grape Strike. I argue that, although publicly neutral, the Ad Hoc Committee, in actuality, possessed a profarmworker bias.

17. John Dart, "Diocesan Paper that Supported Chavez to Fold: Publication to End July 20; Fresno Unit's Labor Views Angered Catholic Growers," *Los Angeles Times*, June 19, 1972.

18. Ibid.

19. Bishop Ricardo Ramirez, "What Cesar Chavez Believed," *Origins*, May 27, 1993, 19.

20. Sean B. Flanagan, "Catholic Social Principles and Chavez: A Case Study" (Master's thesis, Loyola University of Los Angeles, 1971), 60.

21. "*Twin Circle*, New National Catholic Paper, To Be Launched in November," National Catholic News Service, August 30, 1967.

22. "Personal Opinions," *Twin Circle*, January 4, 1970. *Twin Circle* specifically supported the farmworkers right to organize and be included in the NLRA. *Mater et Magistra* quote taken from George G. Higgins with William Bole, *Organized Labor and the Church: Reflections of a "Labor Priest"* (New York: Paulist Press, 1993), 87.

23. Daniel Lyons, "Sour Grapes," *Twin Circle*, January 4, 1970.

24. Edith Myers, "Priest-Editor Goes to the Source of the Grape Strike," *Twin Circle*, February 22, 1970.

25. Philip Nolan, "Bishops Break Grape Deadlock," *Twin Circle*, April 19, 1970. Although the article does not directly accuse Chavez of being a communist, the tone appears intended to leave that impression.

26. George Higgins to Joseph F. Donnelly, July 10, 1970, Box 129/91, folder: Farm Labor File 1970, GHC.

27. Ibid.

28. "Editorial," *Twin Circle*, March 15, 1970.

29. Daniel Lyons, "Editorial," *Twin Circle*, May 10, 1970.

30. Ibid.

31. George Higgins to Daniel Lyons, May 11, 1970, Box 129/91, folder: Farm Labor File 1970, GHC.

32. Ibid.; and Higgins with Bole, *Organized Labor and the Church*, 95.

33. Higgins with Bole, *Organized Labor and the Church*, 95.

34. George Higgins to Dale Francis, June 23, 1970, Box 129/91, folder: Farm Labor File 1970, GHC.

35. Ibid.

36. Ibid.

37. Cesar Chavez to George Higgins, February 19, 1970, Box 129/91, folder: Farm Labor File 1970, GHC.

38. George Higgins to Cesar Chavez, May 11, 1970, Box 129/91, folder: Farm Labor File 1970, GHC.

39. George Higgins to Joseph Donnelly, July 10, 1970, Box 129/91, folder: Farm Labor File 1970, GHC.

40. Daniel Lyons, "Chavez Reaps Bitter Harvest," *Twin Circle*, July 12, 1970.

41. Ibid.

42. "Bishops' Committee Statement on Grape Worker Editorial," Press Service, U.S. Catholic Conference, July 15, 1970.

43. "Bishops Rap Critic of Role in Boycott," *Fresno Bee*, July 16, 1970.

44. Patrick J. Sullivan, *Blue Collar, Roman Collar, White Collar: U.S. Catholic Involvement in Labor Management Controversies, 1960–1980* (Lanham, Md.: University Press, 1987), 114.

45. "Bishops' Committee Statement."

46. Joseph Donnelly, "The Bishops and the Farm Labor Dispute," interview with Gerald Sherry, National Catholic News Service, July 1970.

47. Ibid.

48. "Protest Newspaper's Position," National Catholic News Service, July 28, 1970.

49. John Dart, "Catholic Newspaper Criticized by 5 Bishops on Grape Strike," *Los Angeles Times*, July 16, 1970.

50. "Twin Circle Editor-Publisher Resigns," National Catholic News Service, August 19, 1970.

51. "Twin Circle Editor Resigns," *Central California Register*, August 21, 1970.

52. Gerald E. Sherry, letter to the editor, *California Farm Labor*, July 2, 1975.

53. Ibid.

54. Jerry Filteau, "Cesar Chavez Dead."

55. Michael Cross, "Priest Picks Lettuce." This document was a "white paper and undated." Box 129/95, folder: Untitled, GHC.

56. Michael L. Cross to John Cardinal Dearden, September 30, 1970, Box 126, folder: October–December 1970, BAHC.

57. Ibid.

58. Cross, "Priest Picks Lettuce."

59. Cross to Dearden, September 30, 1970.

60. Ibid.

61. Ibid.

62. Ibid.

63. Joseph L. Bernardin to Michael L. Cross, November 4, 1970, Box 126, folder: October–December 1970, BAHC.

64. Michael Cross to Joseph Bernardin, November 12, 1970, Box 126, folder: October–December 1970, BAHC.

65. The note does not have an addressee. Box 126, folder: October–December 1970, BAHC.

66. "Bishop Reprimands Priest Crossing 'Salad Bowl' Picket Line," National Catholic News Service, September 4, 1970.

67. Ibid.

68. "Priest Continues Attack on Church Role in Farm-Labor Dispute," National Catholic News Service, September 11, 1970.

69. "Interference Charge Unjust, Committee Consultant Says," National Catholic News Service, September 28, 1970.

70. "Priest Continues Attack."

71. "Father Cross Criticizes Church's UFWOC Grant," *Salinas Californian*, May 15, 1971.

72. Gerald Costello, "Committee Members Disagree with Anti-Chavez View," National Catholic News Service, March 30, 1973.

73. "California Church Official Supports Document Assailing Farm Workers Union," National Catholic News Service, November 3, 1972.

74. Gerald Costello, "Lettuce Boycott: California Priests Oppose Boycott," National Catholic News Service, March 29, 1973.

75. Thomas J. Earley to "The priests of the United States," October 1972, Box 126, folder: October 1972, BAHC.

76. George Higgins to Thomas Earley, November 1, 1972, Box 126, folder: November 1972, BAHC.

77. Ibid.

78. Ibid.

79. Ibid.

80. Ibid.

81. Ibid.

82. Robert Raimonto, "Priest Was 'Used' in Lettuce Dispute, Bishop Says," National Catholic News Service, November 16, 1972.

83. Costello, "Lettuce Boycott."

84. Ibid.

85. Ibid.

86. Ibid.

87. George Higgins to James Rausch, February 25, 1974, Box 126, folder: February 1974, BAHC.

88. Ibid.

89. Philip Maxwell to B. V. Gajda, November 30, 1973, Box 126, folder: October–December 1973, BAHC.

90. Ibid.

91. Stephen Sosnick, *Hired Hands: Seasonal Farm Workers in the United States* (Santa Barbara, Calif.: McNally, 1978), 360.

92. Linda Majka and Theo Majka, *Farm Workers, Agribusiness, and the State* (Philadelphia: Temple University Press, 1982), 240.

93. Sosnick, *Hired Hands*, 357.

94. Ibid.

95. Philip Maxwell to B. V. Gajda, November 30, 1973.

96. Ibid.

97. Ibid.

98. George Higgins to James Rausch, March 1, 1974, Box 126, folder: March 1974, BAHC.

99. James Rausch to Philip Maxwell, February 28, 1974, Box 126, folder: February 1974, BAHC.

100. Philip Maxwell to James Rausch, March 4, 1974, Box 126, folder: March 1974, BAHC.

101. Harry Clinch to James Rausch, March 4, 1974, Box 126, folder: March 1974, BAHC.

102. James Rausch to Harry Clinch, March 8, 1974, Box 126, folder: March 1974, BAHC.

103. James Rausch to Philip Maxwell, March 8, 1974, Box 126, folder: March 1974, BAHC.

104. Harry Clinch to James Rausch, March 8, 1974, Box 126, folder: March 1974, BAHC.

105. Ibid.

106. Philip F. Maxwell to James Rausch, March 8, 1974, Box 126, folder: March 1974, BAHC.

107. Ibid.

108. Ibid.

109. Ibid.

110. Ibid.

111. Ibid.

112. Ibid.

113. Ibid.

114. Roger Mahony to Joseph Donnelly, November 4, 1970, Box 129/91, folder: Farm Labor File 1970, GHC.

115. Ibid.

116. Ibid.

117. Ibid.

118. Ibid.

119. Ibid.

120. David Luna to Timothy Manning, May 31, 1970, Box 126, folder: January–June 1970, BAHC.

121. Mike Farley to Timothy Manning, June 4, 1970, Box 126, folder: January–June 1970, BAHC.

122. The Priests' Senate of the Diocese of Fresno to Hugh A. Donohoe, September 2, 1970, box 126, folder: September 1970, BAHC.

123. Statement by the Senate of Priests, Archdiocese of San Francisco, June 8, 1970, box 126, folder: January–June 1970, BAHC.

124. Richard P. McBrien to Joseph F. Donnelly, November 10, 1970, box 126, folder: October–December 1970, BAHC.

125. Ibid.

126. Timothy Manning's proposed draft copy of a statement on migratory labor from the bishops of California, April 19, 1968, box 80, folder: Departmental Committees: Social Development: Farm Labor 1968–1969, BAHC. In this document, Manning refers back to Donohoe's 1966 statement.

127. Ibid.

128. Marjorie Hyer, "Chavez Calls Lettuce Boycott Ban Violation of First Amendment," National Catholic News Service, November 30, 1970.

129. Cesar Chavez to Joseph L. Bernardin, August 3, 1968, box 80, folder: Departmental Committees: Social Development: Farm Labor 1968–1969, BAHC.

130. Gerald Costello, *Without Fear or Favor: George Higgins on the Record* (Mystic, Conn.: Twenty-Third Publications, 1984), 101–2.

131. Higgins with Bole, *Organized Labor and the Church*, 90.

132. Ibid.

133. George Higgins to Edward O'Rourke, October 25, 1968, box 80, folder: Departmental Committees: Social Development: Farm Labor 1968–1969, BAHC.

134. Joseph F. Donnelly to Joseph L. Bernardin, October 28, 1968, box 80, folder: Departmental Committees: Social Development: Farm Labor 1968–1969, BAHC.

135. George Higgins to Joseph L. Bernardin, October 31, 1968, box 80, folder: Departmental Committees: Social Development: Farm Labor 1968–1969, BAHC.

136. John Frederick Dalton, *The Moral Vision of César Chávez* (New York: Orbis Books, 2003), 56.

137. Proposed NCCB Statement on Farm Labor, October 31 1968, box 80, folder: Departmental Committees: Social Development: Farm Labor 1968–1969, BAHC.

138. Ibid.

139. Ibid.

140. Flanagan, "Catholic Social Principles and Chavez: A Case Study," 52.

141. Dalton, *The Moral Vision of César Chávez*, 56.

142. Gerald M. Costello, "The Farm Labor Movement," *U.S. Catholic Historian* 19, no. 4 (fall 2001): 36.

143. George Higgins to Joseph F. Donnelly, July 10, 1970, box 129/91, folder: Farm Labor File 1970, GHC. In this letter, Higgins provided Donnelly answers to Gerry Sherry's series of questions on the farm labor problem, and he wrote Donnelly that he could feel "free to edit them or even discard them completely if they don't happen to measure up to your expectations."

144. John Dearden and John Wright to President of the United States, April 18, 1969, box 80, folder: Departmental Committees: Social Development: Farm Labor 1968–1969, BAHC.

145. Majka and Majka, *Farm Workers, Agribusiness, and the State*, 229–30.

146. Statement of George Meany before the Senate Subcommittee on Labor of the Senate Labor and Public Welfare Committee, May 16, 1969, box 80, folder: Departmental Committees: Social Development: Farm Labor 1968–1969, BAHC.

147. George Meany to John Dearden, April 1969, box 80, folder: Departmental Committees: Social Development: Farm Labor 1968–1969, BAHC.

148. Cesar Chavez to John Dearden, October 1, 1969, box 80, folder: Departmental Committees: Social Development: Farm Labor 1968–1969, BAHC.

149. Ibid.

150. John Cosgrove to Hurley, October 17, 1969, box 80, folder: Departmental Committees: Social Development: Farm Labor 1968–1969, BAHC.

151. Draft letter from John Cosgrove to Cesar Chavez, October 17, 1969. Cosgrove sent a draft of this letter to Hurley. Box 80, folder: Departmental Committees: Social Development: Farm Labor 1968–1969, BAHC.

152. Ibid.

153. Ibid.

154. Hurley to John Cosgrove, October 20, 1969, box 80, folder: Departmental Committees: Social Development: Farm Labor 1968–1969, BAHC.

155. Per Hurley's request for a "non-committal" letter, John Cosgrove ended up sending this letter to Chavez instead of the one above. October 27, 1969, box 80, folder: Departmental Committees: Social Development: Farm Labor 1968–1969, BAHC.

156. Draft of a resolution by John Cosgrove to members of the Committee on Social Development, October 30, 1969, box 80, folder: Departmental Committees: Social Development: Farm Labor 1968–1969, BAHC.

157. Joseph Bernardin to John Dearden, November 7, 1969, box 80, folder: Departmental Committees: Social Development: Farm Labor 1968–1969, BAHC.

158. Higgins with Bole, *Organized Labor and the Church*, 90.

159. Ibid.
160. Flanagan, "Catholic Social Principles and Chavez: A Case Study," 65.
161. Ibid., 35.
162. Sullivan, *Blue Collar, Roman Collar, White Collar*, 100.
163. Ibid., 100.
164. Ibid., 92.
165. Roger Mahony to Joseph Donnelly, November 4, 1970, box 129/91, folder: Farm Labor File 1970, GHC. The letter commented on Donohoe's ill health and disappointment "over the financial events of the Diocese" due to the Church's support for the farmworkers.
166. Sullivan, *Blue Collar, Roman Collar, White Collar*, 100.
167. Flanagan, "Catholic Social Principles and Chavez: A Case Study," 65–66.
168. Ibid.
169. Ibid.
170. Ibid., 66.
171. George Higgins to John Cosgrove, February 27, 1970, box 129/94, folder: Mahony Reports—1970, GHC.
172. Ibid.
173. Flanagan, "Catholic Social Principles and Chavez: A Case Study," 67–68.
174. Jacques E. Levy, *Cesar Chavez: Autobiography of La Causa* (New York: W. W. Norton, 1975), 304.
175. Flanagan, "Catholic Social Principles and Chavez: A Case Study," 68.
176. Ibid., 69.
177. Higgins with Bole, *Organized Labor and the Church*, 90.
178. Costello, "Farm Labor Movement," 36.
179. Dalton, *The Moral Vision of César Chávez*, 57.
180. Report of Ad Hoc Committee on the Farm Labor Dispute, April 21–23, 1970, box 126, folder: January–June 1970, BAHC.
181. "Confidential Memorandum" from Roger Mahony to Timothy Manning and Hugh Donohoe, April 1969, box 80, folder: Departmental Committees: Social Development: Farm Labor 1968–1969, BAHC.
182. Ibid.
183. Flanagan, "Catholic Social Principles and Chavez: A Case Study," 66.
184. Ibid.
185. Higgins with Bole, *Organized Labor and the Church*, 91.
186. Levy, *Cesar Chavez: Autobiography of La Causa*, 304.
187. Higgins with Bole, *Organized Labor and the Church*, 91.
188. Ibid.
189. Report: Bishops' Ad Hoc Committee on the Farm Labor Dispute to the Administrative Board National Conference of Catholic Bishops, September 14, 1970, box 126, folder: September 1970, BAHC.
190. Ibid.
191. Ibid.
192. Levy, *Cesar Chavez: Autobiography of La Causa*, 305.
193. Ibid.
194. Ibid.
195. Henry Weinstein, "New Rows to Hoe: Cesar Chavez Now Looks to Other Crops," *Wall Street Journal*, July 31, 1970.
196. Costello, "Farm Labor Movement," 36.

197. Bishop Donnelly to members of Ad Hoc Committee on Farm Labor Dispute, March 2, 1970, box 129/94, folder: Mahony Reports—1970, GHC.

198. Ibid.

199. Ibid.

200. Report on week of March 2, 1970, by Joseph Donnelly, March 11, 1970, box 126, folder: January–June 1970, BAHC.

201. Steven Roberts, "First Grapes with Union Label Shipped to Market from Coast," *New York Times*, May 31, 1970.

202. Ibid.

203. Bill Boyarsky, "Handshakes Seal Pact Ending Grape Boycott," *Los Angeles Times*, July 30, 1970.

204. Higgins with Bole, *Organized Labor and the Church*, 91–92.

205. "How It Happened: Timetable of Grape Workers' Unionization Struggle," *Sacramento Bee*, July 30, 1970.

206. Report: Bishops' Ad Hoc Committee on the Farm Labor Dispute.

207. Ibid.

208. Confidential memo from John E. Cosgrove to Joseph Donnelly, February 4, 1970, box 126, folder: January–June 1970, BAHC.

209. Ron B. Taylor, *Chavez and the Farm Workers* (Boston: Beacon Press, 1975), 242.

210. Ibid., 243.

211. Higgins with Bole, *Organized Labor and the Church*, 91.

212. Ibid., 92.

213. Confidential memo from Cosgrove to Donnelly.

214. William Bole, "The Ministry of Presence," *U.S. Catholic Historian* 19, no. 4 (fall 2001): 7.

215. Harry Bernstein, "Chavez Revolt Catching Fire Across State," *Los Angeles Times*, June 14, 1970.

216. Ibid.

217. William Bole, "Ministry of Presence," 7.

218. "H. Roberts Near Pact with UFW: Largest Farm Contract Seen," *Bakersfield Californian*, June 10, 1970.

219. Bernstein, "Chavez Revolt Catching Fire."

220. Bole, "Ministry of Presence," 7.

221. Ibid.

222. Ibid.

223. Gerald E. Sherry, managing editor, *Fresno Central California Register*, to editor of *Time* magazine, August 6, 1970, box 126, folder: October–December 1970, BAHC.

224. "How It Happened."

225. George Higgins to Joseph Bernardin, May 13, 1970, box 126, folder: January–June 1970, BAHC.

226. Ibid.

227. Roger Mahony to Ad Hoc Committee on Farm Labor, National Conference of Catholic Bishops, May 22, 1970, box 126, folder: January–June 1970, BAHC.

228. Ibid.

229. Ibid.

230. Ibid.

231. Ibid.

232. Ibid.

233. "How It Happened."

234. Report: Bishops' Ad Hoc Committee on the Farm Labor Dispute.

235. Statement by Joseph F. Donnelly, May 21, 1970, box 126, folder: January–June 1970, BAHC.

236. Ibid.

237. George Higgins to Joseph L. Bernardin, June 4, 1970, box 126, folder: January–June 1970, BAHC.

238. Report: Bishops' Ad Hoc Committee on the Farm Labor Dispute.

239. Roger Mahony to Ad Hoc Committee on Farm Labor National Conference of Catholic Bishops, June 17,1970, box 126, folder: January–June 1970, BAHC.

240. Ibid.

241. Report: Bishops' Ad Hoc Committee on the Farm Labor Dispute.

242. Ibid.

243. Roger Mahony to Ad Hoc Committee on Farm Labor National Conference of Catholic Bishops, July 23, 1970, box 126, folder: July 1970, BAHC.

244. Report: Bishops' Ad Hoc Committee on the Farm Labor Dispute.

245. Dick Meister, "Grape Growers and Workers Reach Accord," *San Francisco Chronicle*, July 29, 1970.

246. "Clergy Will Retain Labor Role," *Fresno Bee*, July 30, 1970.

247. Ibid.

248. Ron Taylor, "Chavez, Flushed With Strike Victory, Pledges to Make Grapes Sweet Again," *Sacramento Bee*, July 30, 1970.

249. Ron Taylor, "Chavez: Union Will End Boycott, Help Sell Grapes," *Fresno Bee*, July 30, 1970.

250. Boyarsky, "Handshakes Seal Pact."

251. Report: Bishops' Ad Hoc Committee on the Farm Labor Dispute.

252. Patrick Mooney and Theo Majka, *Farmers' and Farm Workers' Movements: Social Protest in American Agriculture* (New York: Twayne, 1995), 163–64.

253. Report: Bishops' Ad Hoc Committee on the Farm Labor Dispute.

254. Statement by Joseph Donnelly on the farm labor dispute, August 10, 1970, box 126, folder: August 1970, BAHC.

255. Boyarsky, "Handshakes Seal Pact."

256. "Clergy Plans to Maintain Role in Farm Labor," *Fresno Bee*, July 30, 1970.

257. Ibid.

258. Costello, *Without Fear or Favor*, 109.

259. Taylor, *Chavez and the Farm Workers*, 297.

260. Costello, *Without Fear or Favor*, 110.

261. Ibid.

262. Ibid.

263. Ronald Goldfarb, *Migrant Farm Workers: A Caste of Dispair* (Ames: Iowa State University Press, 1981), 193.

Chapter 3. Hasta La Victoria, Onward To Victory

1. George G. Higgins with William Bole, *Organized Labor and the Church: Reflections of a "Labor Priest"* (New York: Paulist Press, 1993), 97.

2. Ibid., 99.

3. Ibid.

4. Linda Majka and Theo Majka, *Farm Workers, Agribusiness, and the State* (Philadelphia: Temple University Press, 1982), 183.

5. Supplementary NCCB/USCC Agenda Documentation, Subject: Ad Hoc Committee on Farm Labor Dispute, box 126, folder: October–December 1970, BAHC.

6. Patrick J. Sullivan, *Blue Collar, Roman Collar, White Collar: U.S. Catholic Involvement in Labor Management Controversies, 1960–1980* (Lanham, Md.: University Press, 1987), 89.

7. Majka and Majka, *Farm Workers, Agribusiness, and the State*, 201.

8. Ibid.

9. Supplementary NCCB/USCC Agenda Documentation.

10. Ibid.

11. Majka and Majka, *Farm Workers, Agribusiness, and the State*, 201.

12. Ibid.

13. Patrick Mooney and Theo Majka, *Farmers' and Farm Workers' Movements: Social Protest in American Agriculture* (New York: Twayne, 1995), 170.

14. California Migrant Ministry flier in support of UFW struggle against the Teamsters, August 4, 1970, box 126, folder: August 1970, BAHC.

15. Frederick John Dalton, *The Moral Vision of César Chávez* (New York: Orbis Books, 2003), 16–17.

16. Stephen Sosnick, *Hired Hands, Seasonal Farmworkers in the United States* (Santa Barbara, Calif: McNally, 1978), 329.

17. Mooney and Majka, *Farmers' and Farm Workers' Movements*, 167.

18. Ibid.

19. Majka and Majka, *Farm Workers, Agribusiness, and the State*, 202.

20. Mooney and Majka, *Farmers' and Farm Workers' Movements*, 167.

21. Majka and Majka, *Farm Workers, Agribusiness, and the State*, 202.

22. Sosnick, *Hired Hands*, 329.

23. George Higgins to Joseph L. Bernardin, August 10, 1970, box 126, folder: August 1970, BAHC.

24. Ibid.

25. Ibid.

26. Roger Mahony to Ad Hoc Committee on Farm Labor, National Conference of Catholic Bishops, August 10, 1970, box 126, folder: August 1970, BAHC.

27. Sosnick, *Hired Hands*, 330.

28. Higgins to Bernardin, August 10, 1970.

29. Statement by George Higgins, Wednesday, August 12, 1970, box 126, folder: August 1970, BAHC.

30. Sosnick, *Hired Hands*, 330.

31. Ibid.

32. Majka and Majka, *Farm Workers, Agribusiness, and the State*, 201.

33. Sosnick, *Hired Hands*, 330.

34. Mooney and Majka, *Farmers' and Farm Workers' Movements*, 167.

35. Dalton, *The Moral Vision of César Chávez*, 17.

36. Mooney and Majka, *Farmers' and Farm Workers' Movements*, 167.

37. Ibid.

38. Roger Mahony to Joseph F. Donnelly, November 12, 1970, box 126, folder: October–December 1970, BAHC.

39. Ibid.

40. Ibid.

41. Majka and Majka, *Farm Workers, Agribusiness, and the State*, 207.

42. Mooney and Majka, *Farmers' and Farm Workers' Movements*, 167.

43. Sosnick, *Hired Hands*, 331.

44. Mooney and Majka, *Farmers' and Farm Workers' Movements*, 167.

45. Ibid.

46. Ibid.

47. Sosnick, *Hired Hands*, 331.

48. Ibid.

49. George Higgins to A. Garnett Day Jr., January 15, 1971, box 129/96, folder: Untitled, GHC.

50. George Higgins John Cosgrove January 15, 1971, box 126, folder: January 1971, BAHC.

51. Higgins to Day, January 15, 1971.

52. George Higgins to Joseph Donnelly, February 10, 1971, box 126, folder: January 1971, BAHC.

53. "Priest Says Workers Better Off Under Growers, Not Union," National Catholic News Service, February 12, 1971.

54. Higgins to Donnelly, February 10, 1971.

55. Ibid.

56. Ibid.

57. Ibid.

58. Ibid.

59. George Higgins to Theodore Hesburgh, February 11, 1971, box 126, folder: January 1971, BAHC.

60. Michael Garvey, "Monsignor George G. Higgins to Receive the 2001 Laetare Medal," March 23, 2001, University of Notre Dame Web site: www.nd.edu/7Ehlrc/MsgrHiggins%20Laetare.htm.

61. Higgins to Hesburgh, February 11, 1971.

62. Ibid.

63. William T. Cavanugh, letter to the editor, *Notre Dame Magazine* Online, spring 2000, University of Notre Dame Web site: www.nd.edu/7Endmag/letsu00.htm.

64. Garvey, "Monsignor George G. Higgins to Receive the 2001 Laetare Medal."

65. Majka and Majka, *Farm Workers, Agribusiness, and the State*, 206.

66. Ibid.

67. Ibid., 207.

68. Ibid., 180.

69. Sosnick, *Hired Hands*, 345.

70. Ibid.

71. Ibid., 346.

72. Ibid., 347.

73. Ibid., 348.

74. George Higgins to Joseph L. Bernardin, April 17, 1971, box 126, folder: April 1971, BAHC.

75. Ibid.

76. Ibid.

77. Ibid.

78. Ibid.

79. Ibid.

80. Ibid.

81. Roger Mahony to U.S. Catholic Bishops' Ad Hoc Committee on Farm Labor, May 8, 1971, box 126, folder: May 1971, BAHC.

82. Ibid.

83. Roger Mahony to Cesar Chavez, June 4, 1971, box 126, folder: April 1971, BAHC.

84. Mahony to Ad Hoc Committee on Farm Labor, June 11, 1971.

85. George Higgins to Joseph L. Bernardin, June 25, 1971, box 126, folder: June 1971, BAHC.

86. Roger Mahony to Ad Hoc Committee on Farm Labor, July 10, 1971, box 126, folder: July 1971, BAHC.

87. Ibid.

88. George Higgins to Joseph L. Bernardin, August 2, 1971, box 129/94, folder: August 1971, GHC.

89. Roger Mahony to Ad Hoc Committee on Farm Labor, National Conference of Catholic Bishops, August 20, 1971, box 126, folder: August 1971, BAHC.

90. Ibid.

91. Roger Mahony to Ad Hoc Committee on Farm labor, National Conference of Catholic Bishops, November 5, 1971, box 126, folder: November 1971, BAHC.

92. Ibid.

93. Hugh Donohoe to Joseph F. Donnelly, August 30, 1971, box 126, folder: August 1971, BAHC.

94. Hugh Donohoe to Allen Grant, June 25, 1971, box 126, folder: June 1971, BAHC.

95. Mahony to Ad Hoc Committee on Farm Labor, November 5, 1971.

96. Hugh Donohoe to Jack T. Pickett, October 5, 1971, box 126, folder: October 1971, BAHC.

97. Statement on the financial support of farmer or farm worker organizations by the Catholic Church, by Hugh A. Donohoe, October 1971, box 126, folder: October 1971, BAHC.

98. Ibid.

99. Sosnick, *Hired Hands*, 332.

100. Ibid.

101. Roger Mahony to Ad Hoc Committee on Farm Labor, National Conference of Catholic Bishops, March 15, 1972, box 126, folder: March 1972, BAHC.

102. John E. Cosgrove to George Higgins, March 20, 1972, box 126, folder: March 1972, BAHC.

103. Ibid.

104. John E. Cosgrove, George Higgins, John McRaith, and Paul Sedillo Jr. to president of the United States, March 24, 1972, box 126, folder: March 1972, BAHC.

105. Ibid.

106. Cesar Chavez to Robert Dole, May 5, 1972, box 129/91, folder: Farm Labor File 1972, GHC.

107. Ibid.

108. John Cosgrove to Joseph Bernardin, June 16, 1972, box 126, folder: June 1972, BAHC.

109. Joseph Bernardin to John Krol, June 22, 1972, box 126, folder: June 1972, BAHC.

110. Ibid.

111. Ibid.

112. Draft of "A Statement by the Committee on Social Development," United States Catholic Conference, June 15, 1972, box 126, folder: June 1972, BAHC.

113. George Higgins to Cesar Chavez, August 24, 1972, box 129/5, folder: Chavez, Cesar 1970–1973, GHC.

114. Ibid.

115. Cesar Chavez to John E. Cosgrove, September 15, 1972, box 126, folder: September 1972, BAHC.

116. "Remarks of George Higgins to the Clergy Conference," June 21, 1972, box 126, folder: June 1972, BAHC.

117. Ibid.

118. Article from the *Catholic Messenger* of Davenport, Iowa, July 27, 1972, box 126, folder: July 1972, BAHC.

119. Roger Mahony to the Ad Hoc Committee on Farm Labor, National Conference of Catholic Bishops, July 20, 1972, box 126, folder: July 1972, BAHC.

120. Ibid.

121. Article from the *Catholic Messenger* of Davenport, Iowa, July 27, 1972.

122. Ibid.

123. Ibid.

124. Ibid.

125. Ibid.

126. "Farm Labor Efforts Earn Papal Praise," *Fresno Bee*, October 3, 1972.

127. Ibid.

128. Susan Ferris, Ricardo Sandoval, and Diana Hembree, eds., *The Fight in the Fields: Cesar Chavez and the Farm Workers Movement* (New York: Harcourt Brace, 1997), 180.

129. Jacques E. Levy, *Cesar Chavez: Autobiography of La Causa,* (New York: W. W. Norton, 1975): 472–73.

130. Ibid., 473.

131. Majka and Majka, *Farm Workers, Agribusiness, and the State*, 213.

132. Ibid., 210.

133. James Vizzard, "Proposition 22: Opposing Viewpoints," *Fresno Bee*," September 10, 1972.

134. Harry Bernstein, "Prop 22: Two Sides of the Farm Labor Issue," *Los Angeles Times*, September 21, 1972.

135. Ibid.

136. George Baker, "Growers, Workers Split on Prop. 22: NLRB Model or Death to Unions," *Fresno Bee*, September 11, 1972.

137. Ron Taylor, "Prop. 22 Struggle Holds Off Chavez, Teamsters 'Warfare,'" *Fresno Bee*, September 19, 1972.

138. Majka and Majka, *Farm Workers, Agribusiness, and the State*, 210.

139. "The Clerics against Prop. 22," *San Francisco Chronicle*, September 1, 1972.

140. Majka and Majka, *Farm Workers, Agribusiness, and the State*, 210.

141. William Farr, "Fraud Found in Prop. 22 Case, Busch Reports: Farm Labor Petitions Misrepresented, He Says, Brown May Go to Court," *Los Angeles Times*, September 10, 1972.

142. Ibid.

143. George Murphy, "Prop. 22 Petitions—Probe Expanded," *San Francisco Chronicle*, September 14, 1972.

144. Ibid.

145. "Political Motive Hint: Reagan Raps Brown on Prop. 22 Furor," *Fresno Bee*, September 16, 1972.

146. Majka and Majka, *Farm Workers, Agribusiness, and the State*, 210.

147. "Bishops Oppose Prop. 22," *San Francisco Examiner*, September 24, 1972.

148. "Catholic Bishops Attack Farm Labor Initiative," *Los Angeles Times*, September 24, 1972.

149. Ibid.

150. Majka and Majka, *Farm Workers, Agribusiness, and the State*, 210.

151. Ibid., 215.

152. Ibid.

153. Sosnick, *Hired Hands*, 335.

154. Ibid.

155. Ibid.

156. Ibid.

157. James Rausch to John Krol, January 10, 1973, box 126, folder: January–June 1973, BAHC.

158. George Higgins to Joseph F. Donnelly, July 17, 1973, box 126, folder: July 1973, BAHC.

159. John Krol to James Rausch, January 15, 1973, box 126, folder: January–June 1973, BAHC.

160. Cesar Chavez to George G. Higgins, February 1, 1973, box 129/91, folder: Farm Labor File 1973, GHC.

161. Cesar Chavez to George G. Higgins, February 6, 1973, box 129/91, folder: Farm Labor File 1973, GHC.

162. Cesar Chavez to George G. Higgins, February 21, 1973, box 129/91, folder: Farm Labor File 1973, GHC.

163. Press conference of George Meany, Miami Beach, Florida, February 20, 1973, box 129/91, folder: Farm Labor File 1973, GHC.

164. George G. Higgins to James Rausch, February 21, 1973, box 126, folder: January–June 1973, BAHC.

165. "Hoffa Predicts Chavez Will Lose Lettuce Fight," *Fresno Bee*, February 21, 1973.

166. Majka and Majka, *Farm Workers, Agribusiness, and the State*, 215.

167. Higgins with Bole, *Organized Labor and the Church*, 97.

168. Ibid.

169. Sosnick, *Hired Hands*, 337.

170. Ibid.

171. Ibid.

172. Majka and Majka, *Farm Workers, Agribusiness, and the State*, 212.

173. Sosnick, *Hired Hands*, 326.

174. Ibid.

175. James Vizzard, "Chavez and the Teamsters: David vs. Goliath?" *America* (1973): 234–38.

176. George Higgins to Gerald M. Costello, April 6, 1973, box 129/91, folder: Farm Labor File 1973, GHC.

177. Ibid.

178. Ibid.

179. Ibid.

180. George Higgins, "Time and Public Opinion Favor Farm Workers," box 126, folder: January–June 1973, BAHC, written as "Yardstick" column.

181. John O'Brien, "George G. Higgins and the 'Yardstick' Columns," *U.S. Catholic Historian* 19, no. 4 (fall 2001): 99.

182. Higgins with Bole, *Organized Labor and the Church*, 98.

183. Gerald M. Costello, "The Farm Labor Movement," *U.S. Catholic Historian* 19, no. 4 (fall 2001): 39.

184. Higgins with Bole, *Organized Labor and the Church*, 97.

185. Levy, *Cesar Chavez: Autobiography of La Causa*, 401.

186. Higgins with Bole, *Organized Labor and the Church*, 97.

187. Sosnick, *Hired Hands*, 343–45.

188. Ibid., 345.

189. Ibid.

190. Harry Bernstein, "Duel in the Sun Union Busting, Teamster Style," *The Progressive*, July 1973, 38. The figures for both Chavez and Fitzsimmons are from 1972.

191. Gerald Costello, *Without Fear or Favor: George Higgins on the Record* (Mystic, Conn.: Twenty-Third Publications, 1984), 113.

192. Higgins with Bole, *Organized Labor and the Church*, 99.

193. Costello, *Without Fear or Favor*, 112.

194. Higgins with Bole, *Organized Labor and the Church*, 97.

195. Ibid., 99.

196. Ibid., 98.

197. Frank E. Fitzsimmons to George Higgins, April 11, 1973, box 129/91, folder: Farm Labor File 1973, GHC.

198. George Higgins to Frank E. Fitzsimmons, April 13, 1973, box 129/91, folder: Farm Labor File 1973, GHC.

199. Ibid.

200. Frank Fitzsimmons to George Higgins, August 14, 1973, box 6–26, folder: U.S. Catholic Conference 1973, UFW Work Department, CLUA.

201. Ibid.

202. George Higgins to Frank Fitzsimmons, August 17, 1973, box 6–26, folder: U.S. Catholic Conference 1973, UFW Work Department, CLUA.

203. Ibid.

204. "Resolution on Farm Labor Dispute," adopted by the Committee on Social Development and World Peace of the United States Catholic Conference, May 23, 1973, box 126, folder: January–June 1973, BAHC.

205. George Higgins to James Rausch, July 3, 1973, box 126, folder: July 1973, BAHC.

206. Ibid.

207. Joseph F. Donnelly to George G. Higgins and Roger Mahony, July 17, 1973, box 129/91, folder: Farm Labor File 1973, GHC.

208. Confidential memo from Timothy Manning to John Krol, July 9, 1973, box 126, folder: July 1973, BAHC.

209. Ibid.

210. John Krol to Timothy Manning, July 17, 1973, box 126, folder: September 1973, BAHC.

211. James Rausch to John Krol, July 23, 1973, box 126, folder: July 1973, BAHC.

212. James Rausch to John Krol, July 24, 1973, box 126, folder: July 1973, BAHC.

213. George Higgins to Joseph F. Donnelly, July 17, 1973, box 129/91, folder: Farm Labor File 1973, GHC.

214. George Higgins to Joseph L. Bernardin, April 17, 1971, box 126, folder: April 1971, BAHC.

215. Cesar Chavez to Joseph F. Donnelly, July 25, 1973, box 129/91, folder: Farm Labor File 1973, GHC.

216. Cesar Chavez to Joseph F. Donnelly, July 25, 1973, box 129/91, folder: Farm Labor File 1973, GHC.

217. Cesar Chavez to George Higgins, July 25, 1973, box 129/91, folder: Farm Labor File 1973, GHC.

218. John Egan to James Rausch, August 30, 1973, box 126, folder: August 1973, BAHC.

219. James S. Rausch to John J. Egan, September 10, 1973, box 126, folder: September 1973, BAHC.

220. Cesar Chavez to Joseph Donnelly, November 12, 1973, box 129/94, folder: Mahony Reports 1973, GHC.

221. Report of Joseph F. Donnelly, November 13, 1973, box 126, folder: October–December 1973, BAHC.

222. Ibid.

223. "Resolutions Passed by The National Conference of Catholic Bishops," November 16, 1973, box 129/94, folder: Mahony Reports 1973, GHC.

224. Report of Joseph F. Donnelly, November 13, 1973.

225. George Higgins to Joseph Maguire, June 3, 1974, box 129/96, folder: Untitled, GHC.

226. James Rausch to Giovanni Benelli, November 19, 1973, box 126, folder: October–December 1973, BAHC.

227. Giovanni Benelli to James Rausch, November 12, 1973, box 126, folder: October–December 1973, BAHC.

228. Rausch to Benelli, November 19, 1973.

229. Cesar Chavez to John Krol, November 17, 1973, box 126, folder: October–December 1973, BAHC.

230. Frank Fitzsimmons to John Krol, November 20, 1973, box 126, folder: October–December 1973, BAHC.

231. Memo from Joseph F. Donnelly to members of the NCCB, December 7, 1973, box 129/94, folder: Mahony Reports 1973, GHC.

232. George Meany to John Krol, December 11, 1973, box 126, folder: October–December 1973, BAHC.

233. Ibid.

234. Press Release from the AFL-CIO, November 30, 1973, box 126, folder: October–December 1973, BAHC.

235. William J. Kuhfuss to John Krol, November 21, 1973, box 126, folder: October–December 1973, BAHC.

236. Ibid.

237. Cesar Chavez to George Higgins, November 27, 1973, box 129/94, folder: UFW Headquarters Correspondence, GHC.

238. Memo from Joseph F. Donnelly, December 7, 1973.

239. Dalton, *The Moral Vision of César Chávez*, 58.

240. J. Craig Jenkins, *The Politics of Insurgency: The Farm Worker Movement in the 1960s* (New York: Columbia University Press, 1985), 194.

241. Frank Fitzsimmons to presidents of all international unions affiliated with the AFL-CIO, April 12, 1974, box 129/96, folder: untitled, GHC.

242. George Higgins to Joseph Keenan, March 27, 1974, box 129/96, folder: Untitled, GHC.

243. William Baum to James Rausch, May 30, 1974, box 126, folder: May 1974, BAHC.

244. James Rausch to William Baum, June 17, 1974, box 126, folder: June 1974, BAHC.

245. Statement by Hugh Donohoe on the status of the farm labor dispute, April 16, 1974, box 126, folder: April 1974, BAHC.

246. Ibid.

247. Roger Mahony to Mrs. Kelvin Larson, April 23, 1974, box 129/94, folder: Mahony Reports 1974, GHC.

248. Roger Mahony to the Ad Hoc Committee on Farm labor, National Conference of Catholic Bishops, April 22, 1974, box 126, folder: April 1974, BAHC.

249. Cesar Chavez to George Higgins, April 26, 1974, box 129/94, folder: UFW Headquarters Correspondence, GHC.

250. George Higgins to Joseph Bernardin, May 20, 1974, box 129/96, folder: Untitled, GHC.

251. Susan Sachen to George Higgins, July 30, 1974, box 129/94, folder: UFW Headquarters Correspondence, GHC.

252. George Higgins to F. J. Smyth, November 14, 1974, box 129/91, folder: Farm Labor File 1974, GHC.

253. Ibid.

254. Ibid.

255. Levy, *Cesar Chavez: Autobiography of La Causa*, 525.

256. Ibid., 522.

257. George Higgins to Cesar Chavez, August 5, 1974, box 129/92, folder: Farm Labor Dispute, GHC.

258. Ibid.

259. Ibid.

260. George Higgins to Cesar Chavez, August 6, 1974, box 129/92, folder: Farm Labor Dispute, GHC.

261. George Higgins to Cesar Chavez, September 2, 1974, box 129/92, folder: Farm Labor Dispute, GHC.

262. Cesar Chavez to George Higgins, August 13, 1974, box 129/92, folder: Farm Labor Dispute, GHC.

263. Ibid.

264. Levy, *Cesar Chavez: Autobiography of La Causa*, 522.

265. Ibid.

266. Ibid.

267. Ibid., 523.

268. Ibid.

269. Ibid.

270. Ibid., 524.

271. George Higgins to Seymour Chalfin, October 23, 1974, box 129/92, folder: Farm Labor Dispute, GHC.

272. Higgins with Bole, *Organized Labor and the Church*, 101.

273. George Higgins to Cesar Chavez, October 17, 1974, box 129/92, folder: Farm Labor Dispute, GHC.

274. Ibid.

275. George Higgins to Cesar Chavez, October 23, 1974, box 129/92, folder: Farm Labor Dispute, GHC.

276. George Higgins to Chavez December 7, 1974, box 129/5, folder: Chavez, Cesar 1974–1975, GHC.

277. Cesar Chavez to George Higgins, December 11, 1974, box 129/91, folder: Farm Labor File 1974, GHC.

278. Cesar Chavez to James Rausch, October 31, 1974, box 126, folder: October 1974, BAHC.

279. James S. Rausch to Cesar Chavez, November 5, 1974, box 126, folder: November 1974, BAHC.

280. Ibid.

281. George Higgins to the editor, *Toronto Catholic Register*, January 13, 1975.

282. Ibid.

283. Ibid.

284. Ibid.

285. Ibid.

286. George Higgins to Cesar Chavez, January 25, 1975, box 129/5, folder: Chavez, Cesar 1974–1975, GHC.

287. Roger M. Mahony, confidential report to members, U.S. Catholic Bishops' Ad Hoc Committee on Farm Labor, January 27, 1975, box 129/94, folder: Mahony Reports 1975, GHC.

288. Gilbert Padilla to James Rausch, March 10, 1975, box 126, folder: March 1975, BAHC.

289. George Higgins to James Rausch, March 25, 1975, box 126, folder: March 1975, BAHC.

290. James Rausch to Gilbert Padilla, March 27, 1975, box 126, folder: March 1975, BAHC.

291. Cesar Chavez to George Higgins, July 22, 1975, box 129/96, folder: Untitled, GHC.

292. George Higgins to Martin Farrell, March 13, 1975, box 129/96, folder: Untitled, GHC.

293. Ibid.

294. Hugh Donohoe to Brad Massman, March 20, 1975, box 126, folder: March 1975, BAHC.

295. Ibid.

296. James Rausch to G. Emmett Carter, April 1, 1975, box 126, folder: March 1975, BAHC.

297. Ibid.

298. Robert Pack, *Jerry Brown: The Philosopher-Prince* (New York: Stein and Day, 1978), x.

299. Ibid., xiii.

300. Ibid., x.

301. Jonathan Curiel, "The Reincarnation of Jerry Brown: State's Former Governor Just Keeps on Evolving," *San Francisco Chronicle*, July 4, 2004, *San Francisco Chronicle* Web site: www.sfgate.com.

302. Ibid.

303. Pack, *Jerry Brown: The Philosopher-Prince*, 24.

304. Ibid., 33.

305. Ibid.

306. Ibid., 2.

307. Ibid., 1.

308. Ibid., 23.

309. Ibid., 26.

310. Richard Griswold del Castillo and Richard A. Garcia, *César Chávez: A Triumph of Spirit* (Norman: University of Oklahoma Press, 1995), 127.

311. Pack, *Jerry Brown: The Philosopher-Prince*, xii.

312. Griswold del Castillo and Garcia, *César Chávez: A Triumph of Spirit*, 127.

313. Goldfarb, *Migrant Farm Workers*, 198.

314. Pack, *Jerry Brown: The Philosopher-Prince*, 52.

315. Majka and Majka, *Farm Workers, Agribusiness, and the State*, 296.

316. Pack, *Jerry Brown: The Philosopher-Prince*, 191.

317. Majka and Majka, *Farm Workers, Agribusiness, and the State*, 234.

318. Levy, *Cesar Chavez: Autobiography of La Causa*, 441–42.

319. Daska Slater, "Jerry Brown Gets Real," *Mother Jones*, July/August 1999.

320. J. D. Lorenz, *Jerry Brown: The Man on the White Horse* (Boston: Houghton Mifflin, 1978), 135–39.

321. Ibid.

322. Ibid.

323. Majka and Majka, *Farm Workers, Agribusiness, and the State*, 246.

324. John C. Hammerback and Richard Jensen, *The Rhetorical Career of César Chávez* (College Station: Texas A&M University Press, 1998), 104.

325. Ibid.

326. Pack, *Jerry Brown: The Philosopher-Prince*, 76.

327. Ibid., 77.

328. Ibid.

329. Jenkins, *The Politics of Insurgency*, 196.

330. Ibid., 197.

331. Goldfarb, *Migrant Farm Workers*, 198–99.

332. Pack, *Jerry Brown: The Philosopher-Prince*, 79.

333. Ibid.

334. Jenkins, *The Politics of Insurgency*, 197.

335. Ibid.

336. Ibid.

337. Mooney and Majka, *Farmers' and Farm Workers' Movements*, 174–75.

338. Timothy Manning to James Rausch, May 27, 1975, box 126, folder: March 1975, BAHC.

339. George Higgins to Giovanni Benelli, June 5, 1975, box 126, folder: March 1975, BAHC.

340. Roger Mahony to James Rausch, May 27, 1975, box 126, folder: March 1975, BAHC.

341. "Top 100 Catholics of the Twentieth Century," *Daily Catholic*, August 5, 1999, Web site: www.dailycatholic.org. *Daily Catholic's* readers voted Cardinal Mahony number ninety-one.

342. Roger Mahony to Joseph Bernardin, July 26, 1975, box 129/96, folder: Untitled, GHC.

343. Ibid.

344. Statement by the California Conference of Catholic Bishops on the signing of the Agricultural Labor Relations Act of 1975, June 5, 1975, box 126, folder: March 1975, BAHC.

345. Ibid.

346. Ibid.

347. James Rausch to Joseph F. Donnelly, June 26, 1975, box 126, folder: June 1975, BAHC.

348. "Comment on the UFW Boycott," by Joseph F. Donnelly, July 9, 1975, box 126, folder: July 1975, BAHC.

349. Ibid.

350. Hugh Donohoe to Joseph Donnelly, July 24, 1975, box 126, folder: July 1975, BAHC.

351. Ibid.

352. Ibid.

353. Joseph Donnelly to James Rausch, August 21, 1975, box 126, folder: August 1975, BAHC.

354. Ibid.

355. Joseph Bernardin to Kathleen Keating, September 22, 1975, box 126, folder: September 1975, BAHC.

356. Ibid.

357. George G. Higgins to James Rausch, November 7, 1975, box 126, folder: November 1975, BAHC.

358. Ibid.

359. Cesar Chavez to Joseph Bernardin, November 11, 1975, box 129/96, folder: Untitled, GHC.

360. Ibid.

361. George G. Higgins to M. E. Anderson, November 26, 1975, box 129/96, folder: Untitled, GHC.

362. NCCB "Resolution on Farm Labor," November 20, 1975, box 129/96, folder: Untitled, GHC.

363. George Higgins to the editor, *Toronto Catholic Register*, January 13, 1975.

364. NCCB "Resolution on Farm Labor," November 20, 1975.

365. George Higgins to Cesar Chavez, April 14, 1976, box 129/5, folder: Chavez, Cesar 1976–1977, GHC. The most notable 1976 correspondence between Chavez and Higgins in the archives pertains to Joseph F. Maguire's appointment as coadjutor bishop of the Diocese of Springfield, Mass. Higgins suggested that Chavez send Maguire a note of congratulations since Maguire was a "staunch supporter" of La Causa.

366. Hugh Donohoe to Allen Grant, June 25, 1971, box 126, folder: June 1971, BAHC.

367. Majka and Majka, *Farm Workers, Agribusiness, and the State*, 239.

368. Sullivan, *Blue Collar, Roman Collar, White Collar*, 146.

369. Ibid., 145.

370. Pack, *Jerry Brown: The Philosopher-Prince*, 80.

371. Ibid., 81.

372. Ibid.

373. Ibid.

374. Ibid.

375. Sullivan, *Blue Collar, Roman Collar, White Collar*, 145.

376. Ibid., 148.

377. Goldfarb, *Migrant Farm Workers*, 199–200.

378. California Agricultural Labor Relations Board, *Setting the Record Straight: A Response by the Agricultural Labor Relations Board (CALRB) to Criticisms of Its Operations, and a Statistical Analysis of CALRB Activities and Accomplishments, August 28, 1975 to April 1976* (Sacramento: CALRB, 1976).

379. Ibid.

380. Ibid.

381. "Special Report to the Bishops" on the status of the California Agricultural Labor Relations Board (September 2, 1975–February 6, 1976) from Roger Mahony to U.S. Catholic Bishops, April 23, 1976, box 126, folder: April 1976, BAHC.

382. Jenkins, *The Politics of Insurgency*, 199.

383. George Higgins to James Rausch, February 9, 1976, box 126, folder: February 1976, BAHC.

384. Ibid.

385. Ibid.

386. "Special Report to the Bishops."

387. Ibid.

388. George Higgins to R. S. Beresford, March 4, 1976, box 129/96, folder: Untitled, GHC.

389. George Higgins, untitled article written as "Yardstick" column, February 15, 1976, box 129/95, folder: National Farm Worker Ministry, GHC.

390. Ibid.

391. George Higgins to Joseph Donnelly, April 1, 1976, box 129/96, folder: Untitled, GHC.

392. Ibid.

393. Roger Mahony to Hugh Donohoe, April 7, 1976, box 126, folder: April 1976, BAHC.

394. Mooney and Majka, *Farmers' and Farm Workers' Movements*, 177.

395. "Special Report to the Bishops."

396. Pack, *Jerry Brown: The Philosopher-Prince*, 82.

397. Ibid.

398. Mooney and Majka, *Farmers' and Farm Workers' Movements*, 177.

399. Sosnick, *Hired Hands*, 381.

400. Jenkins, *The Politics of Insurgency*, 199.

401. Mooney and Majka, *Farmers' and Farm Workers' Movements*, 176.

402. Sullivan, *Blue Collar, Roman Collar, White Collar*, 147.

403. Dalton, *The Moral Vision of César Chávez*, 18.

404. Pack, *Jerry Brown: The Philosopher-Prince*, 82.

405. Mooney and Majka, *Farmers' and Farm Workers' Movements*, 178.

406. Goldfarb, *Migrant Farm Workers*, 200.

407. Mooney and Majka, *Farmers' and Farm Workers' Movements*, 178.

408. Sosnick, *Hired Hands*, 381.

409. George Higgins to Joseph Donnelly, April 1, 1976, box 129/96, folder: Untitled, GHC.

410. Mooney and Majka, *Farmers' and Farm Workers' Movements*, 178.

411. Pack, *Jerry Brown: The Philosopher-Prince*, 86.

412. Ibid.

413. Ibid.

414. Majka, *Farm Workers, Agribusiness, and the State*, 245.

415. Pack, *Jerry Brown: The Philosopher-Prince*, 87.

416. Ibid., 87.

417. Majka, *Farm Workers, Agribusiness, and the State*, 246.

418. Pack, *Jerry Brown: The Philosopher-Prince*, 84.

419. Sullivan, *Blue Collar, Roman Collar, White Collar*, 153.

420. "Special Report to the Bishops."

421. Ibid.

422. Mooney and Majka, *Farmers' and Farm Workers' Movements*, 192.

423. Ibid.

424. Ibid., 193.

425. Ibid., 196.

426. Jenkins, *The Politics of Insurgency*, 202.

427. Majka, *Farm Workers, Agribusiness, and the State*, 246.

428. Sosnick, *Hired Hands*, 382. The three reasons are courtesy of Stephen Sosnick.

429. Majka, *Farm Workers, Agribusiness, and the State*, 246.

430. Ibid.

431. Sosnick, *Hired Hands*, 382.

432. Hammerback and Jensen, *The Rhetorical Career of César Chávez*, 144.

433. Allan Grant to James Rausch, May 19, 1976, box 126, folder: May 1976, BAHC.

434. Ibid.

435. Joseph L. Bernardin to Allan Grant, May 25, 1976, box 126, folder: May 1976, BAHC.

436. Ibid.

437. Thomas Kelly to Ad Hoc Committee on Farm Labor, August 23, 1977, box 126, folder: August 1977, BAHC.

438. James Rausch, address to the Biennial Convention of the UFW in Fresno, August 26, 1977, box 126, folder: August 1977, BAHC.

439. Ibid.

440. Ibid.

441. Ibid.

442. George Higgins to Joseph Donnelly, April 1, 1976, box 129/96, folder: Untitled, GHC. In his letter to Donnelly, Higgins recalled an encounter with Chavez where the two discussed the UFW's need to "tighten up [its] administrative procedures." Higgins reported that he left the meeting "convinced that Chavez is now willing to admit that the union must assume at least 50% of the responsibility for making the system work effectively."

443. James Rausch, address to the Biennial Convention of the UFW, August 26, 1977.

444. Thomas Kelly to Monsignor Lally, December 11, 1981, box 126, folder: December 1981, BAHC.

445. Ibid.

446. "Top 100 Catholics of the Twentieth Century."

447. John Roach to Roger Mahony, December 16, 1981, box 126, folder: December 1981, BAHC.

448. Roger Mahony to John Roach, December 23, 1981, box 126, folder: December 1981, BAHC.

449. Thomas Kelly to Ad Hoc Committee on Farm Labor, December 29, 1981, box 126, folder: December 1981, BAHC.

Epilogue

1. Patrick Mooney and Theo Majka, *Farmers' and Farm Workers' Movements: Social Protest in American Agriculture* (New York: Twayne, 1995), 189.

2. Gerald Costello, *Without Fear or Favor: George Higgins on the Record* (Mystic, Conn.: Twenty-Third Publications, 1984), 116.

3. Mooney and Majka, *Farmers' and Farm Workers' Movements*, 186.

4. Ibid.

5. J. Craig Jenkins, *The Politics of Insurgency: The Farm Worker Movement in the 1960s* (New York: Columbia University Press, 1985), 205.

6. George G. Higgins with William Bole, *Organized Labor and the Church: Reflections of a "Labor Priest"* (New York: Paulist Press, 1993), 103.

7. Jenkins, *The Politics of Insurgency*, 206.

8. Ibid.

9. Ibid.

10. Mooney and Majka, *Farmers' and Farm Workers' Movements*, 188.

11. Jenkins, *The Politics of Insurgency*, 204.

12. Richard J. Jensen and John Hammerback, eds., *The Words of César Chávez* (College Station: Texas A&M University Press, 2002), 89.

13. Linda Majka and Theo Majka, *Farm Workers, Agribusiness, and the State* (Philadelphia: Temple University Press, 1982), 274.

14. Jenkins, *The Politics of Insurgency*, 206.

15. Jensen and Hammerback, *The Words of César Chávez*, 145.

16. Frank Bardacke, "Decline and Fall of the UFW: Cesar's Ghost," *The Nation*, July 26/August 2, 1993, 133–34.

17. Jenkins, *The Politics of Insurgency*, 206.

18. Ibid.

19. Mooney and Majka, *Farmers' and Farm Workers' Movements*, 164–165.

20. Higgins with Bole, *Organized Labor and the Church*, 104.

21. Jensen and Hammerback, *The Words of César Chávez*, 89.

22. Mooney and Majka, *Farmers' and Farm Workers' Movements*, 190–191.

23. Jensen and Hammerback, *The Words of César Chávez*, 111.

24. Ibid., 118.

25. Ibid.

26. Bardacke, "Decline and Fall of the UFW: Cesar's Ghost," 131.

27. Ibid., 130.

28. United Farm Workers Web site: www.ufw.org/asrbio.htm.

29. Ibid.

30. Matt Weiser, "UFW's New Path: Help Millions," *Rural Migration News*, May 12, 2004, Web site: http:/migration.ucdavis.edu/rmn/more.php?id=854þ0þ8þ0

31. Ibid.

32. Nancy Cleeland, "Farm Workers Urge Davis to Sign Binding Arbitration Bill," *Los Angeles Times*, August 11 2002, United Farm Workers Web site: www.ufw.org/lat81102.htm

33. Stephen Sosnick, *Hired Hands, Seasonal Farm Workers in the United States* (Santa Barbara, Calif.: McNally, 1978), 351–52.

34. Jenkins, *The Politics of Insurgency*, 206.

35. Colin Austin, "The Struggle for Health in Times of Plenty," in *The Human Cost of Food: Farmworkers' Lives, Labor and Advocacy*, Charles D. Thompson Jr. and Melinda F. Wiggins, eds. (Austin: University of Texas Press, 2002), 212.

36. Higgins with Bole, *Organized Labor and the Church*, 106.

37. Jenkins, *The Politics of Insurgency*, 207.

38. Sosnick, *Hired Hands*, 350.

39. Jenkins, *The Politics of Insurgency*, 209.

40. Ibid.

41. Ricardo Ramirez, "What Cesar Chavez Believed," *Origins* 23 (May 1993): 19.

42. United Farm Workers Web site.

43. Ibid.

44. Ibid.

45. Presidential Medal of Freedom Web site.

46. Costello, *Without Fear or Favor*, 70.

47. Patrick J. Sullivan, *Blue Collar, Roman Collar, White Collar: U.S. Catholic Involvement in Labor Management Controversies, 1960–1980* (Lanham, Md.: University Press, 1987), 163.

48. Ibid.

49. Joseph L. Bernardin to Joseph O'Brien, October 24, 1978, box 14/27, folder: Controversy—Retirement of Msgr. George Higgins 1978, ACPC.

50. Thomas Kelly to Joseph O'Brien, October 20, 1978, box 14/27, folder : Controversy—Retirement of Msgr. George Higgins 1978, ACPC.

51. Bernardin to O'Brien, October 24, 1978.

52. George Higgins to Ernest J. Primeau, October 17, 1978, box 14/27, folder: Controversy—Retirement of Msgr. George Higgins 1978, ACPC.

53. Joseph O'Brien to Joseph Bernardin, November 27, 1978, box 14/27, folder: Controversy—Retirement of Msgr. George Higgins 1978, ACPC. In the correspondence, O'Brien expresses appreciation for the NCCB-USCC's decision to retain Higgins.

54. Costello, *Without Fear or Favor*, 57.

55. Jerry Filteau, "Msgr. George Higgins, America's 'Labor Priest,' Dead at 86," *Denver Catholic Register*, May 15, 2002, Web site: www.archden.org/dcr/archive/20020515/2002051505wn.htm

56. Ibid.

57. Costello, *Without Fear or Favor*, 57.

58. Ibid.

59. George G. Higgins to Cesar Chavez, September 21, 1981, box 129/96, folder: Untitled, GHC.

60. Ibid.

61. Ibid.

62. Ibid.

63. Cesar Chavez to George Higgins, October 21, 1981, box 129/96, folder: Untitled, GHC.

64. Ibid.

65. Ibid.

66. Ibid.

67. Ibid.

68. George Higgins to Cesar Chavez, July 21, 1983, box 129/96, folder: Untitled, GHC.

69. George Higgins to Cesar Chavez, August 16, 1985, box 129/96, folder: Untitled, GHC.

70. George Higgins to Cesar Chavez, May 7, 1987, box 129/96, folder: Untitled, GHC.

71. Higgins with Bole, *Organized Labor and the Church*, 102.

72. Ibid.

73. From a United Farm Workers of America banner in The Catholic University of America Archives, February 23, 1994.

74. Ibid.

75. George Higgins to Joseph L. Bernardin, April 17, 1971, box 126, folder: April 1971, BAHC.

76. "UFW Mourns Msgr. George Higgins, One of Cesar Chavez's Greatest Champions," United Farm Workers Web site: www.ufw.org/5302mh.htm.

BIBLIOGRAPHY

Primary Sources

ACPC   Association of Chicago Priests Collection. Archives of the University of Notre Dame. University of Notre Dame, South Bend, Ind.

BAHC   Bishops' Ad Hoc Committee on Farm Labor Papers, 1968–1980. U.S. Conference of Catholic Bishops' Archives, Washington, D.C.

CLUA   Collections of Labor and Urban Affairs—United Farm Workers. University Archives. Wayne State University, Detroit, Mich.

GHC   Msgr. George G. Higgins Collection. The American Catholic History Research Center and University Archives. The Catholic University of America, Washington, D.C.

Secondary Sources

Bardacke, Frank. "Decline and Fall of the U.F.W.: Cesar's Ghost." *The Nation*, July 26/August 2, 1993.

Bernstein, Harry. "Duel in the Sun Union Busting, Teamster Style." *The Progressive*, July 1973.

Betten, Neil. *Catholic Activism and the Industrial Worker*. Gainseville: University Presses of Florida, 1976.

Bole, William. "The Ministry of Presence." *U.S. Catholic Historian* 19 (fall 2001): 3–10.

"The Bracero Program." Handbook of Texas Online, University of Texas at Austin, www.tsha.utexas.edu/handbook/online/articles/view/BB/omb1.html.

Burns, Jim. "Bill Proposed To Name Cesar Chavez 'Hero.'" *CNSNews.com*, September 25, 2001.

California Agricultural Labor Relations Board. *Setting the Record Straight: A Response by the Agricultural Labor Relations Board (CALRB) to Criticisms of Its Operations, and a Statistical Analysis of CALRB Activities and Accomplishments, August 28, 1975 to April 1976*. Sacramento: CALRB, 1976.

Cavenaugh, William T. Letter to the editor. *Notre Dame Magazine Online*, spring 2000, University of Notre Dame Web site, www.nd.edu/7Endmag/lets400.htm.

Costello, Gerald. "The Farm Labor Movement." *U.S. Catholic Historian* 19, no. 4 (fall 2001): 33–40.

———. *Without Fear or Favor: George Higgins on the Record*. Mystic, Conn.: Twenty-Third Publications, 1984.

Curiel, Jonathan. "The Reincarnation of Jerry Brown: State's Former Governor Just Keeps on Evolving." *San Francisco Chronicle*, July 4, 2004. *San Francisco Chronicle* Web site, www.sfgate.com.

Curran, Charles E. "George Higgins and Catholic Social Teaching." *U.S. Catholic Historian* 19 (fall 2001): 59–72.

Dalton, Frederick John. *The Moral Vision of César Chávez*. New York: Orbis Books, 2003.

de Toledano, Ralph. *Little Cesar*. Washington, D.C.: Anthem Books, 1971.

Dunne, John Gregory. *Delano*. New York: Farrar, Straus and Giroux, 1971.

Ferris, Susan, Ricardo Sandoval, and Diana Hembree, eds. *The Fight in the Fields: Cesar Chavez and the Farm Workers Movement*. New York: Harcourt Brace, 1997.

Filteau, Jerry. "Msgr. George Higgins, America's 'Labor Priest,' Dead at 86." *Denver Catholic Register*, May 15, 2002, www.archden.org/dcr/archive/20020515/2002051505wn.html

Flanagan, Sean B. *Catholic Social Principles and Chavez: A Case Study*. Master's thesis, Loyola University of Los Angeles, 1971.

Fones, Ken. *Trade Union Gospel: Christianity and Labor in Industrial Philadelphia, 1865–1915*. Philadelphia: Temple University Press, 1989.

Fox, Geoffrey. *Hispanic Nation: Culture, Politics, and the Constructing of Identity*. Tucson: University of Arizona Press, 1996.

Freeman, Joshua. *In Transit: The Transport Workers Union in New York City, 1933–1966*. New York: Oxford University Press, 1989.

Fuechtmann, Thomas, *Steeples and Stacks: Religion and Steel Crisis in Youngstown*. New York: Cambridge University Press, 1989.

Garvey, Michael. "Monsignor George G. Higgins to Receive the 2001 Laetare Medal." March 23, 2001. University of Notre Dame Web site, www.nd.edu/7Ehlrc/MsgrHiggins%20Laetare.htm.

Gillis, Chester. *Roman Catholicism in America*. New York: Columbia University Press, 1999.

Goldfarb, Ronald. *Migrant Farm Workers: A Caste of Despair*. Ames: Iowa State University Press, 1981.

Gonzales, Juan L., Jr. *Mexican and Mexican American Farm Workers: The California Agricultural Industry*. New York: Praeger, 1985.

Greeley, Andrew. "A Man for All Seasons." *U.S. Catholic Historian* 19 (fall 2001): 11–15.

Griffith, David, et al. *Working Poor: Farmworkers in the United States*. Philadelphia: Temple University Press, 1995.

Griswold del Castillo, Richard, and Richard A. Garcia. *César Chávez: A Triumph of Spirit*. Norman: University of Oklahoma Press, 1995.

Guerin-Gonzales, Camille. *Mexican Workers and American Dreams: Immigration, Repatriation, and California Farm Labor, 1900–1939*. New Brunswick, N.J.: Rutgers University Press, 1996.

Gutierrez, David G. *Walls and Mirrors: Mexican Americans, Mexican Immigrants and the Politics of Ethnicity*. Berkeley: University of California Press, 1995.

——, ed. *Between Two Worlds: Mexican Immigrants in the United States; The Immigration Debate 1968–1978*. Lanham, Md.: SR Books: 1996.

Gutierrez, Gustavo. *A Theology of Liberation*. New York: Orbis Books, 1988.

Hammerback, John C., and Richard Jensen. *The Rhetorical Career of César Chávez*. College Station: Texas A&M University Press, 1998.

Heineman, Kenneth. *A Catholic New Deal: Religion and Reform in Depression Pittsburgh*. University Park: Pennsylvania State University Press, 1999.

Higgins, George G., with William Bole. *Organized Labor and the Church: Reflections of a "Labor Priest."* New York: Paulist Press, 1993.

Jenkins, J. Craig. *The Politics of Insurgency: The Farm Worker Movement in the 1960s*. New York: Columbia University Press, 1985.

Jensen, Richard J., and John Hammerback, eds. *The Words of César Chávez*. College Station: Texas A&M University Press, 2002.

Knight, Alan. *The Mexican Revolution: Porfirians, Liberals and Democrats*. Lincoln: University of Nebraska,Press, 1986.

Levy, Jacques E. *Cesar Chavez: Autobiography of La Causa*. New York: W. W. Norton, 1975.

Lorenz, J. D. *Jerry Brown: The Man on the White Horse*. Boston: Houghton Mifflin, 1978.

Los Angeles Times. June 14, 1970–August 22, 2002.

Lyons, Daniel. "Chavez Reaps Bitter Harvest." *Twin Circle*, July 12, 1970.

Majka, Linda, and Theo Majka. *Farm Workers, Agribusiness, and the State*. Philadelphia: Temple University Press, 1982.

Maldonado, Carlos S. *Colegio Cesar Chavez, 1973–1983: A Chicano Struggle for Educational Self Determination*. New York: Garland, 2000.

Marty, Martin. *An Invitation to American Catholic History*. Chicago: Thomas More, 1986.

Massaro, Thomas, and Thomas Shannon, eds. *American Catholic Social Teaching*. Collegeville, N.J.: Liturgical Press, 2002.

Matsumoto, Valerie J. *Farming the Home Place: A Japanese American Community in California, 1919–1982*. Ithaca: Cornell University Press, 1993.

Matthiessen, Peter. *Sal Si Puedes: Cesar Chavez and the New American Revolution*. New York: Random House, 1969.

McGreevy, John T. *Parish Boundaries: The Catholic Encounter With Race in the Twentieth-Century Urban North*. Chicago: University of Chicago Press, 1996.

Meagher, Timothy, John Shepherd, and Joseph Turrini. "Laboring for Justice: Archival Resources for the Study of George Higgins and Catholic Action at the Archives of the Catholic University of America." *U.S. Catholic Historian* 19 (fall 2001): 51–56.

Miller, Kerby. *Emigrants and Exiles: Ireland and the Irish Exodus to North America*. New York: Oxford University Press, 1985.

Mitchell, Don. *The Lie of the Land: Migrant Workers and the California Landscape*. Minneapolis: University of Minnesota Press, 1996.

Monroy, Douglas. *Rebirth: Mexican Los Angeles from the Great Migration to the Great Depression*. Berkeley: University of California Press, 1982.

Montejano, David. *Anglos and Mexicans in the Making of Texas, 1836–1986*. Austin: University of Texas Press, 1987.

Mooney, Patrick, and Theo Majka. *Farmers' and Farm Workers' Movements: Social Protest in American Agriculture*. New York: Twayne, 1995.

Myers, Edith. "Priest-Editor Goes to the Source of the Grape Strike." *Twin Circle*, February 22, 1970.

National Catholic News Service. August 30, 1967–April 28, 1993.

Nelson, Bruce. *Divided We Stand: American Workers and the Struggle for Black Equality*. Princeton: Princeton University Press, 2001.

Nolan, Philip. "Bishops Break Grape Deadlock." *Twin Circle*, April 19, 1970.

O'Brien, David J. *American Catholics and Social Reform: The New Deal Years*. New York: Oxford University Press, 1968.

——. *Public Catholicism*. New York: Orbis, 1996.

O'Brien, John J. *George G. Higgins and the Quest for Worker Justice: The Evolution of Social Thought in America*. Lanham, Md.: Rowman and Littlefield, 2005.

——. "George G. Higgins and the 'Yardstick' Columns." *U.S. Catholic Historian* 19 (fall 2001): 87–101.

Pack, Robert. *Jerry Brown: The Philosopher-Prince*. New York: Stein and Day, 1978.

"Personal Opinions." *Twin Circle*, January 4, 1970.

Raleigh (N.C.) News and Observer. July 29, 2000.

Ramirez, Bishop Ricardo. "What Cesar Chavez Believed." *Origins* 23 (May 1993): 19–20.

Ross, Fred. *Conquering Goliath: Cesar Chavez at the Beginning.* Keen, Calif.: Grafico, 1989.

Rosswurm, Steve. *The CIO's Left-Led Unions.* New Brunswick, N.J.: Rutgers, 1992.

Rothenberg, Daniel. *With These Hands: The Hidden World of Migrant Farmworkers Today.* New York: Harcourt Brace, 1998.

Ruiz, Ramon Eduardo. *The Great Rebellion: Mexico 1905–1924.* New York: W. W. Norton, 1980.

Sanchez, George J. *Becoming Mexican American: Ethnicity, Culture and Identity in Chicano Los Angeles, 1900–1945.* Oxford: Oxford University Press, 1993.

Schatz, Ronald. *The Electrical Workers: A History of Labor at General Electric and Westinghouse, 1923–60.* Chicago: University of Illinois Press, 1983.

Schultheis, Michael J., Edward P. DeBerri, and Peter J. Henriot. *Our Best Kept Secret: The Rich Heritage of Catholic Social Teaching.* Washington, D.C.: Center of Concern, 1987.

Seaton, Douglas. *Catholics and Radicals: The Association of Catholic Trade Unionists and the American Labor Movement, from Depression to Cold War.* Lewisburg, N.J.: Bucknell University Press, 1981.

Segal, Sean. *Early Church Involvement in U.S. Farm Labor.* Senior thesis, The Catholic University of America, 2000.

Sherry, Gerald. "Farm Labor Battle: Church's Involvement Outlined." National Catholic News Service, December 17, 1973.

Slater, Daska. "Jerry Brown Gets Real." *Mother Jones*, July/August 1999.

Slayton, Robert. *Back of Yards: The Making of a Local Democracy.* Chicago: University of Chicago Press, 1986.

Sosnick, Stephen. *Hired Hands, Seasonal Farm Workers in the United States.* Santa Barbara, Calif.: McNally, 1978.

Sullivan, Patrick J. *Blue Collar, Roman Collar, White Collar: U.S. Catholic Involvement in Labor Management Controversies, 1960–1980.* Lanham, Md.: University Press, 1987.

Sweeney, John J. "Reflections on Monsignor George Higgins." *U.S. Catholic Historian* 19 (fall 2001): 17–26.

Taylor, Ron B. *Chavez and the Farm Workers.* Boston: Beacon Press, 1975.

Tentler, Leslie, "Present at the Creation: Working Class Catholics in the United States." In Rick Halpern and Jonathan Morris, eds., *American Exceptionalism? U.S. Working Class Formation in an International Context.* London: Macmillan, 1997.

———. *Seasons of Grace: A History of the Catholic Archdiocese of Detroit.* Detroit, Mich.: Wayne State University Press, 1990.

Thompson, Charles D., Jr., and Melinda F. Wiggins, eds. *The Human Cost of Food: Farmworkers' Lives, Labor and Advocacy.* Austin: University of Texas Press, 2002.

"UFW Mourns Msgr. George Higgins, One of Cesar Chavez's Greatest Champions." United Farm Workers Web site, www.ufw.org/5302mh.htm.

U.S. Catholic Conference Press Service. July 15, 1970–November 29, 1973.

Vera Cruz, Philip. "The Farm Workers and the Church." *The Catholic Worker*, September 1970.

Weiser, Matt. "UFW's New Path: Help Millions." *Rural Migration News*, May 12, 2004.

INDEX

Actists. *See* Association of Catholic Trade Unionists (ACTU), 16

AFL-CIO: alliance with the USCC/NCCB, 51–52; and farmworker unions, 11–12, 28; support for UFW, 90, 98, 105, 107, 111, 112, 130–131; Teamsters' interaction with, 95, 106; UFW as an affiliate of, 6, 92, 133

agricultural industry in California, 7, 63, 69

agriculturalists. *See* growers

Agricultural Workers Organizing Committee (AWOC), 11, 12, 26, 27

Alien Land Law, 8

Alinsky, Saul, 24, 25, 33, 34

American Farm Bureau Federation. *See* Farm Bureau

Antle, Bud, Inc., 67, 68, 129

Association of Catholic Trade Unionists (ACTU), 15, 16

Battle of the Salad Bowl: Ad Hoc Committee's role in, 3, 5, 47, 94, 98; Catholic growers in, 84; end of, 130; intra-clergy debate regarding, 35–36, 38; origins of, 65–67; Teamster-grower involvement in, 75, 92, 93, 128; Vatican's interest in, 103

Benelli, Most Reverend Giovanni, 103, 109, 110

Berman, Howard, 118

Bernardin, Cardinal Joseph, 37, 54, 110, 121, 129–130, 140

Bird, Rose, 118

"Bird of Passage" myth, 9

Bishops' Ad Hoc Committee on Farm Labor: and CALRA, 119, 120, 121; Chávez bias in favor of, 49, 70, 73, 74, 82, 98; critics of, 33–45, 63, 75, 77; disengage-

ment from the UFW, 6, 80, 123, 129, 130, 139, 140; formation of, 4, 54, 56, 58–59; hierarchy's support for, 32–33, 47, 76, 77; as mediator, 3, 5, 59, 62, 69, 78–79; neutral façade of, 20, 76, 77, 83, 123; neutral façade removed, 66, 84, 90–91, 93, 99–100; personnel changes in, 89; press conference at end of the Delano Strike, 65; professionalism of, 60; Hollis Roberts and, 61

boycott: AFL-CIO's endorsement of, 107; bishops' debate on, 50, 52–58, 102–105, 111, 113, 114–115, 120–121, 123; CALRA and, 118; Catholics divided over, 31, 39, 41–42, 46, 86; Chávez seeks bishops' endorsement of, 48, 52, 102, 122; Chávez's strategy central to, 28, 29, 61, 90, 106, 127, 129, 137; economic pressure on grape growers, 5, 59–60; of Gallo, 112; grape boycott ends, 64; of Heublein, 78–79; Higgins's support for, 49, 96, 98–99; Nixon's opinion of, 82–83; prohibitions against, 71, 81, 87–88; Reagan's opinion of, 29–30

Bracero Program: braceros under, 11, 26–27; Chávez's opposition to, 25; Higgins's opposition to, 12, 17–19; Mitchell Committee's opinion of, 20; origins of, 10; termination of, 3, 92. *See also* Public Law 78

Brown, Jerry: and CALRA, 113, 117–119, 122; and CALRB nominations, 123–124; Catholic influence on, 116; Chávez's alliance with, 6, 92, 111, 116–117; critics of, 117; defeat in Senate race, 136; "Moonbeam" moniker, 115–116; presidential campaign of, 125–126; and Proposition 14, 127; and Proposition 22, 87–88, 116

Brown, Pat, 27, 87, 116, 117

California Agricultural Labor Relations Act
(CALRA): Ad Hoc Committee's support
of, 119, 123, 127, 130, 139; description of,
80; enactment of, 115, 117–119; subversion of, 121–122, 126, 128; UFW's contri-
bution to, 138
California Agricultural Labor Relations
Board (CALRB): Ad Hoc Committee's
involvement with, 123, 129; funding crisis
of, 125–127; Mahony as chairman of,
127–128; purpose of, 118; staffing of,
123–124; subversion of, 121, 128
California Farmer, 80
California Supreme Court, 71
Campaign for Human Development, 80
Carter, Bishop G. Emmett, 114
Catholic News Service, 17, 31
Catholic social teaching: *Gaudium et Spes*,
13; *Mater et Magistra*, 12, 33; *Octogesima
Adveniens*, 13; *Quadragesimo Anno*, 12,
14, 50; *Rerum Novarum*, 12, 13, 50
Catholic University of America, 13, 17, 131,
141, 145
Catholic Worker, 15–16
Catholic Worker Movement, 15–16
Central California Register, 32, 55, 84–85
Chatfield, LeRoy, 118, 123–124, 125
Chávez, César: as administrator, 6, 60, 72,
114, 131, 133–135; alleged to be Communist, 33, 61; boycott strategy of, 28, 29, 61,
90, 106, 127, 129, 137; and Jerry Brown,
6, 92, 111, 116–117; and Catholic hierarchy, 4–5, 48, 52, 66, 81, 102, 121–122;
contributions, 138–139; CSO years, 24–
25; death of, 138; dividing the Church,
31–32; early years of, 22; faith of, 3, 13,
23–24, 28; fasting by, 29; and Monsignor
Higgins, 22, 141–145; incarceration of,
71; marches by, 27–28; and media, 27, 95;
NFWA years of, 26–27; and non-violence,
23, 28; in Oxnard, 25; and Paul VI, 108–
110; political decline of, 136–137, 139;
and Presidential Medal of Freedom, 138;
and Teamsters, 67, 69, 74
Chávez, Helen Fabela, 23
Chávez, Manuel, 61
Chinese Exclusion Act, 7
Citizens Committee for Agriculture, 70
Civil Rights Movement, 3, 26, 31, 92

Clinch, Bishop Harry, 37, 40, 41, 43, 44, 45
Clinton, Bill, 138
Cody, Cardinal John Patrick, 114
Cohen, Jerry, 24, 62, 70, 134, 141–142
Community Service Organization (CSO),
24–25, 26, 143
cortito (short-hoe), 138
Cosgrove, John, 53, 54, 61, 71, 81, 82, 83
Costello, Gerald, 92–93
Cross, Father Mike, 35–40, 45, 70
Curtis, Bishop Walter, 56, 89

Day, Dorothy, 15–16
Dearden, Cardinal John, 36–37, 51–56
Delano Grape Strike: Chávez's march to Sacramento, 28; end of, 4, 30, 64–65; as intrafaith conflict, 3, 31–33, 51; origins of, 26–
27; violence against UFW during, 28–29
Deukmejian, George, 6, 128, 136–137
Donnelly, Bishop Joseph: as Ad Hoc Committee chairman, 56, 58; bias, 34, 49, 73,
82, 84, 91–93, 99–101; and boycott, 102,
104, 120; and critics, 35, 39; death of, 130;
at Delano press conference, 65; as mediator, 62–63, 69
Donohoe, Bishop Hugh: and Ad Hoc Committee's creation, 54, 56; and boycott, 48,
53, 55, 103, 114, 121; concern about farm
labor dispute, 46, 58, 80–81; financial concerns of, 47, 55, 79, 83–85, 86; Pope Paul
VI's praise for, 85–86
Dwyer, Archbishop Robert, 35

Earley, Monsignor Thomas, 38–40, 45
Egan, Monsignor John, 101–102

Farm Bureau, 39, 79, 86–88, 105, 129
Farm Placement Service (FPS), 25
Farm Services Agency, 78–79
farmworkers: Anglo, 10; Chinese, 7; Japa-
nese, 8; and Mexican Revolution, 8
Farm Workers Service Center, 80–81, 138
Fighting for Our Lives (film), 113
Fitzsimmons, Frank "Fitz": Chávez's antipa-
thy toward, 86–87; critics of, 92, 95; and
Monsignor Higgins, 66, 95–98; and
Nixon, 86; protests Church involvement,
104–105
Fleming, Herbert, 73

1969 conference of, 54–58; as successor organization to the NCWC, 48
U.S. Conference of Catholic Bishops (USCCB), 3, 37, 131
U.S. Department of Defense, 82

Vatican II, 20–21, 47, 85, 92, 141
Vizzard, Father James, 92–93

Wagner Act. *See* National Labor Relations Act
Willinger, Aloysius J., 32
Woodcock, Leonard, 96, 98

"Yardstick" column, 17, 22, 89, 93, 97

Zambrano, Aristeo, 135

ABOUT THE AUTHOR

Marco Prouty earned his PhD in U.S. history from The Catholic University of America. He holds an MA in religion from Pepperdine University, a BA in international studies from the University of Washington, and an AA from Peninsula College. He is a former career foreign service officer of the U.S. Department of State. He has served as a vice consul in the Dominican Republic, as desk officer for Barbados and the Eastern Caribbean, and as chief of the Political and Economic Section at the U.S. Embassy in Belize.